Practice with Purpose

Literacy Work Stations for Grades 3–6

Debbie Diller

Stenhouse Publishers
Portland, Maine

Pembroke Publishers Limited
Markham, Ontario

To all the children with the "gift of struggle,"
and to the teachers who have taught me
how to make practice purposeful

Stenhouse Publishers
www.stenhouse.com

Library of Congress Cataloging-in-Publication Data
Diller, Debbie, 1954–
    Practice with purpose : literacy work stations for grades 3–6 / Debbie Diller.
        p. cm.
        Includes bibliographical references.
        ISBN 1-57110-395-3
        1. Language arts (Elementary) 2. Classroom learning centers. 3. Group work in education. I. Title.
LB1576.D4647 2005
372.6'044—dc22   2005043793

Published in Canada by
Pembroke Publishers Limited
538 Hood Road
Markham, Ontario L3R 3K9
ISBN 1-55138-194-X

Cover and interior design by Martha Drury
Icon illustrations by Wes Rowell

Manufactured in the United States of America on acid-free paper
11 10 09 08 07 06   9 8 7 6 5 4

Contents

Acknowledgments

Readers are often curious about where authors get ideas for their books. The ideas recorded in *Practice with Purpose* originated in the classrooms of hundreds of teachers with whom I've worked over the past five years. My friend John O'Flahavan has told me that our teaching improves when we open the doors of our classrooms to watch each other teach. That has been my great privilege. It is impossible for me to note the name of every teacher who has spoken with and questioned me about literacy work stations for upper grades over the years. But to each of them, I offer my heartfelt thanks. And to John, thanks for encouraging me to carve out time for writing.

It has been my honor to work with many inspirational educators over my teaching career. Special thanks to Betty Best for knowing that I could teach third grade (even though my only desire at the time was to teach kindergarten), and for suggesting that I become a consultant and share my ideas with others. I'm also grateful to Gerry Haggard for asking me to teach migrant students in grades 6 through 10, knowing that I could make a difference. Thank you

to Judy Wallis for her vision and for exposing me to some of the best minds in the field of education and beyond, including Regie Routman. Thanks for inviting me to present with you at International Reading Association in Reno. And to Janine Hoke, my wonderful principal, who saw what I could do and gently pushed me out of the nest—I am eternally grateful.

Several teachers allowed me to visit their classrooms to study how to make literacy stations work in upper grades, and I am grateful to them: Heather Tate, fifth-grade teacher at Herod Elementary in Houston Independent School District; Shawn Verow, sixth-grade teacher at Miller Intermediate School in Alief Independent School District; and Lizzy Evers, who teaches fifth grade, and Aracely Soto, Jennifer Taylor, and Jen Bateman, all third-grade teachers at Meadow Wood Elementary in Spring Branch I.S.D. Thanks for all the photos (and video) they let me take of their kids at work, and for their brainstorming sessions after school.

A special thanks to all my friends in West Virginia who treated me like family as I worked in their schools over the past few years: Jeanie Bennett, Libby Bucy, Barb Godwin, Beverley Kingery, Becky Mattern, Cynthia Nesselroade, Greg Pancione, Roy Wager. Thanks to all the upper-grade teachers in Hampshire, Harrison, and Upshur counties who let me walk through and teach in their classrooms, who attended numerous training sessions with me, and who asked me the tough questions. Thanks, too, to the principals who joined us there. I appreciate my new friends in the Chicago area who also had me visit their schools and work on an ongoing basis with their teachers on literacy work stations, especially Barb Kurth.

Thank you to all the administrators in the Houston area who invited me into their schools to work with teachers and students on literacy work stations in grades 3 through 6 on a continuing basis, including Cathy Airola, Georgia Bartlett, Liz Chambers, Gabe Coleman, Susan Cornell, Debbie Denson, Brenda Emanuel, Janie Evans, Jim Goggin, Kathy Heath, Noel Gray, Nancy Harn, Holly Hughes, Julia Kerr, Dedrick Martin, Debbie Phillips, Pat Shoffit, Carol Suell, Carolyn Weige, and Keith Yost.

A big thanks to Elisa Farris, the visionary principal of Alexander Elementary in Katy I.S.D. for opening her school to me and my camera at any and all times, especially over the last few months as this book neared production. Also, I appreciate Karen Muller, her literacy coach, my tour guide and photo assistant at Alexander. Many thanks to Kim Czubara, Susie Gutierrez, Debby Johnson, Diane Nicodemus, and Kelly Sobieski for the impromptu pictures I shot in their rooms. And to Kelly Jackson, principal extraordinaire in Alvin I.S.D., who saw my ideas for primary grades work so well that she trusted me to extend them into the upper grades.

The photos of kids working at stations in this book would not be possible without the permissions that several teachers helped me obtain. Thanks to Lisa Campbell, Jody Johnson, Patty Malcolm, Karla Klyng, Stacey Markley, and Chris Ware.

To the wonderful folks at Stenhouse who so kindly helped me craft this book, a huge thanks! To Philippa Stratton, who is a delight and a wonder . . . I'm so glad you remembered our title! To Brenda Power for encouragement and pushing me higher . . . you made this book so much better! To Tom Seavey, for wisdom and good business sense. To Martha Drury, for her stunning designs.

For all who supported me on the home front, I express my gratitude to Tangye Stephney and Karla Pitts, my dear friends and prayer partners; my teacher friends Patty Terry and Pam House, who always help me when I get stuck; Lisa Gregory and Pat Marshall for helping me problem-solve; Wade Lee, Paul Reyes, and Alex Rivas, who helped me think about science; Betsy Franco for poetry help; Nancy Considine for title advice; Jan Tucker for guidance and direction; and Janette Smith, my assistant, with whom I could never have made any of this happen.

Finally, hugs to my mom and dad, who inquire often about my work; to Jon and Jess, whom I love dearly and who have taught me so much; and to my patient husband, Tom, who waited many nights and weekends while I sat at my computer writing, who had to sit at home with our Great Dane because the kids had gone off to college and I was consulting around the country. It's finished! Let's hit the road!

1

What Is a Literacy Work Station?

You enter the classroom. Students are working with partners all around the room doing all kinds of reading, writing, listening, and speaking. Yes, they are talking, but they're actually talking about what they're reading and writing! All twenty-seven are engaged in their work and look like they're happy to be at school. How did the teacher orchestrate this? She must have bribed them with a reward, like a pizza party. The room isn't very large, but every part of it is being used. You thought you needed a huge room to do this, but this teacher has managed to make it work, even though she teaches in a small space. You notice that some kids are using the whiteboard and the overhead; others are gathered in small groups at their desks; some sit on the floor; several are in a corner classroom library space. Surely they aren't on-task!

But as you walk around and talk to the kids, you find that they really know what they're supposed to be doing and why, and they are in fact doing it. You see a pair of students doing independent research at computers, using Web sites their teacher has book-

Kids work in pairs at buddy reading, newspaper, and word study stations in a sixth-grade classroom.

marked. Two more are sitting on the floor listening to a story from the basal reader on a tape recorder; they tell you that after they listen, they use comprehension task cards to guide their discussion and help

1

Two students work at the geography station while two others are at the word study station.

prepare them for the state reading test. In a corner two students are curled up in the classroom library, reading magazines and books. Two others are seated at a small table at the writing station, helping each other edit pieces from their writing folders from writing workshop. Another pair of students sits at two desks writing a news article for the class newspaper; all their materials are housed in a notebook labeled "Newspaper Station." Two students create poems with magnetic words on the side of the teacher's file cabinet. They show you how they use a rhyming dictionary as a reference tool, since they've chosen to write a poem with couplets. A pair of students is seated on the floor nearby with a small basket of books labeled "Buddy Reading"; they read and discuss a chapter from a novel the teacher has helped them select from the choices in the basket.

Two students stand by the whiteboard and test each other on this week's spelling words. A pair of students is in the content-area station working on a social studies project; they are reading about the Civil War and taking notes for the song they're composing together. At a group of desks, four students meet in a literature circle/book club to discuss a book they've been reading during independent reading time. Meanwhile, their teacher works with a group of five students, guiding their reading and helping them comprehend a nonfiction piece on skateboarding.

How can their teacher keep up with all that they're doing? Isn't this a lot of work for the teacher? Where are her worksheets? you wonder. Actually, this teacher has less paperwork to do than she used to. She is using literacy work stations effectively in her upper-grade classroom. When asked, she explains that this type of teaching is much easier than she had thought—mostly because the students are so engaged, and she can actually teach a small group while the others independently practice things related to what she's already taught. She has less grading of busywork and more time to spend planning meaningful instruction.

What Is a Literacy Work Station?

Isn't this like centers? I thought they were for kindergarten. There's no time for this in upper grades. I have too much to teach! These are comments I've heard from teachers in grades 3–6 as they've pondered using literacy work stations. What is a literacy work station?

I define a literacy work station as "an area within the classroom where students work alone or interact with one another, using instructional materials to explore and expand their literacy. It is a place where a variety of activities reinforce and/or extend learning, often without the assistance of the classroom teacher. It is a time for students to practice reading, writing, speaking, listening, and working with letters and words" (Diller 2003).

Let's break down this definition and take a closer look at each part of what constitutes a literacy work station.

An Area Within the Classroom

One problem teachers usually mention is that they don't have enough space in their classrooms for centers. Literacy work stations use existing classroom furniture and don't take up much extra room. For example, if you have an overhead projector, you have an overhead work station. Your tape recorder becomes your listening station. Your computers make up your computer station. Literacy work stations use classroom space effectively. They are not an extra; they are an integral part of instruction. The following chapters include space-saving instructions on how to set up each literacy work station.

Storing a tape recorder and supplies on the bottom of an overhead cart saves space.

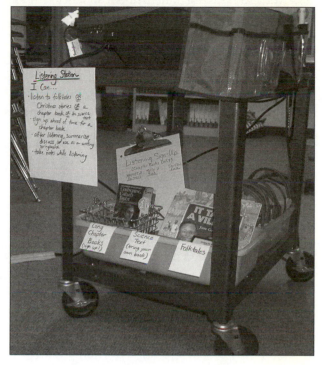

Working Alone or with Partners

Many teachers also tell me that their classrooms will get too noisy if they use this type of active learning. I often suggest reducing the number of students working together to decrease the noise level and to increase student engagement. In literacy work stations, most students work in pairs, especially at the start of the school year. Sometimes I allow kids to work alone. Some actually prefer working solo and are less distracted when doing so. Remember that there are other times during the day for small-group work, such as in a social studies project, a science experiment, or a game in P.E.

Using Instructional Materials

Instructional materials already used in teaching are placed at the work stations. The emphasis is on the teacher modeling with materials first, working with the students to be sure they understand how to use them, and then moving the materials into the literacy work stations for independent practice. I used to make and use lots of games with file folders, but I found that the kids who were most successful with them were usually the ones who didn't need the practice. Today I prefer teaching a strategy in a large or small group as part of my instructional time and then moving it into the work station for independent practice.

Variety of Activities

Choice is a big part of making literacy work stations successful. A station should include a variety of things for students to choose from, but not so many that it becomes overwhelming. I call this "controlled choice." It seems to work well when the teacher introduces several choices within one work station from which learners can select. Any of the activities there should provide the practice the student needs, but because the student has a choice, he or she actually learns more. In the following chapters are ideas for developing "I Can" or "I Will" lists, which help the teacher and students work together to negotiate a list of possible choices for activities at

The "I Can" list provides directions for third graders at buddy reading.

each work station. Some teachers put a colored dot or a star beside each activity that is a "have-to" and should be done first.

Time for Students to Practice

The emphasis at literacy work stations is on practice—meaningful, independent practice without the teacher's assistance. It is a time for students to practice all that the teacher has been modeling. Thus, activities placed at the literacy work station grow out of what the teacher has done during read-aloud, shared reading, modeled writing, shared writing, small-group instruction, content-area instruction, and so on. Things aren't put into the work stations just to keep students busy.

Literacy Work Stations Versus Traditional Learning Centers: The Benefits

A literacy work station is fundamentally different from a traditional center in several ways, as shown in Figure 1.1. The emphasis in literacy work stations is on teacher modeling and students' responsibility for their own learning. In traditional centers, the teachers often did too much of the work. They would, for example, think of ideas for the materials, make the materials, laminate them, cut them out, explain them, explain them again, and clean up after they were used. In addition, they would decide when to change the materials (usually every Friday afternoon) and what would be done with them.

In literacy work stations, students share in the decision-making process. They help decide when to change materials, and they negotiate ideas for what they'd like to do to practice at each station. No longer does the teacher change the centers weekly. This process is explained in more detail in Chapter 2. When setting up work stations, upper-grade students can help determine where to place them. They can even help write the directions for the

Figure 1.1 **Differences Between Literacy Work Stations and Traditional Learning Centers**

Literacy Work Stations	Traditional Centers
Materials are taught with and used for instruction first. Then they are placed in the work station for independent use.	New materials were often placed in the center without first being used in teaching. The teacher may have shown how to use the center once, but it was often introduced with all the other new centers at one time.
Stations remain set up all year long. Materials are changed to reflect students' reading levels, strategies being taught, and topics being studied.	Centers were often changed weekly to go with units of study. Materials often changed every week.
Stations are used for students' meaningful independent work and are an integral part of each child's instruction. All students go to work stations daily as part of their "work."	Centers were often used by students when they "finished their work." Centers were used for fun and motivation, for something extra.
Practice materials are differentiated for students with different needs and reading levels.	All students did the same activities at centers. There was not usually much differentiation.
The teacher and students write directions for activities together to share and build ownership.	The teacher wrote all the directions and prepared everything beforehand.
The teacher works with small groups during literacy work stations (doing guided reading, word study, and/or literature circles/book clubs) and differentiates instruction within each small group.	If the teacher met with small groups, each group often did the same task.

activities in the station, as well as create signs, management boards, and labels to keep things organized and running smoothly.

There are several differences between primary and intermediate literacy work stations, as noted in Figure 1.2. Transitional and fluent readers have special needs. These students are gaining in fluency as they learn to read and write with greater ease. However, as they move to longer, more complex texts, their fluency may decrease. At these levels, they often have good decoding skills but may lack comprehension. Or they may have difficulty with decoding longer words or certain vowel combinations. They also must learn to pay attention to new words and acquire specialized vocabulary in content areas. They need to learn to sustain interest and attention when reading longer books and writing longer pieces. They are reading silently most of the time and learning to do more revising and

A student checks out a book from the classroom library to read for an extended period during independent reading later in the day.

Figure 1.2 **Transitioning Between Primary and Intermediate Grades with Literacy Work Stations and Meaningful Independent Work**

K–2 Work Stations	Transitions	3–6 Work Stations
Independent Reading as a separate time from literacy work stations	Moving to longer period of time for independent reading and response writing	Independent Reading as part of independent work time (quiet versus active part); might work with one reading group during about twenty minutes of this time
Classroom Library	Move to silent reading for a longer period of time and include expanded responses to books read; use genres (like articles and nonfiction) they'll need for taking state reading tests	Classroom Library
Listening Work Station	Provide tapes for students who need extra support; expand to include social studies and science texts	Listening Work Station
Writing Work Station	Give students a longer chunk of time to practice writing strategies and include genres they'll need for taking state writing tests	Writing Work Station
ABC/Word Study Work Station	Transition to more investigative word study work with complex word patterns/etymology, vocabulary, and so on, especially as related to their own reading and writing	Word Study/Spelling Work Station
Drama Work Station	Provide opportunities for students to practice fluent reading with reader's theater scripts as well as develop comprehension through dramatizations and improvisations	Drama/Reader's Theater Work Station
Poetry Work Station	Move to more interpretation of poems, focusing more on inference	Poetry Work Station
Overhead Work Station	Can use overheads for cursive handwriting, grammar, and state test practice	Overhead Work Station
Social Studies and Science Work Stations	Become places for inquiry/research of topics related to science, social studies, and health	Content-Area Work Stations
Guided Reading Groups/Literature Circles	More students are moving into literature circles, sometimes combined with guided reading	Guided Reading Groups/Literature Circles

editing. They need to expand their reading and writing to a variety of genres.

As students move into higher and higher levels of reading and writing, your work stations will have to change to reflect their needs. You might have students go to just one work station a day, compared with primary classrooms, where they often go to two or three work stations daily. Students will probably stay at the stations longer than they did in the primary grades, because their reading and writing stamina are increasing. Independent reading time also expands in intermediate grades and is part of the independent practice time. Students often read and then write responses to what they read, sometimes in preparation for literature circles or book clubs.

Guaranteeing Independence

One huge benefit of using literacy work stations in your classroom is that students will be more motivated to work independently. However, to help students learn how to take on more independence, several conditions must be in place. Teachers must model appropriate behavior, allow for a gradual release of responsibility, provide a risk-free environment and a proper independent work level, and communicate clear, explicit expectations.

Modeling

Teacher modeling helps ensure independent learning. Students need to see many demonstrations of how to use materials or do tasks before they can do them well on their own. Simply showing something once isn't enough for most learners, even adult learners. Brian Cambourne's Conditions of Learning model (1988) identifies demonstration as an important prerequisite for language learning. I have found that the most successful work stations are those using materials and activities that teachers have modeled most.

Gradual Release of Responsibility

The best way to guarantee success at literacy work stations is through lots of modeling, with teachers gradually releasing more responsibility to the students. Pearson and Gallagher's Gradual Release Model of Instruction (1983) outlines this principle (see Figure 1.3). My favorite example of how I used the gradual release model to teach a new behavior is when I taught my teenage daughter how to do the laundry. First, she needed to learn about the materials to be used and to know what it looked like to do the laundry. She'd had fourteen years of "modeled laundry," so it was on to the next step! Next, we did "shared laundry." While we sorted the clothes together, I explained how to separate dark colors from white and told her why that was important. I set the temperatures while she watched, and explained why I used each temperature. (Because she bought some of her own clothes, she had a vested interest in the "whys.") In a few weeks we moved on to "guided laundry." Now she sorted and I checked; she set the temperature on the washer and dryer, and I checked; she hung the all-cotton pieces on hangers to dry, and I checked. When I was satisfied with her performance, she finally moved to "independent laundry." I was sure she could do it on her own, because I had *gradually* released the responsibility to her.

To best train students for literacy work stations, teachers do the same thing. They begin by modeling—showing students how to do something such as use a graphic organizer while reading. For example, during large-group time I might do a read-aloud of a newspaper article, such as the "Shortcuts" feature, available in the Sunday comics. Each week's edition is about a different topic, such as earthquakes, roller coasters, or electricity. I set the purpose for listening, instructing students to listen for interesting facts about and new words related to the topic, the Galapagos Islands. After reading, we create and fill out a chart

Figure 1.3 **Gradual Release of Responsibility Approach, Pearson and Gallagher 1983**

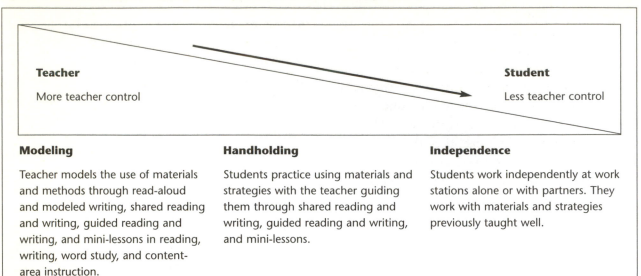

Teacher

More teacher control

Student

Less teacher control

Modeling

Teacher models the use of materials and methods through read-aloud and modeled writing, shared reading and writing, guided reading and writing, and mini-lessons in reading, writing, word study, and content-area instruction.

Handholding

Students practice using materials and strategies with the teacher guiding them through shared reading and writing, guided reading and writing, and mini-lessons.

Independence

Students work independently at work stations alone or with partners. They work with materials and strategies previously taught well.

The teacher models how to use the materials for the newspaper station with the whole class gathered around. Two students help with the modeling.

recording this information. We might use this same type of informational text graphic organizer to map out information from material read in social studies or science several times (see Appendix D). I then move the blank chart to the "Shortcuts" newspaper station and make it available to students for independent practice.

Risk-Free Environment

Another of Cambourne's Conditions of Learning is referred to as *approximations*. Students are encouraged to "have a go" at tasks as they practice them. Students learn best in a classroom where they feel safe and secure. They often learn more when working with a peer to practice something new. Eric Jensen (1998) explains how the brain learns best when threats are removed. Grading everything students practice can be threatening for some, because they are just learning how to do certain tasks. Use grades judiciously at work stations. Carefully select products to grade after students have had opportunities to practice. Students still must be held accountable for their practice time, but there are better ways to do that. Each of the following chapters has a section on "How to Assess/Keep Kids Accountable," as well as "How This Station Supports Student Performance on State Tests."

Independent Work Level

Sometimes students get into trouble at a work station when they cannot do a task independently because it's too difficult for them. I see this often in classrooms, and it is common in the classroom library. Often when students are playing around here, it's because they have chosen books that are either too hard or not interesting to them. Helping them choose books that are at their independent level will make this station run more smoothly. See Chapter 3 for ideas on this.

Russian psychologist Lev Vygotsky (1978) explained that student learning takes place during the student's "zone of proximal development" or ZPD. Activities in the ZPD are just a little beyond the student's independent level (or what the student can do totally on his or her own), things the student can do with the support of a peer. Sometimes the ZPD is explained as what students can do with support today that they can do on their own tomorrow. Social interaction is used to further the learning within the student's ZPD. Just a bit beyond a student's ZPD lies frustration. If you closely examine students who get into trouble in class, chances are you'll find that some of them are being asked to function at a level above their current ZPD. This is why differentiation at literacy work stations is so critical.

Clear, Explicit Expectations

When I observe in classrooms, I sometimes notice stations that aren't working well at all. I ask the students what they're supposed to be doing at that station. Many times they don't know. For example, in one fifth-grade classroom the word study work station was very noisy. I asked the students to tell me about what they were doing there. They said, "We're supposed to be playing this game, but we've never played it before and aren't sure how to do it." That's why they were arguing and talking off-task. I sat down with them and played a few rounds of the game until they knew how to play it; after that they worked fine on their own. If the teacher had shown them how to play the game first (perhaps in a small group, particularly for her struggling students), rather than just telling them to read the directions and play it, they would have been more successful and probably wouldn't have disrupted the class.

In this book you will find suggestions for an "I Can" or "I Will" list to post at each work station. The list outlines what students can do at the station, which helps clarify expectations. Because the lists are developed with the students, they will better understand what to do at each work station. These lists, combined with teacher modeling, will head off many potential problems.

Directions made with the class for the culture station help students practice what they're learning about in social studies.

When working with upper-grade students, an alternative to the "I Can" list is to write directions for the station *with* your class. This promotes buy-in and clarification of what you expect kids to do when working independently. Have materials gathered that you want students to use in the station, talk about how to use them, and then write the directions together as a class. Post them with the station materials.

Why Should I Use Literacy Work Stations?

This book is dedicated to all the students who had "the gift of struggle." This is a term I first heard Ellin Keene, co-author of *Mosaic of Thought* (1997), use in a workshop I attended. I thought of my daughter, Jessica, who had trouble learning to read. It was a struggle for her, but it was also a gift. As a beginning reader she said to me, "Mommy, my brain is not wired for reading. You're going to have to make me practice every night." This difficulty became a gift as Jessica learned to be patient with herself as a learner, as she practiced diligently and became

more and more skilled. Today she is a college student focusing on her strength as a learner in the field of biology; she learned how to study and work at something important to her; she's an excellent reader and reads both fiction and nonfiction well. Her struggle turned out to be a gift, because it taught her to persevere. The gift of struggle can be helpful to you as a teacher, too. Whenever I have worked hard to help a student solve a problem, I have learned as much as the child.

Literacy work stations help meet the needs of *all* students, especially those who struggle with traditional pencil-and-paper tasks. I still remember the names of those I had trouble reaching in my third-grade classroom more than twenty-five years ago . . . Michael, Adam, and Lance. Reading was difficult for them, and they had trouble staying in their seats doing the "packets" I assigned them for independent work. They needed more hands-on work with manipulatives, more opportunities to read and talk with a partner, more chances to work beyond their desks. A little movement would have done them good! I don't beat myself up for what I didn't provide for them (I did the best I could with the knowledge I had at the time); instead I think of these students as a reminder of all the kids who need literacy work stations.

Eric Jensen writes about getting the brain's attention in his book *Teaching with the Brain in Mind* (1998). He suggests that to increase students' intrinsic motivation and keep their attention, teachers should provide choices, make learning relevant and personal, and make it engaging (emotional, energetic, physical). These are exactly the factors that make literacy work stations successful.

Jensen writes that a change in location is one of the easiest ways to get the brain's attention. At literacy work stations, students move to various places in the classroom to participate in learning with partners for a short time. He also suggests that teachers provide a rich balance of novelty and ritual. In contrast to seatwork, literacy work stations provide novelty as students partake in a variety of tasks around the classroom. In each chapter that follows I show how to maintain novelty in work stations and thus engage students (and reduce behavior problems). Refer to the sections called "Ways to Keep the Station Going Throughout the Year."

Teachers can do much to set up success for students by considering what students pay attention to and what engages them. To increase students' attention to tasks, have them try one of the following:

- Play a game.
- Make something.
- Talk with a partner.
- Tell a story.
- Be a recorder (have a job to do).
- Move.
- Act it out.
- Do something new.

Literacy work stations provide all of the above and more.

Two students choose from a variety of word study games to reinforce vocabulary and spelling.

Making It Personal

As you read this book, make it personal. Feel free to write notes in the margins. Ask questions that pop into your mind as you read, and discuss them with a colleague. If what you're already doing in your classroom is working effectively to meet the needs of every student, keep doing it. Use the parts of this book that make sense to you and that seem like they will engage students in more meaningful independent practice. Remember, there is no one way that will help everyone. Follow the lead of your kids. Ask for their input. They will show you the way.

Reflection and Dialogue

1. Share your new ideas about literacy work stations with a colleague. Discuss the definition of work stations provided earlier in this chapter.
2. Think about your students and their level of engagement. What specific things most engaged them recently? Make a list and plan similar kinds of activities.
3. Try using the gradual release of responsibility approach. Think about something new you've learned to do and how you probably went through a similar process. Plan for your first work stations using this model.
4. Work with a colleague to write a note to parents explaining literacy work stations. Include how and why you'll use them this year. Taking the initiative with parents will head off many questions about what you are doing in your classroom.
5. Take baby steps. Choose one or two stations in this book that seem comfortable for you to start with. Use equipment and materials you already have in your classroom and can work with easily.

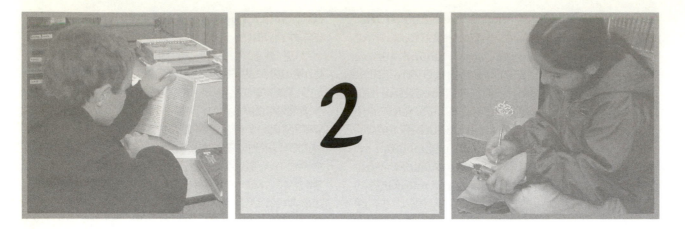

Management of Independent Work Time

Most upper-grade teachers I've worked with have found success using a combination of quiet and active structures for independent work time. Many start the year by establishing a silent, independent reading time that eventually becomes a time for teacher conferences with students and/or small-group reading with one group.

If you want to use literacy work stations in your classroom, think of this as a more active time when students have the opportunity to move somewhere other than their assigned seats to participate in purposeful independent practice with a partner. How to make literacy work stations work effectively for you and your students is the focus of this chapter and the remainder of this book.

Quiet Independent Practice

You might begin your independent practice time with a quiet period in which students do independent reading, followed by response writing. Intermediate students should be able to sustain

their silent reading of self-selected books for a minimum of twenty to thirty minutes. Chapter 3 goes into detail about how to teach for and maintain productive independent reading time. Chapter 4 discusses teaching students how to write high-quality responses to their independent reading.

Fourth graders read independently during the quiet independent practice time before literacy work stations.

These procedures will not happen by chance in most classrooms. After this routine is well established (about three weeks or so), you might begin working with a small group during quiet independent practice time. You might also choose to meet with individuals and confer with them about their reading.

Active Independent Practice

You will probably want to have literacy work stations, the time for more *active* independent practice, after the quiet independent practice time. After training students on routines for literacy work stations, this will also be a time you might work with a small group. Again, take three or four weeks at the start of the school year to establish procedures, so students know exactly what to do and won't interrupt you when you start working with small groups. You might work with guided reading groups and/or literature circles once literacy work stations are established.

Pairs of students work around the room on a variety of literacy tasks while the teacher monitors at the start of the year.

How Do I Get Started with Literacy Work Stations?

Plan for Space

Begin by planning for space in your classroom. Literacy work stations are not an "extra" for students who finish their work. They are part of the students' independent practice, which includes independent reading and writing and practicing what you've already taught. Think about where you want students to work independently. Use every area you can think of, including space on the floor, on the walls, in the corners of your classroom, and at desks or tables. You'll need to plan for three to four feet of space between each work station so students will be able to work quietly and not bump into each other.

Use existing furniture, such as your computers (computer work station), overhead (overhead work station), pocket chart stand or file cabinet (vocabulary or poetry work station), bulletin boards (writing work station), and chalkboards or whiteboards (spelling or grammar work station). Some literacy work stations can be portable and stored on shelves,

This writing work station is set up on a built-in counter with a bulletin board behind it in a portable classroom.

Figure 2.1 **Classroom Planning Map**

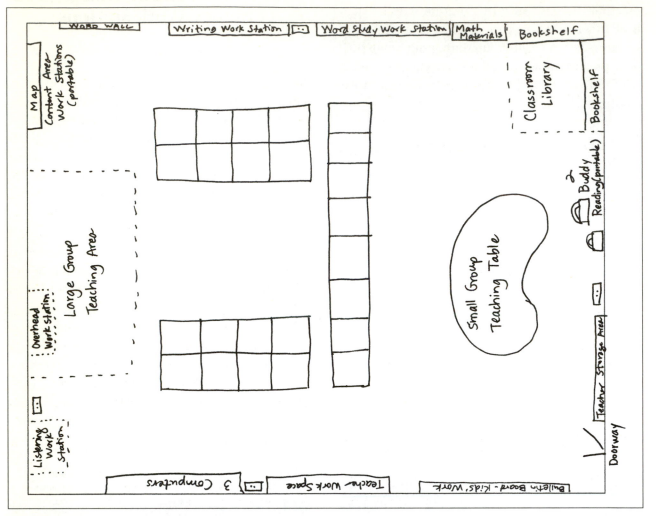

including buddy reading baskets (filled with two copies of several books) or word study games (such as Scrabble, Jr. or homonym matching cards). Put a tape recorder on the floor for a listening station. You don't need to use a table; it takes up too much space. Put several books and tapes in a basket by the tape recorder. If you have a TV cart, set up the listening station on the bottom of the cart. If you have built-in counters, you can place materials for work stations there. Some teachers have set up work stations inside cabinets, using a shelf or two and posting directions on the inside of the cabinet doors, with a literacy work station sign on the out-

side. Try to designate a corner of the room for your classroom library. Consider the one where you now might have your teacher desk. Or place bookshelves at a 90-degree angle from the wall to create a cozy nook. See Chapter 3 for ideas on setting up the classroom library.

You might want to chart out your classroom space on a piece of paper first, using notes to show where you will place each work station (see Figure 2.1). Sketch in doors, windows, built-in cabinets, computer connections, and so forth to help you plan around these permanent fixtures. Plan with the following spaces and ideas in mind:

- Large-group teaching area (perhaps a rug on the floor)
- Small-group teaching area (table that seats four to six students)
- Classroom library (corner if you have one)
- Publishing/writing area
- Word wall (see Chapter 6 for ideas)
- Places for students to work independently (around the perimeter of the room)—include quiet and active spaces
- Display spaces for student work
- Individual spaces for students (desks and cubbies or lockers)
- Teacher space
- Storage spaces (for supplies, math manipulatives, etc.)
- Traffic flow

Be flexible with your classroom space. You might assign several students the job of "furniture mover" to create a variety of physical setups as needed during the school day. For example, have these helpers move a few desks to create a large-group area for read-aloud; then replace the desks for independent learning time.

Plan for Time

A question I am always asked is How do I schedule this into my day? Julie Morgenstern, author of *Organizing from the Inside Out* (1998) and *Time Management from the Inside Out* (2000), recommends that you focus on getting space under control before you attempt to manage time. She says that you can *see* space, but that you can't see time. How true!

If you value independent practice, you'll find a way to build it into your day. Some teachers have difficulty finding time for literacy work stations at first, because they continue doing what they've always done, as well as add on this new routine. However, there simply won't be enough time in the day. See Figure 2.2 for a sample schedule. Look critically at your current schedule. There may be inef-

Figure 2.2 **Intermediate Language Arts Schedule Integrating Literacy Work Stations**

(Two and a half hours for language arts instruction—self-contained classroom)	
8:00–8:15	Classroom jobs/self-select books for independent reading and writing topics
8:15–8:35	Read-aloud/shared reading with mini-lesson on reading/writing strategy
8:35–9:00	Independent reading/response writing
	Guided reading with one group or individual reading conferences
9:00–9:45	Music, art, P.E.
9:45–10:15	Guided reading/literacy work stations—one group/one rotation
10:15–10:30	Word study/spelling
10:30–11:30	Writers' workshop
11:30–12:30	Lunch/recess
12:30–1:30	Math
1:30–2:10	Social studies
2:10–2:50	Science
2:50–2:55	Reflection—write about you learned today in your journal

fective or inefficient things you've been doing for years that you could do in a more meaningful and integrated way. For example, at one school I worked with, the fifth-grade teachers were spending fifteen minutes on spelling, twenty minutes on grammar, and fifteen minutes on handwriting each day. I showed them how to integrate grammar and handwriting into their writing lessons, which gave them more time in the day since they weren't chopping their curriculum into little bits.

Teachers with block scheduling have even less time. You might choose not to do literacy work stations daily, but to include them several times a week for independent practice. See Figure 2.3 for a sample block schedule that integrates literacy work stations.

Figure 2.3 **Block Scheduling (90 minutes each for Block A and Block B)**

Reading Workshop

Monday/Wednesday/Friday		Tuesday/Thursday	
Block A		*Block A*	
8:30–8:45	Mini-lesson and read-aloud/shared reading	8:30–9:00	Independent reading/response journals
8:45–9:15	Small-group instruction (guided reading or literature circles) and literacy work stations	9:00–9:15	Class sharing/book talks
Block B		*Block B*	
10:30–10:45	Mini-lesson and read-aloud/shared reading	10:30–11:00	Independent reading/Response journals
10:45–11:15	Small-group instruction (guided reading or literature circles) and literacy work stations	11:00–11:15	Class sharing/book talks

Writing Workshop

Monday/Wednesday		Tuesday/Thursday		Friday	
Block A		*Block A*		*Block A*	
9:20–9:30	Mini-lesson	9:20–9:50	Writing and conferring	9:20–9:45	Writing and conferring
9:30–10:00	Writing and conferring	9:50–10:00	Sharing	9:45–10:00	Class sharing/weekly reflection
Block B		*Block B*		*Block B*	
11:20–11:30	Mini-lesson	11:20–11:50	Writing and conferring	11:20–11:45	Writing and conferring
11:30–12:00	Writing and conferring	11:50–12:00	Sharing	11:45–12:00	Class sharing/weekly reflection

Look realistically at what you can handle. If you have always used worksheets for independent practice, gradually wean yourself off. You might have half your students at literacy work stations while the other half are doing seatwork. This will actually cut your seatwork in half automatically (and you'll have fewer papers to grade and more time to enjoy life).

Plan for Grades

One of the biggest fears teachers share with me is that they won't get enough grades using literacy work stations. I've never seen this happen. If anything, upper-grade teachers have an overabundance of grades.

Begin by determining how many reading (or language arts) grades you really need by the end of

the six- or nine-week grading period. Check with your administrators about expectations; some school systems have minimum requirements, such as twelve grades per each nine weeks in reading. Don't give more grades than you actually need. Also think about what you want those grades to communicate. Be sure your reading and writing grades accurately reflect how students are doing as readers and writers. Continue to assign some grades in traditional ways, such as on test and quiz scores and assigned projects. Some of the things students do at literacy work stations can be graded as well. For example, writing done at the writing work station is a product that can be graded. Book reviews written at the classroom library might be assigned a score. But don't feel that you must grade *everything* students do. You will wear yourself out! Remember that literacy work stations are for *practice*. You do not need to grade everything that students practice. Grades are for evaluation *after* kids have practiced for a time.

If I don't grade it, they won't do it, I'm often told by upper-grade teachers. If you have this problem in your classroom, reevaluate what you're asking students to do for practice. If students are enjoying their work and learning from it, you won't have to hold the accountability ax over their heads every minute of the day. Work that is satisfying provides its own intrinsic rewards. I have found that most students really enjoy the type of practice provided at literacy work stations because it is more interesting to them than mounds of traditional worksheets. Use the ideas at the end of each chapter under "How to Assess/Keep Kids Accountable," and the sharing time question cards provided in Appendix A.

Using Mini-Lessons with Literacy Work Stations

Literacy work stations should always be connected to what you've already taught. They are set up for practice linked to instruction. Beginning literacy work stations time with a brief mini-lesson, or model, will provide focus and direction to the day's independent practice and help students' work be more meaningful. During a mini-lesson, you can show students exactly what you expect them to do at a literacy work station. Whenever you introduce a new strategy, task, or tool, take a few minutes to show and tell kids how they can use it during independent work time. The key to successful mini-lessons is that they are *short* and *focused*, no more than about ten minutes long.

There are three different times to use a mini-lesson: when you're introducing the work station, when you're adding something new to a station, and when you're reviewing or reteaching a station activity. Teachers often assume that they can introduce an activity just once or give students written directions and have them be successful. This is a

mistake; most learners need multiple models on an ongoing basis.

Mini-Lessons at the Beginning of the School Year

At the start of the school year, the mini-lessons you will need to conduct are different from those you'll do later in the year. You might teach one of the mini-lessons suggested below daily for the first two weeks of school. (For more ideas, refer to the "How to Introduce the Work Station" and "What the Teacher Needs to Model" sections in the following chapters.) *Do not assume that students who have used work stations in third grade will know exactly what you expect them to do in fourth grade!*

Begin by having students sit in the large-group teaching area. Tell them explicitly what you expect them to do. Then have two students role play while

Two students help demonstrate a new activity for the spelling station while the class watches during the mini-lesson.

the rest of the group observes. Have the observers tell what they noticed. For example, after you have modeled and explained to students how to use the buddy reading basket with follow-up "Test-Taking Questions" cards found in Appendix D, have two students show the rest of the class what it would look like if they were at that station.

The students modeling might sound something like this:

Student 1: Let's read Chapter 1 of *The Adventure of the Buried Treasure*. It's the one Mrs. Diller read to us this morning during read-aloud.

You're doing a quick model here, so use a book that you have two copies of and that you read aloud earlier that day to save reading time for your demonstration.

Student 2: Okay. Here's a sticky note for you. Be sure to put your name on it, so we can mark where we are in the book when we finish.

Buddy reading basket with task cards.

Both students read silently for a minute or so. Because the teacher has read this particular book aloud already, they are familiar with it. To save time, the teacher tells them to pretend they've finished reading.

Student 1: Let's use the cards to talk about what we just read.

Student 2: (*taking a card from a ring of "Test-Taking Questions" cards*) "Choose a main character. How did he/she feel throughout the story?"

Student 1: One character is Puddles. He's a dog. He sniffs the yard and finds a strange bone buried in his yard. I think he feels excited and curious.

Student 2: Susie is the other main character. She loves her dog, Puddles, and calls him Puds for short. She feels very close to her dog.

Student 1: There are two more characters—Annie and Megan. They try to help Susie dig up the bone and something rusty. The ground is really hard, so they wet the ground and get all muddy while digging. They feel hopeful and determined.

Student 2: What about the big orange cat, Fluffo? Do you think that's a main character?

Student 1: I think Fluffo isn't as important as the others. But I think Fluffo and Puds are going to get into a fight.

The rest of the class listens in and watches these two students read and discuss the first chapter. Then they have a chance to tell what they noticed that the role-modeling students did. Comments might include the following: "They read silently and didn't bother each other." "They used the cards and did a good job of answering the questions." "They took turns talking and looked at each other." "When they were finished, they put their sticky notes with their names in the books to mark their places." Thank all the students for their participation and remind the class to do exactly what they saw modeled when they work at this station.

Here are some examples of what you might say in a variety of role-playing scenarios:

■ *How to use the equipment/materials.* "You'll be using atlases at the Geography Station. Turn the pages carefully and use the table of contents and index to help you find what you need fast. If you're using a map pencil and it breaks, don't sharpen it and disturb others. Instead, place it in the container by our pencil sharpener that says 'needs sharpening.' The materials manager will take care of it at the end of the day. Use a crayon or another colored pencil instead."

■ *How to share materials.* "There are plenty of materials, but you will have to share. If somebody wants a material you're using, use a problem-solving strategy. Ricardo and Stephan, pretend you both want to choose the same book from the classroom library. What can you do?"

■ *How to solve a problem.* "Sometimes a problem may come up at your work station. Maybe a listening tape breaks or you run out of paper at the writing station or someone tries to grab something out of your hand. There are many ways to solve a problem. If something breaks or you run out of something, ask a materials manager for help. If someone is bothering you, tell that person to stop and why. If that person won't stop, take your work to your seat and finish it there until it is time to switch stations. If your problem has to do with taking turns, remember the ways we have to solve that problem." In addition to having students role play solving problems that may come up, you might also write a chart together that explains what to do in a given situation.

■ *How to take turns.* "You will be working with a partner, so you will have to take turns. Decide who will go first and then let the other one

Two students role play how to solve a problem. Work stations rules written by the class are in the background.

go. Switch back and forth. If one of you goes first today, let the other one go first tomorrow. Or play Rock, Paper, Scissors, or flip a coin. Or you could both write your name on a scrap of paper and pull one name to see who goes first. If you're having trouble with someone taking too long, use an egg timer. Then let the other one have a turn. Steph and Louis, please show us what it would look like if you were having trouble taking turns and solved your problem."

■ *Where can I go for help?* "If you need help with materials or something breaks, ask a materials manager. If you have trouble with the computer, ask the computer expert. Or reboot the computer. Or write what happened on a sticky note, and do the alternative activity I've placed there. Don't ask me for help while I'm working with a small group. That will interrupt the others there. LaShonda and Van, please show us what it might look like if you're having a problem at one of the stations. Show us how to get help without interrupting me." Debbie Miller, in *Reading with Meaning* (2002) notes a great solution that her students came up with for the "how do I get help" problem. If there's something that only the teacher can help with, they suggested, write her a note and stick it on the dry-erase board by her table so that when she is free, she can read it.

■ *How to put things away.* "Let's make labels for things that have certain places we need to return them to, so you can always find what you need at the station. It's important to return things where they belong, so the next people can find and use them. Keep materials neat and organized, and be considerate of the people who will be using this station next. Especially think about where you're placing books in the classroom library. We are organizing the books by genre so you can easily find what you want. We'll also have a materials manager who will check on literacy work stations when we're finished to be sure everything's where it needs to be."

Mini-Lessons Later in the Year

You may have to repeat some of the mini-lessons throughout the year for reinforcement. If you notice that students are having trouble settling a dispute, for example, make a note to do a mini-lesson on that the following day. Remember, much modeling produces better behavior at work stations.

In addition, you will be doing other kinds of mini-lessons later in the year. These may consist of quick reviews of how to use particular materials you've already used instructionally. You'll simply remind students of how to use them on their own in the literacy work stations.

For example, you may have used a transparency of a writing sample to demonstrate subject-verb agreement. Tell students you will place this transparency in the "Overhead Materials" notebook for them to use independently at the overhead work station today. Remind them how to use and care for

the materials (including the vis-à-vis or dry-erase pen to edit) and how to put them away neatly. It is a good idea for students to review the procedures that they will use at this work station. Assume nothing and model everything!

Each time you place new materials in a work station, tell the students you have done so. This prepares them for the new task—and heads off any questions they may have that they'd be tempted to interrupt you with while you're working with a small group. You can mention during a writing lesson, for example, that you're placing the list of strong verbs you brainstormed today in the writing work station for them to refer to while they're writing. Remind them that you'll be looking for strong verbs in their writing. Expect to see what you're teaching practiced independently at literacy work stations.

Mini-Lessons Before Quiet Independent Time

You may choose to do mini-lessons before students read independently. Tell students you expect them to try this strategy while reading silently, as well as in the reading they're doing at literacy work stations. For example, you might model how to preview a book, looking at the title, illustrations, and summary on the covers. Be sure to model this several times in read-aloud and shared reading. See the chart of Sample Reading Strategies to Model Before Independent Reading in Figure 2.4.

Management Boards

Many types of management boards can be used for literacy work stations. I've found that classrooms are generally more successful when a teacher uses a management board, although some highly skilled teachers manage without them. The key is for students to know where they're supposed to be, when they're supposed to be there, and what they're supposed to be doing and why.

Figure 2.4 Sample Reading Strategies to Model Before Independent Reading

Note: Choose just one at a time as the focus for your lesson. Stick with that one for a while until you see students applying it!

Before Reading Strategies

- Previewing a book (front and back covers): looking at title, heading, illustrations, summary
- Thinking about what you already know about a topic
- Making predictions about what will happen in the book
- Making a connection to other related stories
- Asking yourself questions about what you might find out in the book

During Reading Strategies

For Comprehension:

- Checking on predictions made about a book
- Creating an image of the story, visualizing
- Making a connection to other related stories
- Asking questions about what is happening
- Predicting what a word will be, based on the first, middle, and last sounds and thinking about what makes sense

For Decoding:

- Breaking a word into parts
- Relating the word to a familiar word
- Skipping the word and going on

- Reading on to get more information on what a word might be
- Reading on to see whether predictions make sense

For Monitoring:

- Self-correcting when something does not make sense
- Seeing whether the sentence sounds right (grammar)
- Rereading a difficult passage, getting another running start

For Fluency:

- Reading faster for momentum and fluency
- Reading the first line of a paragraph and skimming the rest
- Reading what you don't understand slowly and what you do quickly
- Reading parts so they sound like talking; using different voices for different characters

After Reading Strategies

- Looking up really important words in the dictionary
- Creating a metaphor or analogy to understand the story
- Stopping at certain points to think and predict
- Asking yourself questions about what is happening
- Talking to someone else who has read the story
- Paying attention to what's new to you

A pocket chart holds student names and icons for a flexible management board.

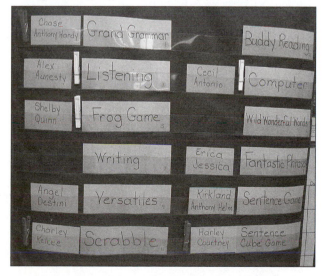

The simplest type of management board is a basic pocket chart. Simply write or type each student's name on a card and place two names on the left-hand side in each row. To the right of each pair of names, place one or two icons to show where those children are to go during literacy work station time. The icons in Appendix A can be reduced to fit in a pocket chart. At the end of each day, move the icon down to the next space so that the students' activities change the next day. This way you don't have to keep extra charts to be sure everyone gets to go to every station. This method ensures that they do. You also don't have to worry about getting all the work stations "done" in one week. You simply rotate kids from station to station; over time, they automatically get to do everything.

Velcro, construction paper, and posterboard are needed to make this simple management board in a third-grade classroom.

This management board was made by a group of fifth graders. Each group chose something with eight legs, because they had eight stations to choose from.

Kid-made icons show students where to go on this management board.

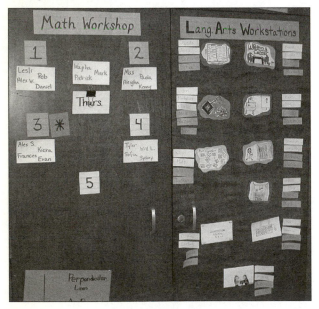

If you don't have a pocket chart or have no room for one, you might set up a space divided into squares on a magnetic chalkboard or make a similar chart with Velcro dots. If you use a magnetic chalkboard space, put a small piece of magnetic tape on the back of each card and icon. If you use a Velcro dot chart, put a Velcro dot on the back of each card.

Some upper-grade teachers I know worked with their students to create a class management board as a problem-solving exercise. Plus, it saved the teacher's time in having to create the board! Kids created their own icons for the work stations, then divided into small groups and created a rotation that would work for the whole class.

A management board showing literacy work stations, independent project work, and a small reading group for one day.

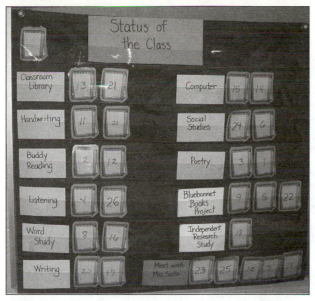

In one classroom, we devised a management board where some students go to work stations, some do independent projects (with prior teacher approval), others are in book clubs or literature circles, and the teacher meets with one small group.

Regardless of how you set up your management board, begin by having students go to one work station daily. Eventually, you may decide to have students go to two a day, depending on your grade level and schedule. You'll need two copies of each icon if students go to two stations a day, so more than one group can use that same station. If you have students go to two stations daily, simply place two different icons beside the pair of students' names to show where they will go first and second. Students can read the board and know where to start and where to move to for their second station. Again, simply move the icons down to the next row beside the next pair of names daily.

Don't worry too much about getting the management board to work perfectly at first. You'll be able to work it out with your students. Just know that you might have to do a bit of tweaking along

the way. All the teachers I've worked with have come up with a system that fits both their needs and the needs of their kids. And these boards look different from classroom to classroom.

Work Stations Time

Each day after independent reading time, let students review the management board and move right into their work stations. Or place the icon for independent reading time on your management board as the first one for each group, followed by the icon for the literacy work station where you'd like them to work. In that case, you'd do a mini-lesson followed by independent reading time and literacy work stations time. Students should know what to do and get busy right away because of the modeling you have done. At the beginning of the year, while students are learning to use the work stations, you should circulate, observe, and give guidance as needed. Only when classroom management is under control will you be able to focus on good small-group teaching. Invest the first month or so of school in teaching routines to your students and watching them practice at literacy work stations so that you will be able to work with small groups in the following months. Once you have begun small-group instruction, you must remain aware of what students are doing at work stations. Suggestions for how to accomplish this are given in upcoming chapters in the sections called "How to Assess/Keep Kids Accountable."

Sharing Time

After independent reading and work stations time, it is useful to have a brief sharing time with the class. This provides an opportunity for students to reflect on what they've done that day and deepen their learning. During sharing time, gather the students in your large-group teaching area, much as you did during the mini-lesson. This time, lead a short, focused discussion about what they did and

Sharing time follows independent reading and literacy work stations time.

learned during independent reading, in small groups, and at literacy work stations. You might find it useful to post one specific question to reflect on each day. Some teachers put the questions on individual cards and have a student choose one for the focus each day. See Appendix A for sample cards. Here are some possibilities for sharing:

■ What did I learn during independent time today?

■ What did I enjoy doing during independent time today? Why? What did I learn there?

■ What didn't I like during independent time today? Why not?

■ What did I do to help myself be a better reader today?

■ What did I do to help myself be a better writer today?

■ What did I learn about word study today? New words? A new strategy?

■ What do I think we should change at work stations? Why?

■ What else would I like to do at work stations? What and how would that help me learn?

■ How did I solve a problem at work stations today?

■ How did I help someone else solve a problem at literacy work stations?

Frequently Asked Questions

As you read the following questions, keep in mind that there is no one right answer to any of them. Management styles are as varied as classroom teachers. There is no one ideal way of managing literacy work stations that will solve all problems. The best advice I can give is to use your common sense in dealing with challenges that arise.

How many students should work together at a station?

Most problems that occur in work stations are interpersonal. The troubles are usually among the students working there: kids don't share, they argue, they get too loud, they get physical with each other. Many teachers I've worked with have found that having only two students at a work station reduces noise and behavior problems dramatically. The old saying "Two's company, three's a crowd" seems to hold true. You may want to start the year like this, then adjust accordingly. It is your choice. Do what seems to work best in your classroom.

How many work stations should I have? How often should I change them?

You must decide how many stations you and your students can handle. Some teachers have just three or four kinds of stations but more than one kind of each. For example, you might have two different listening stations, three social studies stations stored in different clear plastic shoe boxes, and two buddy reading stations, along with the classroom library and a writing station.

Many teachers who use work stations effectively have eight to ten stations (including some stationary and some portable ones) that they use all year long. Set up a classroom library and writing station first. (See Chapters 3 and 4.) Then think about adding the ones that are easy to set up, such as listening, buddy reading, spelling, handwriting, computer, and newspaper stations. Ideas for these are in Chapter 5. The teachers who use a wide variety of stations do not change activities every Friday, so having this many is not as much work as it might sound. The practice activities that are moved into the work stations are things that the students have already learned to do with the teacher during instruction. Students practice them during work station time. A variety of work stations keeps kids'

interest high. You don't have to be tied into a Monday–Friday rotation, so don't worry about making sure every student gets to every work station in a week. Each chapter lists "Ways to Keep This Station Going Throughout the Year" to help you keep the stations novel and interesting.

Some teachers have half their students do seatwork while others are at work stations to reduce the number of stations when they are first making the transition. If you choose this option, you will need fewer work stations. Remember that you might have multiples of a station, such as two buddy reading stations or two listening stations, as mentioned above. You might have four students working at two computers. Also, once students are working in small groups, you will not need as many work stations. You might have a group or two in a literature circle as well as a group working with you in guided reading.

Throughout the year, you may replace some of your earliest stations with ones that require more thinking. For example, you might open a drama or poetry station. You might set up a word study station, as well as one for content areas (see Chapters 6 through 9).

Which stations are best for me to set up in my classroom?

Think about what you're teaching and what your students' needs are. Always consider the combination of curriculum as well as your kids. Know that your stations may change throughout the year. You may want to start with some of the easy-to-set-up stations from Chapter 5, and then, as you get to know your students, substitute some different stations to best meet their needs. Use the charts in Appendixes B and C to help you thoughtfully choose a variety of literacy work stations that build comprehension, fluency, phonics, vocabulary, and writing.

Where do all the materials come from?

Begin with materials you already have in your classroom. Look at your teaching resource materials,

Half the class reads at their seats while the other half goes to work stations.

including teachers' guides, professional books, and supplemental materials. You may have out-of-adoption resources that can be adapted. Or you might be the parent of older children who have outgrown books and games that are stored in your attic or basement. Check with other teachers on your grade level and share resources. You might be surprised by how much you already have that can be used.

Should my students do work stations every day?

If you want work stations to become part of your classroom routine, it is best to have students work at them at least three days a week. Some upper-grade teachers run literacy stations daily and work with small groups during this time; in these classrooms students know what's expected of them and work well independently (most days). Having work stations on Fridays is not often enough to provide much valuable practice time, and students may

treat them like "indoor recess." You don't want this to happen!

How long should work station time last?

Most teachers have their students stay at a work station for about twenty to thirty minutes. If your students can sustain working there longer, use more time. Remember that you might have students doing independent reading for twenty to thirty minutes, followed by work stations time of the same length. If you choose to have students go to two work stations daily, this will double the time they spend there.

If you let kids stay too long in one work station, behavior problems often begin to occur. It's a good idea to keep an eye on the time and move students to a new activity before trouble starts. Many teachers keep a timer by their small-group reading table and set it for the number of minutes that students will be at a station. When the bell rings, students know to clean up and/or switch stations.

How do I decide who should work with whom?
There are many ways to pair students. Probably the most important starting consideration is that the partners get along with each other. If they don't, work stations are doomed to fail. Decide on your purposes for the grouping before deciding who will work together. For example, if you want students to practice activities on the cutting edge of their development, if you want them to do things that are just a little challenging but within their range of accomplishing, then you might pair students at a similar level who need practice with the same type of thing.

Some teachers pair students heterogeneously so they can help each other. This has its place, too. For example, if you're working on fluency, you might pair a child who is a bit more fluent with one who is not as fluent to provide a good model.

At times, you might want students to choose their own partners. This may motivate some learners because of the added choice provided.

Think carefully about how you set up your grouping at work stations, and be flexible. Vary the partners occasionally to keep interest high.

Should the students decide or should I choose which stations they will go to?
Research has shown that choice helps motivate students. However, when it comes to classroom management, many teachers do better initially giving students "controlled choices" at literacy work stations. It is generally easier to start the year by assigning students where you'd like them to go and eventually turning over more of the choice to them than to begin by letting everyone go wherever they'd like and ending up with chaos!

Provide choice within each literacy work station by having several open-ended tasks children can choose from. This allows students to have some choice in a controlled way, which will help estab-

lish a predictable routine. For example, at the listening station there may be three different tapes and several types of response sheets for students to choose from. (See Appendix D for samples.) If you include some nonfiction as well as fiction tapes, as well as a variety of response forms, students must apply their understanding of which graphic organizer (response sheet) matches the type of text (fiction or nonfiction selection). Put out more than one task to prevent the problem of "early finishers." Make sure there are always plenty of things to do at one station so students don't have to interrupt you to find out what to do next because they finished before everyone else.

What if some students finish before everyone else? What if someone isn't finished when it's time to switch to another work station?
If the activities in the station are varied, openended, and interesting, students generally won't finish early. (If they do, look at what you put in that station. Perhaps it doesn't have enough depth to it.) However, some students may become engaged in an activity and not be ready to move on to the next station. Be flexible! Allow the student to take his or her work to a desk to finish, and skip that rotation for that student. One exception to this is the computer station, because some students will never want to move to another station.

What if students misbehave during literacy work station time?
Students sometimes don't do what they're expected to do during work station time. They should be made aware beforehand of what they are supposed to do and what will happen if they break the rules. I use the "one strike and you're out" rule in literacy stations. This time is highly motivating to most of the class, and they don't like to miss it, so if they know the teacher means business, they are more likely to do what is expected. I simply tell students, "This is what you may do at the stations. This is what you may *not* do. If you break the rules, you

will have to leave the station at once." I don't give idle threats or warnings. I tell them what I expect and then follow through.

If you have students who on occasion can't handle the "freedom" of going to literacy work stations, you might have them do traditional seatwork instead. When they see how much fun their peers are having learning together, they may be motivated to get their behavior back on track.

Some teachers have a chair or two by their small-group table for students who have not behaved appropriately during work stations. This sometimes works better than sending those students back to their desks, where they act out to keep trying to get the teacher's attention. They often tend to pay attention to the reading lesson and sometimes even learn something from the vicarious learning experience.

Other teachers have misbehaving students write a note of apology to anyone they've interrupted and tell what they will do differently next time they go to that work station. Some have students draw a picture to show how their behavior will change when they return to that station.

If you find the same students having to be removed from work stations day after day, take a look at them. You may want to design an individualized plan for those students' independent work to help them practice what they can be successful with.

How do I get started?

Most intermediate teachers begin with getting independent reading and writing responses going well during the first couple of weeks of school. To do so, they set up a classroom library and a writing station as their first work stations; then they move into teaching literacy work stations routines. You could introduce one station per day for a week, gradually presenting tasks that you've taught with and creating "I Can" lists or directions for each station with your class. Or open two a day if you and your kids can manage it. Start with easy-to-set-up stations,

such as those suggested in Chapter 5. At the end of a week, have students go to just one station for ten to fifteen minutes. You might put four students per station, assigning each a partner, to begin. Or you could have half your students go to stations while the other half works independently at their seats; then have them switch.

Gradually introduce additional stations over the next week or so until you have enough to engage all students in meaningful tasks. Begin using a management board when you have introduced enough work stations to warrant one (at least five stations). Students will catch on easily to how this works, especially if they have done it in previous grades. Be sure to end independent work time with sharing time, so you can problem solve with the class and keep them accountable. Add new tasks and extend the time at literacy work stations accordingly. For example, move from ten minutes to twenty as there is more for students to do there.

Solving Ongoing Problems

Problems students mention during sharing time can become the next day's mini-lessons. For example, when one third grader said she had trouble at the writing work station because she couldn't think of a topic, we reviewed how writers get ideas in the next day's mini-lesson and began to create a "Writing Ideas" chart. Later, I suggested to her teacher that she place this chart in the writing station so students could refer to it for help. In another classroom students were not using the newspaper station materials correctly. They were playing around with the vis-à-vis pens and not being productive. Instead of suggesting to this teacher that she close the work station because students weren't acting appropriately, I showed her how to do a maintenance mini-lesson on how to use the *Mini Pages* newspaper, a nationally syndicated news supplement for students, in this station. The teacher had assumed the students would know how to use these materials and had never really taught any lessons on how to use them. In the mini-lesson the class brainstormed an "I Can" list. They came up with the following:

I Can . . .

- Read the news articles first.
- Circle the main idea of one article. Write a one-paragraph summary about it.
- Then use the pens to do the activities on the last page.
- If you finish, choose another *Mini Pages* to read.
- Clean up when finished. Close the pen tightly.

These ideas were posted at this station and behavior improved. The teacher also added paper for students to record their work so she could see what they'd done.

Although good teaching should head off many problems, trouble will still brew from time to time. When a problem arises at work stations, begin by looking at what could have caused it. The first place to look is at your own teaching. (Ouch!) I used to look at the students first until I realized that many problems were related to my instruction. Ask yourself these questions:

- How did I model this new task or use of materials? Did I model at all? Did I model enough? Should I remodel?
- How long has this material or task been in the work station? (It might be time to replace it to keep interest high.)
- Are the materials at the work station well organized and easy to use?
- Have I recently had students change partners? Is it time for new partners? Would someone work better alone?
- Is there an "I Can" list or directions written with the students posted in the station? Does it need to be updated?

- Is there enough for students to do at this station? What materials need to be changed or added?
- Is this activity or task at the student's independent level? Is it too hard or too easy? How can I create more differentiation at this work station?
- Is the activity or task interesting and meaningful to the student? If not, what can I change to make it so?

Reflection and Dialogue

Consider the following:

1. Work with a partner to plan your classroom space. Use suggestions from this chapter.
2. Work with your team to look at scheduling and how you can carve out time for literacy work stations.
3. Discuss how you will get grades with your team. Have a plan in place before starting literacy work stations.
4. Pick the stations that you'll introduce during the first week. Choose ones that look easier to set up. You might work with a partner to do this.
5. Plan several mini-lessons for these work stations with a colleague. Think about everything that kids might possibly not do right, and include those things in a mini-lesson. That way students will know exactly what you expect. You might videotape a mini-lesson and share it with other teachers from your grade level. Discuss how this mini-lesson helped your students.
6. Choose a literacy work station from your classroom that you've had trouble with. Brainstorm with a colleague what to do to improve the work station.
7. With a colleague, develop a plan for behavior during literacy work stations. Let students know exactly what will happen if they don't

follow the rules. Meet with that colleague on a weekly basis to discuss your plan until the students' behavior is well established. Readjust your plan as needed.

8. Create a management board. Go on a "field trip" to other teachers' rooms to see their management board ideas.

Independent Reading and the Classroom Library

As students enter this classroom first thing in the morning, three of them head for the classroom library to choose new books for independent reading. Laurie sits by the tub labeled "Biographies." She thumbs through the titles there and pulls out *Milton Hershey*. She reads the front and back covers and tells her friends sitting beside her, "I think I'd like reading about this guy's life. He did a lot with chocolate."

"I'm looking for a book on desert plants. I'm learning about the saguaro cactus for my inquiry project and am ready to take notes. Have you chosen your topic yet?" adds Ricardo as he reaches for the "Life Science Books" tub. He browses through the indexes of several books and chooses two that interest him. He shows them to Sarah, who also decides to look for a book for her inquiry project.

"Which basket would have books about germs in it?" she asks.

"They should be in the 'Life Science Books' tub, too. It's the one I've been using," Ricardo tells her. He hands the book basket to Sarah, and she finds two books: *Germs Make Me Sick!* and *Achoo! The Most*

A well-designed classroom library helps kids choose appropriate books.

Interesting Book You'll Ever Find About Germs. She browses through them and signs them out in the Book Checkout notebook. Then she looks through the "Historical Fiction" tub. This is her favorite

A checkout system makes keeping track of classroom library books easy.

genre, and she just finished reading *Sarah, Plain and Tall* yesterday. She chooses *Little House in the Big Woods* and adds it to the stack of books she wants to read next.

About thirty minutes later it's independent reading time; these same students are reading the books they chose from the classroom library. Everyone is seated around the room reading silently while their teacher confers with individual students about their reading. On each student's desk is a "next read" stack of books; the classroom library is closed during this time. Students are expected to choose books ahead of time for independent reading to minimize interruptions.

After independent reading time, it's time for literacy work stations. The classroom library has reopened. Now two other boys lie on pillows here. One is leafing through a tub of books labeled "Earth Science Books." The other is reading a *Cricket* magazine and occasionally showing an interesting part to his partner. Eventually, the first boy chooses *Eyewitness Explorers: Rocks and Minerals* and begins

to read. They lie on the floor reading silently for the next fifteen minutes while the rest of the students are involved at a variety of other literacy work stations.

Why Have a Classroom Library?

Many upper-grade teachers I've worked with tell me they don't have space in their classrooms for a classroom library. I tell them they can't afford not to make space for one if they want their students to become avid independent readers. I wonder where children will go to get books. Having a classroom library makes books accessible to students. When we surround students with books in the classroom, they are enticed to sample them and find out for themselves how wonderful the world of literacy can be. We can no longer guarantee that students will go home and read like we may have been able to ten or twenty years ago. We have to make children want to read by surrounding them with an irresistible environment that encourages them to come and explore there.

Can't students just use the school library? I'm often asked. Of course, students should be encouraged to use resources in the school library, too. But it's not always convenient to send children to the library, and it's hard to monitor their choices there. By having a classroom library, you are available to overhear conversations there and conveniently aid students in their book selections. If you expect students to do independent reading, you must have books available for them to use. Relying on the school library or books from home won't provide the resources all children need to participate actively in independent reading. At one of the schools I work with, teachers in grades 3–6 had no classroom libraries at first. But when they added excellent classroom libraries, their students began to thrive as independent readers. Student talk about books increased in the classroom, and students could often be seen in the classroom library sharing books with each other.

What Students Do in the Classroom Library

The classroom library is a place where students are expected to browse books and choose reading materials both for independent reading time and for inquiry projects. You should also see and hear students talking with each other about the books they've read. It isn't necessarily silent all the time; rather it's a spot in which students read, write, and talk about books. You should see your students engaging in the following kinds of activities at the classroom library:

■ *Reading, writing, and talking about authors.* Author studies help generate interest in books written by those authors. Series books are especially appealing to intermediate students, so highlight some authors of series books, such as Mary Pope Osborn (*Magic Tree House*), Jean Craighead George (*Julie of the Wolves* and others), and Gary Paulsen (adventure stories such as *Hatchet*). Studying authors also helps students understand where writers get ideas

for their books and strengthens connections between reading and writing. Bookmark some author Web sites to create interest. Post the author Web site on the tub containing those books, along with a photo of the author if you can print one off the Internet. For a list of favorite author Web sites for intermediate students see Appendix B.

■ *Using a "How to Choose Books" chart to choose books for independent reading and inquiry.* The teacher creates this chart with students to help them select books that are "just right" for reading independently. See the mini-lesson in this chapter for help with doing this.

■ *Reading and recommending books to others.* Students should be encouraged to talk with each other about the books they are reading and have read. You should overhear "book talk" in your classroom library. Some recommendations might also be written as notes to classmates. Others might be posted on a "graffiti board" made of bulletin board paper.

Labeled tubs in a classroom library highlight and picture authors.

A chart made with a third-grade class is posted in the classroom library to help kids with book choice.

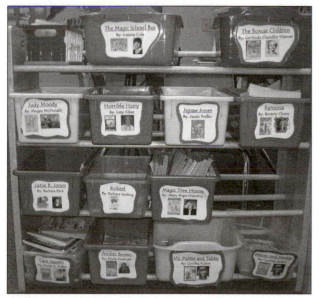

Fourth graders write book recommendations and place them in library pockets matching the genre in the classroom library.

Students write book recommendations on sticky notes and put them on a chart in the classroom library.

- *Reading independent-level books.* With teacher guidance, students should learn to choose books they can read independently. This is important so students can sustain their reading for longer periods of time, thus getting more practice.
- *Writing and posting book reviews of classroom library materials.* Students enjoy reading each other's book reviews, written to inform and influence others to read the books they've read. These are not book reports, which are usually written to "prove" to teachers that they've read books. Instead, these reviews encourage peers to read more.
- *Writing their thinking about books on sticky notes as they read classroom library books.* Place pads of sticky notes in the classroom library so students can jot down their connections, questions, and other thinking as they read. These sticky notes can then be used in students' discussions about the books they've read. Another idea is to have students jot down notes about a book on a sticky note and fasten it on a chart or to the front of a book to encourage others to read it.
- *Marking favorite pages with bookmarks.* See Appendix B for sample bookmarks on which

students might record their thinking as they read. These thoughts can be shared in student discussions about the books they're reading.

- *Recording titles of books read and books they'd like to read* in individualized reading logs. See the mini-lesson section in this chapter called "How to Keep a Reading Log" for ideas.
- *Checking out classroom library books to take home.* Use a checkout system such as a notebook with a page for each student to write the date and title of books checked out to help you keep up with where the books are. This is a good way for students to have appropriate books to take home for practice reading.
- *Returning materials to labeled containers when finished with them.* Having students help set up the library at the start of the year will enable them to do a better job of keeping your classroom library well organized. Expect students to put materials back where they belong as they use the classroom library.

How to Set Up the Classroom Library

Begin by finding a space that will stand out to students and other visitors to your classroom. If you value reading, your classroom should show it. A corner works well for a classroom library. If you can't find a corner, create one by positioning a

An inviting library draws kids in to read.

bookshelf at a 90-degree angle against a wall to create a nook. Just be sure you have a full view into the classroom library! Choose sturdy bookshelves or even line the floor along the walls with tubs of books. Most excellent classroom libraries have at least two bookshelves. Some teachers build shelves with cinder blocks and boards under chalkboards to create space for a classroom library. Others use built-in bookshelves (that were already in their rooms) and plan their library around them. Some teachers use rain gutters attached under the chalkboard to create display areas for books. You may also use a metal spinning bookcase, which is perfect for paperback novels.

Put an attractive rug in the classroom library to define the space and make the area comfortable for sitting and browsing. Add colorful matching pillows for students to snuggle up to while reading. Place comfortable seating in the area, too. A beanbag chair or two, a small bench, or even a small sofa or rocker makes this space inviting. A silk ficus tree or clay pots of inexpensive brightly colored silk flowers breathes life into the space. Adding clip-on or table lamps creates an ambience and shows the students that you care enough to make this a beautiful place for them.

Pay attention to the wall area (or a bulletin board) surrounding your classroom library. You'll want some space devoted to displays to motivate and support readers. At the start of the year you

This library is loved by the students with autism who work in this special education resource room.

might leave this wall space empty to make room for your students' response writing, newspaper clippings about current events, library rules, and other charts that you'll write with your students. Throughout the year, these displays will change based on what your students are saying about and doing in the classroom library.

You might consider creating a genre wall as part of this display. Build the genre wall with your students as you read aloud to them throughout the year. Begin with labels for a fiction side and a nonfiction side of the wall. You might even color-code these signs with, for example, white for fiction and blue for nonfiction. If you do this, color-code your library book storage tubs as well, using white labels on tubs for fiction and blue labels on tubs for nonfiction. Make labels for various kinds of fiction, including "historical fiction," "humorous fiction," "mystery," "realistic fiction," and "fantasy." Also make labels for various kinds of nonfiction, includ-

ing "biography," "news articles," "physical science," "reference books," "geography," and "history."

Choose powerful examples of each new genre to read aloud. After you read each book, scan its cover and display it as a reminder or exemplar of that genre. Or place the book in a zippered plastic bag stapled to your bulletin board. Show students how to use the genre wall to think about the kinds of books they'd like to read as well as how to return books to the proper bins on the bookshelves. Record what you're learning about each genre, too.

Other wall displays for your classroom library might include charts made with your students. For example, at the start of the year, create charts on classroom library rules and book checkout procedures. These charts can be made simply with 9-by-12-inch construction paper and markers, so they don't take up too much space (or time in making them). It's best not to plaster your walls with reading posters from commercial sources. Students tend

This "genre wall" is placed near the classroom library. Books read aloud to introduce the genre are placed in labeled zippered plastic bags to visually "anchor" kids' learning about different kinds of text.

to ignore these over time as they become like wall-paper.

The next thing you'll need is some plastic tubs to put the books in. Measure your shelves carefully so the tubs fit well. I prefer clear plastic shoe boxes because the books usually fit nicely into them. Remember that an important part of a classroom library is its organization. How would you like to shop in a bookstore with books shelved in random order? The containers will help you organize books in a variety of ways. They might be arranged by genre, topic, author, series, and/or reading level. The best way to get students to use the library in the way you'd like them to is to organize the books *with* them. See the section called "How to Introduce the Classroom Library" in this chapter for more information.

Materials

An excellent classroom library may include the following materials:

- Sturdy bookshelves, labeled "fiction" and "nonfiction," to store books and help define the space.
- Spinning bookrack for displaying series books, books by a highlighted author, or theme-related books.
- A wide variety of books and other print materials, consisting of about one-third fiction, one-third informational text, and one-third other kinds of reading materials, such as magazines, newspapers, poems, plays, biographies, and how-to books.
- Books and other print materials written by students, including class-made books and student-authored text in both fiction and nonfiction.
- Containers that hold sorted books and are labeled by the students.
- Comfortable seating (beanbag chairs, small sofa, and/or large pillows).

- A silk or real plant(s) to enliven the space.
- A lamp.
- A rug.
- A tape recorder (for playing soft music).
- Book reviews written by the class and by individual students.
- A book checkout system.
- Forms and paper with pencils attached on clipboards for writing responses and book reviews.
- Bookmarks.
- Sticky notes.
- Discussion cards to use after reading (*52 Fabulous Discussion-Prompt Cards for Reading Groups* by Laura Robb has premade card stock cards that you can teach with and then move to the classroom library for after-reading discussion).
- "How to Choose a Book" chart made by the class.
- "How to Check Out a Book" chart made by the class.
- "Classroom Library Rules" chart made by the class.

How to Introduce the Classroom Library

After you have set up your classroom library, you'll want to introduce it to your students so they will know how you expect them to behave in this area. Don't assume that because they've been to the school library or have had a classroom library in another grade level that they will behave as you'd like them to in *your* classroom library.

Gather the students in or near this area and point out the way you have thoughtfully planned the space. Or plan it with them if you don't have it set up yet. Show them the comfortable seating you've provided and tell them how you expect them to take care of the materials there. Explain how you'd like the rug positioned and how to put books and other materials back when they've finished with them. (If you don't have your library set up yet, ask for ideas and possible donations from your class.) Tell your class why you want them to use the classroom library and when it will be appropriate for them to do so. Expect them to care for and manage the library, so it will remain an inviting space. You might create a "Rules for the Classroom Library" chart *with* them so they will have ownership for this space.

You may choose to sort the books and categorize them in tubs before students arrive at the beginning of the year. Many teachers tell me they don't have time to do this, and they cringe at the thought of sorting all their books because they have so many. If so, I recommend that you sort the books *with* your students. This is a great way to teach them about genre as well as to familiarize them with the books available for independent reading. Remember that you don't have to put every book you own in your classroom library to begin. Start small so you and your students don't feel overwhelmed. Organizing the books *with* your class may also help get the books returned to the correct tubs!

For ideas on how to organize your library, take your students on a quick "field trip" to the school library. Have them look for the ways the school librarian organizes the books there. You might take them on a guided tour. Or you might give clipboards to pairs of students and have them jot down ways they see that the library is organized. When you return to class, share ideas such as the categories found in the school library (nonfiction categories such as animals, plants, and machines; biography; picture books; reference; and so forth). Make a list of these possibilities. Then show students how to sort books into two stacks: fiction and nonfiction. Point out what makes a book fiction or nonfiction. You might have students work in pairs to sort books. Give them a few minutes and then ask for all fiction books to be put into one container, such as a tote tray or cardboard box labeled "fiction." Do the same with nonfiction.

A veteran teacher I met recently had lots of old books she couldn't bear to part with, so we sorted books into a third category: "icky" books. Students had to tell why the book was icky—it was outdated, produced in black and white with no color, had missing pages, and so on—before it was placed in this category. This helped the teacher pare down her overcrowded library and provide better choices for the students. She plans to donate the books to children in a foreign land who don't have many books.

On another day, work as a class again to sort the nonfiction books into categories. Look at your col-

Kids helped sort books and decide on category names in this student-organized classroom library.

lection and have students decide on categories. Have students create labels for your book tubs. Some possible categories are plants, animals, rocks and minerals, weather, planets, reference, poetry, math, biography, human body, explorers, wars, magazines, and newspapers.

On a final day, you could sort your fiction books. Categories might include award winners, easier chapter books, challenging chapter books, animal stories, historical fiction, mystery, fantasy, science fiction, folk tales, Magic Tree House, Boxcar Children, Captain Underpants, Avi, Jean Craighead George, Louis Sachar, and short picture books.

If you don't have time to sort all the books as a class, get the kids started by modeling and doing a few together. Then let pairs of students continue to work on sorting while at the classroom library during work stations time. Place sticky notes in the classroom library for them to use as temporary labels while they sort. Students can make permanent labels after the sorting is completed.

How to Introduce Independent Reading

I always introduce independent reading by pulling students up close to me in a large-group teaching space. If a teacher hasn't designated one, I create one by moving student desks. (Students can always help me move the desks back after the lesson.) I've found that when students sit near me, the proximity increases their attention. I begin by talking with the class about what *independent* means. Usually they respond with something such as, "It's when you do it by yourself." I then write *Independent Reading* on the board and explain that this is what we'll be doing today. Next, I make three columns labeled: "Looks Like," "Sounds Like," and "Feels Like." Then I have students take turns telling me in their own words what they think it should *look like* during independent reading. They say things such as, "You should have your eyes on your own book" and "You look like you're interested in your book."

This "looks like, sounds like, feels like" chart brainstormed by fourth graders clearly defines expectations for independent reading time.

As they make suggestions, I chart their ideas and act them out. When a student says, "Stay in your seat," I wiggle in mine and pretend like I'm going to fall off the chair while reading. The kids begin to laugh. I respond with "Have you ever seen anyone look like that during independent reading time?" They all smile as I explain that I had better *not* see that type of behavior during independent reading today. I also add that I will not allow anyone out of his or her seat to choose a book during independent reading. I expect them to have chosen books that will hold their interest. The first few days of independent reading we might read for only ten to fifteen minutes so that all students can be successful.

Then we move on to the "Sounds Like" column. This is usually summed up in one word, which most of them volunteer: *silent*. I explain that during this time it's very important that they be quiet so they can think about their books as they read. The only exception to this is if I'm working with second-language learners who must often

A teacher confers with individuals during independent reading time.

whisper read quietly so they can better understand what they are reading.

The last column that we fill out together is the "Feels Like" column. I ask the students to think about what it feels like when independent reading is going really well. In one fourth-grade classroom, a student said, "It feels like you're in the book." Another added, "You can see what's happening in your mind. You can hear what's happening, too." Students often say things such as, "Relaxing; exciting; it feels like I'm learning new stuff."

Before I send them to their seats to try independent reading for the first time, we read the chart together. I remind them that this is exactly what I expect to see them doing. Then they return to their desks and begin to read. While they read, I walk around and monitor. I look at the books they've chosen and might take notes about their book choices. This is also a time when I might begin to quietly confer with students about their reading.

Independent Reading as Quiet Independent Work Time

Use independent reading as *quiet* independent work time. Build students' reading over time to at least

twenty to thirty minutes daily. Remember that you can use this time to meet with a small group once this routine is well established. See Chapter 2 for sample daily schedules. Literacy work stations are a more *active* independent work time. They usually follow independent reading. The classroom library is used to help students prepare for independent reading, and it also serves as a station students rotate to during literacy work stations for additional reading practice.

Where to Get Books for the Classroom Library

Teachers new to teaching or new to a grade level may not have many books for a classroom library. Here are some ideas to consider:

- Use book clubs such as Scholastic and Troll to order books. You can earn valuable points redeemable for free books. Back-to-school offers are usually best, with enhanced offers of extra points for orders.
- Purchase books from garage sales. There are often sales at public libraries, too. If covers are worn, have students design their own covers for the books. Glue them on with Tacky Glue, an adhesive found at crafts-supply stores.
- Ask parents for donations. Some teachers post "wish lists" on their classroom doors during open house or holiday times.
- Ask parents to donate used books from home. Perhaps students have "outgrown" some books read when younger. These might be given to a lower grade level or set in a tub for easier reading.
- Ask your principal or parent-teacher organization for classroom library books. 101 Book Challenge is a company that sells classroom library collections to schools.
- Frequent discount bookstores for good buys on children's books.

- Use www.ebay.com or www.amazon.com (used books) to buy discount children's books online. Type in the name of an author or series. Collections of books are often available, as well as individual titles.
- Use some student-made books in your classroom library. Save books, poems, and stories written by last year's class to stock a special tub of "Books by Student Authors."
- Borrow books from your school or local public library. Keep close tabs on these, as they must be returned. Ask the librarian for a printout of books borrowed and keep it in a safe place.
- Share books with another teacher. Put out only part of your book collection at a time and then swap them each month or every semester with a colleague.
- Ask your school librarian for copies of old magazines. These are often discarded after several years.
- Ask parents to donate a magazine subscription to your classroom. By the end of the year, you'll have quite a collection that can be used the next year as well.

What the Teacher Needs to Model

Remember that just because students are older doesn't mean they don't need modeling. They still need models, but the modeling changes in relation to the kinds of tasks students are doing and the kinds of texts they're reading. Sometimes the teacher does the modeling, and at other times students might do some of the modeling.

Sample Mini-Lessons for Independent Reading

How to choose books.
Gather your students in or near the classroom library. Move desks if you need to so you can pull students closer to you. Show them a few books you are reading on your own time. For example, in a recent classroom visit I brought along *Shape* magazine, *The Three Junes,* and a book of quotes I was reading. I showed the students that I often read several kinds of texts at once. I explained that I read magazines when I have just a few minutes and want to relax and read about something specific such as exercising or fashion; I read novels when I have more time and want to think more deeply about what I'm reading; I read the book of quotes for inspiration. Szymusiak and Sibberson (2001) write about the idea of a "next read stack" in their book, *Beyond Leveled Books.* Kids love this idea. I also tell the class why I chose these reading materials. For example, I picked *Shape* magazine because I'm looking for some new exercises to try with my handheld weights; I chose *The Three Junes* because an award sticker was on the cover and the blurb on the back seemed interesting; I selected the book of quotes because I love words and quotes are short and don't take much reading time but provide a lot of fuel for my thinking.

After I show them the books I'm reading and explain how I chose my books, I invite students to start their own next read stacks. Some students bring books and magazines from home; others use books from the school library; many choose reading material from the classroom library. These next read stacks can be kept on the edge of students' desks or in zippered plastic bags inside their desks or in individual storage spaces elsewhere in the classroom, such as tote trays or cubbies.

Create a chart with students on "How to Choose Reading Materials." Begin with ideas on how you chose what you're reading to get the chart started:

- It's about something you want to learn.
- It's about a topic you're interested in.
- It's an award winner.
- It's something short because you don't have much time.

Post this chart in or near your classroom library so students can refer to it easily. It will be a reminder if they're having trouble choosing what to read next. Along with this lesson (which you will probably refer to several times, especially at the start of the school year), teach students how to recommend books to each other. This peer talk about books and reading will do more to help students choose appropriate books than anything.

How to recommend books.

Every day, model for students how to recommend books. Linda Gambrell (1996) calls this the "blessing of the books." Several times a day, pick up a book and tell the students a little bit about it, just enough to get them interested in reading it themselves. "Bless" all kinds of reading materials. For example, say, "I read this newspaper article on new video game technology that's being released and thought some of you might be interested in reading it. It's in the News Clippings notebook in the newspaper tub in the classroom library." Be sure to rec-

ommend easier books for the students in your class who need lower-level reading materials. Don't call them easy books, but make eye contact with the readers who might best benefit from these books as you share them with the class. (This also helps alleviate the problem of students who feel embarrassed about having to read easier books because they have reading difficulties.) Recommend a book such as *Way to Go! Sports Poems* by Lillian Morrison for kids who love playing baseball and basketball. Keep the "blessings" short—just a few brief comments, so you can recommend several books at a time.

As you share books with students, they will begin to follow your model and recommend books and articles to each other. When you allow students access to the classroom library, you will hear them talking with each other about books. This is the best place for recommendations to occur, because the books are right there and they can show them to each other. Provide as many opportunities through the day as possible for "book talk." The more kids talk with each other about their reading, the deeper

Real book reviews from magazines, newspapers, and the Internet are kept in a notebook in the classroom library to provide models for students to write their own.

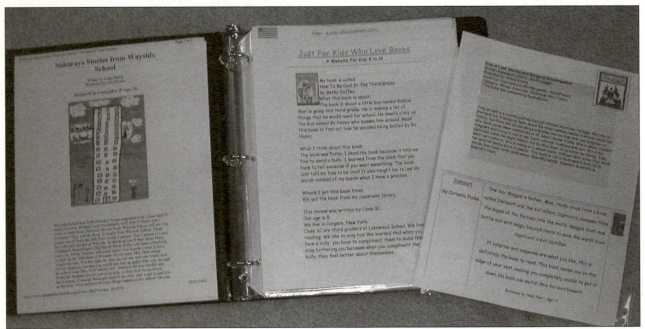

A student records information about a book he just finished reading in his reading log.

their comprehension will be, and the more they'll read.

Teach your class how to write book reviews also. These are in lieu of traditional book reports that are written for the teacher to "prove" that students have read the books. Book reviews, on the other hand, are written for peers so students can give others feedback on what they've read. Bring in sample book reviews from newspapers and magazines. Book order forms from companies such as Scholastic and Troll often have short book reviews on their fliers. You might have a notebook in your classroom library with book reviews in it. Include professional book reviews as well as student ones.

Expose students to online book reviews as well. Go to www.amazon.com and show students how to read and write book reviews. Type in the book title and when the page opens, scroll down to Customer Reviews. You will see an option to Write an Online Review. An option will come up that says Use Our Kid's Review Form. There is a form for students to fill out and submit. This is real-life book reviewing at its best! You might demonstrate how to do this using a computer projection system, if you have one in your classroom. Other Web sites with book reviews written by children include

www.alanbrown.com and www.spaghettibookclub. org.

If students get ideas of books they'd like to read next, they might put them in their reading response folders, explained in more detail in the next chapter. There are forms in Appendix C they can use to record their "Things I Want to Read" ideas and a plan for library visits.

How to keep a reading log.

To model how to keep a reading log, I show students my personal reading log kept simply in a lovely journal. I write down the month, book title, author, and genre whenever I finish a book. I record the information only when I've completed a book. If I wrote down every title I ever started, it wouldn't be as useful to me as a reader. I don't write a summary of every book I've read; if I had to, I'd probably stop using my log. I use my reading log to make recommendations to friends. I like looking through it and chronicling my life according to the books I read; I also set a reading goal to complete one book per month. This log, which I've kept since 1996, is very special to me. Students love seeing it; it shows what real readers do. I don't ask students to do something I wouldn't do as a reader or writer myself.

This sample teacher reading log models the teacher's reading life.

6-03 • Sea Glass by Anita Shreve - realistic fiction	• Girl with a Pearl Earring by Tracy Chevalier - historical fiction
• The Power of Full Engagement by Jim Loehr & Tony Schwartz - nonfiction	• Work Less, Make More by Jennifer White - nonfiction
• Five Quarters of the Orange by Joanne Harris - realistic fiction	• Balzac and the Little Chinese Seamstress by Dai Sijie - fiction
7-03 • Bel Canto by Ann Patchett - realistic fiction	8-03 • A Tree Grows in Brooklyn by Betty Smith - realistic fiction
• Traveling Light by Max Lucado - nonfiction	• Maiden Voyage by Tania Aebi - nonfiction
• Girl in Hyacinth Blue by Susan Vreeland - historical fiction	9-03 • Blessings by Anna Quindlen - realistic fiction
	• Devil Wears Prada by Lauren Weisberger - humorous fiction

In Chapter 4 you will find ideas on how to set up a reading response folder with students. The reading log is one part of that folder. You might use the reproducible reading log pages found in Appendix C. There's also a reproducible page for the folder in Appendix C called Abandoned Books where students can write down titles they started but didn't finish; it is designed to help them identify patterns of poor book choice.

How to Solve Problems That May Arise

To keep your classroom library an attractive, well-used space, below is a list of some possible problems you may encounter, with ideas for solving them.

Differentiating at This Work Station

Think about the various reading levels and interests of students in your classroom, and strive to provide books that match them. One way to differentiate in the classroom library is to have students help you sort through the many chapter books you may have collected. (It seems as though all intermediate students want to read chapter books, even if some of them are too difficult for some members of your class.) Don't "tempt" students to choose books that are too hard by putting too many challenging titles in your classroom library. Instead, you might have students help you sort chapter books into easier chapter books (for most kids in our class) and challenging chapter books (for most

Classroom Library Work Station

Possible Problem	Troubleshooting Ideas
No time to organize your classroom library	Have your class organize the books. Use the suggestions in this chapter.
Messy library	Have students reorganize the book tubs. Determine if it is just one or two students being messy, or if it is a class problem. Assign a student librarian to care for this area. This person might do daily checks to be sure the library stays in order.
Kids playing around and not reading in the classroom library	Post classroom rules made by students, including "Reading only—no playing around." Have students return to their desks if they don't follow the rules.
Kids making inappropriate book choices (too hard or too easy)	Confer with individuals regularly to check what they're reading. Offer help to students needing help with book choice. Encourage students to recommend appropriately leveled books to their classmates. Do mini-lessons with the class on book choice. Create and display charts about how to choose books in this area.
Not enough books	See section on "Where to Get Books for the Classroom Library."
Book hoarders	Have students clean out their desks regularly.
Books disappearing	Use a book checkout system. Limit the number of books students may borrow at a time. They will "police" each other. Have students create "Wanted" posters and post these in the classroom library. Usually, students will watch each other. Have a class meeting to discuss this problem.
Torn or damaged books	Have a container labeled "Book Hospital." Assign student helpers to repair these books. Use book tape (not clear packing tape) on book spines to preserve them. Ask your librarian for some.

Green dots are placed on easier books in this third-grade classroom library to help students who need help with book choice.

kids in our class). Put these books in separate labeled baskets. Or put green stickers on all the easier books in each bin to support book choice for your struggling readers. You will probably have to update these bins several times throughout the year. Remember that most of the independent reading students do should be easier rather than very challenging so they will develop fluency and comprehension.

I don't think it's necessary to level all books in your classroom library. In the intermediate grades, student interest will often provide the fuel needed for a reader to tackle an occasional harder book and succeed. However, some students may need the support of a few tubs of leveled books. If you do decide to level some of your books, you might use Pinnell and Fountas's *Leveled Books for Readers Grades 3–6* for help with leveling. Some teachers use Accelerated Reader levels. Caution: if you do use Accelerated Reader, please *don't* give grades based upon how many points students earn! And don't have most of your classroom library book baskets labeled with Accelerated Reader levels.

Ways to Keep This Station Going Throughout the Year

"My students use the classroom library enthusiastically at first, but lose interest in it over time. What can I do?" is a question I'm often asked. One way to address this issue is to watch what students do there. Ask yourself which tubs are most often pulled off the shelves for browsing. Move less popular choices near the favorites. See which students are excellent at using your library and choosing books. Have them help others. Here are a few more things to try:

- Post student responses and book reviews in the classroom library. You might keep these in a notebook for everyone to read.
- Collect book reviews from Scholastic or Troll book orders. Cut these out and put them in the notebook with student book reviews.
- Read aloud books daily, and add these to the classroom library. Ask for student input about which basket to put them in. Read aloud the first book in a series to evoke interest in that series. Or read aloud a new genre to get students interested in that kind of book. Display the read-aloud book at the front of each basket. Also, do "book blessings" regularly.
- Do author studies with your students. Then prepare baskets of books by the author being studied. Much information can be gleaned from author Web sites. See Appendix B for a list of suggested author Web sites. Change book displays to highlight science, social studies, and health topics being taught. If you are studying rocks and minerals in science, feature those books in your classroom library. You might have a small table or extra student desk on which to display content-area books and materials.

How to Assess/Keep Kids Accountable

Remember that time spent at work stations is practice time, and that you don't need to grade everything your students practice. However, students need to be held accountable for what they're doing at the classroom library to be sure that they are using their time wisely and that they are truly practicing reading, writing, and thinking. Here are some ideas for ensuring accountability at the classroom library:

■ Observe four or five students in the classroom library daily. Jot down notes so you don't forget what you saw and heard them doing.

■ Have students respond in writing to some of the books they're reading. Let them know how many responses you expect and how you will grade them. Sample rubrics can be found in Appendix C.

■ Collect student reading logs weekly. If you have twenty-five students in your class, look at five each day. If you have two classes of students, do the same; however, you'll be able to examine the logs only every other week this way. Look at what students are reading. Are they reading a balance of fiction and nonfiction? Are they reading books that are too easy or too difficult? Confer with students individually to discuss patterns you notice and to find out how their reading is going. Use this information to stock your library with the kinds of books that will best meet your students' needs.

How This Station Supports Student Achievement on State Tests

The classroom library supports independent reading by providing interesting and accessible books and other print materials for *all* students. As students read daily in independent reading, as well as at the classroom library during literacy work stations time, their reading stamina increases. Students need to practice reading for longer chunks of time so they will be prepared for the amount of

reading they must do on state-mandated reading tests. Using a genre wall familiarizes students with a variety of text structures, which will improve reading comprehension. Reading from a series of books also provides support for comprehension as students become familiar with the same characters and settings across several books. Providing test-taking question cards that ask the same kinds of questions as your state reading test will also give students the practice they need to be successful on that test. See Appendix D for sample test-taking question cards. Have students use these after they read books in the classroom library. (These can also be used at the buddy reading work station, as described in Chapters 2 and 5.)

Reflection and Dialogue

Consider the following:

1. Is your classroom library inviting to readers? What could you do to make your library more appealing? Ask your class for suggestions.

2. How are the books organized in your classroom library? Work with a colleague to share ideas on library organization. Visit each other's classrooms and talk about what's working and what needs to be changed.

3. What do you need more of in your classroom library—informational text, biography, historical fiction, reference books, magazines? Take an inventory.

4. What would you like to add to your classroom library—writing materials, an author study, discussion cards? Ask your students for suggestions.

5. Observe your students in the classroom library. How independently do they choose and read books there? What do you learn from their conversations? Use this information to support their choice of books and to help them grow as readers.

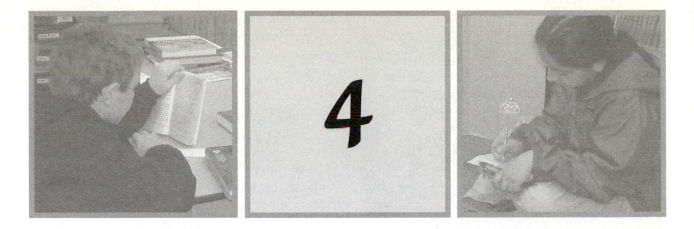

Response Writing and the Writing Work Station

Two students sit at a small table by a bulletin board. They are each writing something different. Maria is completing an adventure story about two fourth-grade friends; she has been writing this short chapter book for about a week and uses her time at the writing work station to continue what she did in writing workshop. Each student has a writing folder stored in a crate under the writing work station table so it is easy for them to access their work. Miguel is working on a poem about hurricanes; he has enjoyed studying this topic in science and is writing about what he learned in this poem. He plans to post his poem at this station when it is finished. Maria refers to the editing suggestions on the nearby bulletin board after she finishes writing her chapter. Then she gives it to Miguel to read for feedback. She is eager to publish this piece so it can be placed in the classroom library. When finished, Miguel asks her to listen to his poem so far. He will put it in the works-in-progress section of his writing folder and work on it next time he comes to the writing work station.

In another classroom down the hall, two students sit on the floor at their writing work station. Their teacher has created a writing space with a tri-fold science project board, which is propped up beside them to create a writing nook. They are reading a list of possible writing ideas on the project board and talking about what they will write about next. They decide to write a ballad about the Oregon Trail, a topic they have recently studied. They look through a notebook of sample ballads the teacher has collected and placed in this station for help. Then they clip a blank piece of paper onto a clipboard and begin to write together. The writing partners periodically refer to their social studies book, which the teacher has placed in a basket labeled "Reference Materials." They also pull out a copy of *The Scholastic Rhyming Dictionary* to help them with word choice.

All these writers have specific purposes and audiences in mind. They are using tools the teacher has provided right there in the writing work station so they have easy access. They are

Two fifth graders sit at an inviting bistro table to write.

using their partners for support, planning, and getting response. They are involved in high-quality writing at well-designed writing work stations. They are practicing what their teachers have modeled during writing time.

Why Have a Writing Work Station?

Setting up a special space for writing shows students, parents, and administrators that you care about writing instruction. It extends the time available in the school day for writing by providing students with the opportunity to experiment with a variety of writing forms, as well as to continue work on pieces from writing workshop. It gives learners a chance to try out different types of writing, such as poems, biographies, news articles, persuasive letters, and book reviews, as well as more traditional stories and reports.

The writing station is a place to display charts developed about good writers and high-quality writing, as well as to store materials writers use, such as dictionaries and thesauri. It provides opportunities for preadolescent writers to use some novel writing supplies such as special stationery, gel pens, and clipboards, which may motivate the most reluctant of them. At the writing station, students

get to talk with other writers about their writing, asking for feedback and planning together. They can display and view writing by fellow student authors.

What Students Do at the Writing Work Station

A wide variety of writing activities should be available at the writing work station throughout the year. A list of ideas follows for you to choose from. Many of these ideas focus on how to get started, which is what most kids have trouble with when sitting at the writing work station and looking at a blank piece of paper. Read on for ideas of what students might do at the writing station. They are listed by categories to help you plan.

Getting Ideas/Getting Ready to Write

■ *Writing a variety of things—letters, lists, character sketches, directions, stories, informational text, news articles, chapter books . . .* Teachers should provide models of how to compose different forms first and gradually post samples in the writing station to help students remember and understand the structure of these forms. It's best to add each new form of writing as you've modeled with it in whole-group instruction.

■ *Writing a description—of a magazine picture, of a classmate, of a teacher, of a pet . . .* Including a folder stocked with magazine pictures, photos of students from your classroom, and pictures of you and your family and pets may provide some students with ideas of what to write about on days when they're stumped. Have blank pages for students to add their own pictures to use as inspiration, too. Post a sample description as a model. Be sure to teach students *how* to write a description before placing these materials here.

■ *Writing to persuade, argue, and request.* This type of writing is often tested on state writing

Samples of different kinds of writing (a book review and a letter) provide models for students at the writing station.

> Dear Miss Taylor, BOOK REVIEW LIT. LETTER
> I read Hatchet chapters 1 to 12 by Gary Paulsen. This is a survival story about a 13 year old boy named Brian. Brian gets stranded in the Canadian wilderness while on a flight to visit his dad for summer vacation. The pilot of the small plane has a heart attack and dies leaving Brian to fly the plane. After surviving a serious plane crash, Brian is using all his strength and wit to cope with his new environment. Up to now, Brian has found shelter, food, water and made fire.
> This story takes the reader on a roller coaster ride of excitement and sadness let downs. I think this is a _____ Story because _____

> 09.14.04 DATE
> Dear Mom & Dad GREETING
> I have great exceptional news! Tonight at 7:30 p.m. is Open House at my school. Everyone will meet in Miss Taylor's room number 252 so we can show our talented work.
> I am so excited enthusiastic to show you our classroom. There is a lot to see. For example, I will show you the Warm Fuzzy chart and jar, my writing binder, and my tote tray. I also want you to see where I sit. Most of all, I want to share the Fantasy Land Brochure I created. I know you will like it.
> I know you have a bunch loads to do, but this is an opportunity you just can't miss. P.T.A. is even providing refreshments. Do you think you can make it?
> Sincerely, CLOSING
> P.S.

A pocket folder holds magazine pictures, writing samples, and other ideas to help students get started with writing.

- *Writing to entertain.* Let students play with writing their own jokes, comics, riddles, and political cartoons. Some will enjoy writing fiction, especially chapter books. Remember that to write good stories, students need to have heard and read lots of stories. Don't force them to write made-up stories. Many students prefer to write nonfiction or personal narratives.
- *Doing "expert writing."* Everyone is brilliant at something. Help students discover their area of expertise. You might keep a list in your classroom of "experts." For example:

Our Areas of Brilliance:

- Denisha—roller hockey
- Paola—computers
- Scott—baseball
- Ruby—rock collecting

Then encourage students to write about what they know a lot about—their area of expertise. For example, suggest that Denisha write about roller hockey. She might write a how-to-skate book or a glossary of hockey terms or a brochure about roller hockey.

- *Exploring author Web sites.* Either bookmark or provide a list of suggested author Web sites for students to visit. (See a list in Appendix B.) Many of these Web sites tell where authors get their writing ideas or other information about the writing process. Students might then create author profiles, telling what they learned

exams, so it's good to provide extra practice at the writing work station. It's also a real-life writing skill, so provide names and addresses of people and places students might write to. Other ideas include your principal, cafeteria staff, parents, local legislators and other government officials, and children's book authors (write to them via their publishers). Leave space for peers to make suggestions of other people to write to as well.

about these writers. Or they may get ideas of what they'd like to write about from the authors' ideas.

- *Using picture books as models for writing.* Periodically, place picture books you've used in read-aloud as models for writing. For example, if you've read Patricia Polacco books to model use of vivid language, you might display a few of them for browsing. You could even have students use highlighter tape to mark favorite words. Glancing at these could provide inspiration for student writers.

- *Compiling notes into outlines, reports, summaries, or time lines.* Students might use content-area information at this work station to create reports or summaries of what they've learned. Of course, this could also be done at content-area work stations. See Chapter 8 for more information.

- *Working on writing weekly responses to books read during independent reading time.* A system for teaching students to write weekly responses to books read during independent time is shared in this chapter. Students might choose to work on their writing responses at the writing station, too.

- *Working on pieces from writing workshop.* Having students' writing folders stored in a crate under or by the writing table will provide easy access to writing begun during writing workshop.

Conferring

- *Collaborating with others to compose, organize, and revise various types of texts.* Students need time and opportunity to work with partners to plan and revise their writing. Post guidelines for peer conferences here. You might also include colored pencils, scissors, and tape for use as "revising" tools.

- *Conferring about writing; editing for conventions, such as capitalization, punctuation, grammar, and spelling.* Students might choose to work with

Peer conference guidelines and a proofreading chart remind students of teacher expectations at the writing station.

partners to edit each other's writing at this station. Procedures for peer editing could be posted here. Include a chart showing proofreading marks. You might post a reminder to students to *not* write on each other's papers, but to make suggestions to the writer, who then makes the changes.

Writing for an Audience

- *Writing messages others can easily read and understand.* Many teachers have classroom mailboxes in their writing station so students can write notes to each other. A hanging shoe bag labeled with one student's name per pocket works well. Students will often take more care with spelling and punctuation when writing a message to someone they care about. Teach two rules here: be encouraging and sign your own name!

■ *Practicing cursive.* You may have a separate handwriting work station, but remember that if you are teaching cursive, students can practice it as they compose at this work station, too. Provide a cursive handwriting chart for students to look at if they need help forming a letter.

Other Writing Ideas

■ *Using reference materials and writing resources, such as dictionaries, thesauri, and word walls.* Model how to use dictionaries and thesauri when you write in front of your students. If they see you using these resources, they may use them, too. Place a variety of dictionaries at this station. Scholastic has several specialized versions, including *The Scholastic Dictionary of Idioms* and *The Scholastic Science Dictionary.*

■ *Publishing writing pieces from writing workshop.* You might have some blank books and/or bookmaking supplies here for students who are ready to publish. Some teachers place pub-

lishing supplies in a caddy for students to use here. Others choose to put art supplies at a separate publishing work station.

■ *Using the computer for writing.* In some classrooms, the teacher places the writing station next to the computer so students can use technology for writing, as well as traditional pens and paper. Another possibility is to have a laptop or portable word processor available at the writing station.

How to Set Up the Writing Work Station

You don't need much space for a writing station, but plan for an area near a bulletin board if possible so you'll have a place to display charts, samples, and student writing. If you have a word wall, try to place the writing area where students can easily see and use those words as a reference. (See Chapter 6 for ideas on upper-grade word walls.) If you have computers, you might set up your writing station beside them so writers can use them for composing, editing, or publishing.

A small table or two student desks might be used to define the space; these also provide hard, smooth surfaces for writing. One teacher I know

Set up near a bulletin board or extra chalkboard at the start of the year to provide a display area that will support student writing.

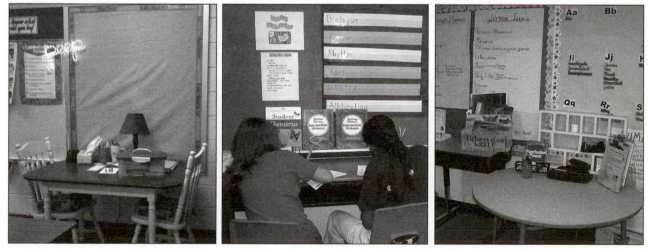

uses a section of her teacher desk for her writing work station (because all she ever did was stack papers on it anyway). Another has students sit on the floor beside a trifold project board; they use clipboards to write on, and their pens and writing materials are stored in a portable caddy. Still another teacher has two tall bar stools pulled up to a bistro table that holds writing supplies so kids can confer about their writing there. Set up the space to provide a comfortable place for students to write and talk about their writing with each other. Be sure to model conversation about writing throughout the day, so students will learn how to talk about their work like writers.

Use stacking trays for storing paper. Put different kinds of paper in each tray and have kids add a label to each to help the area stay neat and organized. Likewise, place writing implements in labeled containers. Intermediate students enjoy writing with a variety of materials, such as gel pens, fancy plumed pencils, and brightly colored paper. Don't put every writing material you own in this space, or it may become overcrowded and difficult for students to manage well. Add things gradually to help retain their novelty and make cleanup easier.

If you're using writing folders for writing workshop, place them in a crate (or two) in this station, possibly under the small table or desks there. This

A well-designed writing station includes help for writing (brainstormed with the students) and interesting supplies that students can easily access.

A help board displayed in the writing station reminds students how they can help themselves as writers.

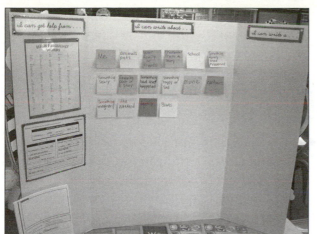 

provides easy access to works in progress and gives students places to store unfinished pieces.

On a nearby bulletin board, display supports for writing. Include charts generated with your students during writing workshop, such as "Where to Get Help for Your Writing" or "How to Have a Peer Conference." Post a chart of proofreading marks and commonly misspelled words. Teach with these charts during writing workshop as well. Leave some space to post high-quality writing samples. One fourth-grade teacher had samples of writing that represented various scores on her state's fourth-grade writing test for students to use as models.

Materials

Remember not to put out too much in the writing work station at a time so students won't be overwhelmed. What follows is a list of what might be used in the writing work station in the course of the entire school year:

Things to Write On

- A variety of paper (such as notebook, blank white, neon brights, black construction paper, card stock folded for cards, and special stationery)

- Notepads (cool ones are often available at discount stores)
- Sticky notes for peer editors' suggestions
- Envelopes (neon brights as well as white)
- Old greeting cards cut in half and used as postcards
- 8 ½ x 11 inch colored paper, cut into smaller sizes for instant stationery
- Stickers to decorate plain paper

Things to Write/Create With

- A variety of writing implements (such as sharpened pencils, gel pens, fancy pens, decorated pencils from discount stores, glitter crayons, and bold-colored markers)
- Colored pencils for editing (have a backup set in case pencil points break)
- Staplers (especially those in interesting shapes and colors), scissors, and tape, used for making books and revising

Things for Storage

- Labeled stacking trays (for paper storage)
- Labeled containers for writing tools (pens, pencils, crayons, etc.)
- Crate filled with students' writing folders from writing workshop

Reference Tools

- A variety of dictionaries (picture, student, foreign language, and college versions)
- A variety of thesauri
- Other writing resource books such as those from Write Source (available at www.thewrite-source.com) and Scholastic, such as the *Scholastic Dictionary of Synonyms, Antonyms, and Homonyms*
- Samples of high-quality student writing
- Samples of a variety of forms of writing (list, letter, poem, outline, time line, research report, news article, etc.)
- Charts made by the teacher and students together intended as aids to student writers (such as strong verbs list, good leads, satisfying endings, and other words for *said*)
- Interesting magazine photos mounted on colored paper and stored in clear plastic sleeves (for ideas); notebook, folder, or box for storing them
- Theme words on cards or charts (according to content-area topics)
- Author-study tubs

How to Introduce the Writing Work Station

Gather the students near you and talk with them about this station. Show them where the materials are and go over your expectations for using them. Explain that this is a place where students may practice different kinds of writing. They may practice writing a particular form of writing you've been modeling, such as letters or editorials or poems; they may work on pieces from writing workshop stored in their writing folders; they may write in their writer's notebooks; or they may confer with each other about their writing. Write an "I Can" list with them. At the beginning of the year, it might look like this:

I Can . . .

- Write letters to friends or family.
- Work on pieces from my writing folder.
- Create a card to celebrate, to congratulate, or to thank someone.
- Read my writing to a partner for response and feedback.

As you teach writing lessons to the class, be sure to add models for writing to this station. For example, if you want to be sure students are doing a good job of writing cards, post sample cards there. Include a variety, such as birthday, congratulations, and get-well cards. Point out features of these cards, including clever greetings, rhymes, designs, and font types. Encourage students to use these models to help them make interesting cards and create verses with more sophisticated language. Do the same for other writing forms, such as letters, ads, poems, persuasive essays, and so on through the year.

You might have students help you organize the writing supplies and have them create labels for materials here. You will probably want labels such as "colored paper," "notebook paper," and "special stationery" for stacking paper-storage trays. You may want to have labels for "pens," "pencils," and "markers" stored in small containers. (A silverware caddy from a discount store works well for this.) Explain that you want to have a special place for each item so students can keep this area neat and orderly and make it easier for them to find what they need as writers.

What the Teacher Needs to Model

To help students develop as writers, you'll need to model often and well. *Writing Through the Tween Years* by Bruce Morgan (2005) provides specific information on teaching writing to eight- to twelve-year-olds and is a helpful teacher resource. The writing work station will be used most effectively if you've modeled the following routines over time:

How to write a (memoir, poem, news article, etc.).
Show students how to write a particular type of writing. Think aloud with them as you compose in front of them. Be explicit about how you got your writing idea, how you choose your words, and how you shape the piece according to the particular structure. For example, a poem looks and sounds different from a news article. Show professional examples of the form, too. For example, if you're teaching how to write a news article, show and display articles from the local newspaper, several kids' magazines, and the Internet. Point out what makes each of them a news article and then encourage students to use these features and techniques as they write. Be sure to post these samples with a label in the writing station. Then add this kind of writing to your "I Can" list there.

How to talk about writing ideas.
Show students how to talk about what they might write about. Model how to choose ideas they know and care about. They might write about topics they have studied in science or social studies; they might write about things that have happened to them. Have students work with partners in class to practice this before you expect them to do this independently at the writing station. You might use a fishbowl model, having two students sit in the middle of a circle and talk about writing ideas while the rest of the class sits around them and observes.

How to choose a topic.
As a class, list ways writers choose topics. Post this list in your writing station. It might include the following:

- ■ Think about what you know a lot about and care deeply about.
- ■ Choose things you've done that are interesting or evoke a lot of emotion for you (something funny, sad, scary, or exciting).

A chart of "things we can write about" brainstormed with students is displayed in the writing station.

- ■ Use ideas you got from reading a book (it reminded you of something that happened to you).
- ■ Remember something you've seen or heard that gives you an idea for a story.
- ■ Consider something you learned about that you want to share with others.

How to use a dictionary or other reference book.
Use a dictionary and other reference books to model for students how to choose words or verify spelling. Use these tools when writing in front of your class. Show students real applications of these materials, so they see real reasons for using them.

How to have a peer conference.
Don't try this at the beginning of the year! It is best to practice this for a while before expecting students to do it independently at this station. It will

take time for them to get to this point. Again, use the fishbowl technique to model peer conferences. Teach students how to listen to each other's writing and offer suggestions. Remind kids not to write on each other's papers but to share ideas and let the writer make changes on his or her own paper.

How to edit.

Again, the writer should make his or her own corrections. A peer may offer suggestions but should not write directly on a partner's paper. Model how to edit in your writing instruction. Show this in your own writing, or in writing your class is doing together. Teach proofreading marks and post a small chart showing them in your writing station.

How to use the computer for writing.

Teach your class how to do word processing. Many students find it easier to revise and edit on a computer because cutting and pasting is so much easier. Students' writing is often easier to read in a typed version, and they may be more apt to return to their writing and improve it in this form.

A notebook at the computer station contains directions on how to do things kids might have trouble with here, such as opening and saving documents, naming documents, and changing fonts.

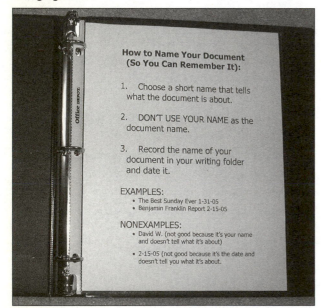

Set up a folder for each student, and teach them how to access it. Show your class how to use the editing tools in the toolbar that accompanies your word processing software. You might do this in your computer lab or in your classroom if you have a computer projection device or a video card that allows you to project the computer screen onto a television. You might also write a how-to with the class on opening and saving documents; copying, cutting, and pasting text; changing fonts; and naming your document to match the content (and remember it). You might have a notebook where each student has a page for recording names of his or her documents and a description of what is in each. See the section on the computer work station in Chapter 5 for more ideas. You might want to post a status-of-the-class sheet at the computer for kids to note where they are with their computer writing so you can keep track of where they are in the process. See Appendix C for a sample form.

How to use authors as mentors.

By doing author studies, you begin to show your class how writers write. Encourage students to try techniques their favorite authors use. For example, Will Hobbs writes outdoor adventure stories. If students go to www.willhobbsauthor.com and click on Favorite Questions, they can find a section called About Writing. There Will tells where he gets his writing ideas, how he revises, and how much he writes each day. Many author Web sites include this type of information. Study some authors as a class, using Web sites and providing tubs of their books in your classroom library. Be sure to include authors of both stories and informational texts. Encourage students to do independent author studies as well. Have them share with each other what they're learning about authors and their styles and writing tips by creating author profiles.

How to write a response to books read during independent reading.

Detailed directions on setting up a reading response folder are included in the next section. These are

Students do independent reading and then write responses in their reading folders in a special education resource room.

along the lines of Nancie Atwell's literary letters (1998). Many teachers like these because of the accountability they provide on a weekly basis.

However, another possibility for writing responses is a simpler, more private type of response. If you choose this option, you'll need to model for students how to jot down thoughts as you're reading. You might keep your own reading journal in a composition book and model how to do this during read-aloud. This type of response is not graded, but it can still be used for gaining considerable assessment information about how students are doing as readers and writers.

How to Introduce Response Writing

Tell your class that sometimes writing about what you read can help you better understand it. Sometimes writing after you've read allows you to tell someone else about what you found out. At other times you might want to write about something you read to help you remember it or to record what it made you think about. Explain that students won't need to write *every* time they read, but

that you would like them to write about their reading once a week (if you're using response folders that will be collected as described below) so that you'll know what they're thinking about the books they're reading.

Show students how to write a response for their folders by doing shared writing with your class after a read-aloud. Start with a short picture book, such as *The Lotus Seed* by Sherry Garland. Before reading, tell students to listen carefully so that they can help you write a letter telling what they thought about the book. (You can share it with a neighboring class so you'll have a sense of audience.) After the read-aloud, compose a letter together on the overhead or on a chart. Tell the students it should have the following attributes:

- Letter format
- Book title and author
- Responses to the book, such as
  This book made me think of . . .
  I wondered . . .
  An example of striking language was . . .
  The part that I really connected to was . . .
  This made me feel . . . because . . .

Write together. Model how to date the letter and write *Dear Friends* followed by a comma. Have students help you compose the letter, beginning with something like *We really enjoyed reading* The Lotus Seed *by Sherry Garland. This book reminded us of . . .* Be sure to give your letter to another class to read.

Teach your class how to write their own responses by doing another read-aloud on a subsequent day and asking them to write you a letter using the same attributes modeled earlier. Write a letter back to the class (on a transparency or on the board) and respond to their writing as a whole. It might look something like this:

Dear Class,

Thanks for your letters about the read-aloud book The Memory String, *by Eve Bunting. I, too,*

A class letter written to the principal about a read-aloud book is posted as an example for kids' reading response writing.

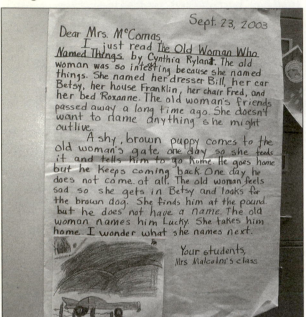

really enjoyed this story. It reminded some of you about things that have happened in your family. It triggered some memories for me, too. It made me think about my grandma who liked to sew and had all kinds of fascinating buttons.

I thought the idea of a memory string was really interesting. In fact, it might be memorable to make one. My children just left for college, so I may take some old buttons off some of their outgrown clothing and make my own! I may write to some relatives and ask them to send me some of their old buttons, too. This book made me wish I'd kept buttons from my wedding dress and my dad's army uniform. Maybe you would like to start a memory string. Let me know if you do.

Thanks for writing. I look forward to receiving more of your letters.

Your teacher,
Mrs. Diller

Read the letter with the class and point out the way you used the same attributes they did. Help

them find interesting words in your letter and encourage them to do the same in their writing.

After you've had students write several response letters after read-alouds and you know they have the gist of this assignment, ask them to write you one letter a week about something they're reading during independent reading time. Tell them that you will help them set up a special folder in which to keep their responses and that you will give them time to write these during independent reading. Explain that they don't have to write every day, but that they will probably want to write when their reading triggers a memory or an idea they want to capture.

Setting Up a Response Folder

If you choose to include this more formal type of response writing to independent reading as described above, specific directions follow. However, if you envision response writing as a periodic private and personal kind of response, you might simply have each child use a composition book for that.

Each student in your classroom will need a pocket folder with metal fastening brads for a reading response folder. Label the folder with a cover, My Reading Folder. On the left inside cover, attach your criteria for writing a response at the top. On the pocket at the bottom, glue your guidelines for independent reading time. Develop these with your students. A sample might look like this:

Guidelines for Independent Reading Time

■ Always be reading a book or writing about what you're reading in your response folder.

■ Work silently so that you and your neighbors can do your best thinking.

■ Have your books preselected. You may NOT go to the classroom library during independent reading time.

■ Choose books you enjoy and can read on your own.

Cover of reading folder for independent reading and response writing.

First divider for "Books I've Read This Year" and following sample reading log.

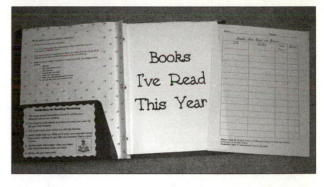

- Keep up with your reading response folder. Record book information when you finish reading a book. Complete your weekly responses on time!

Then use three different-colored pieces of card stock to divide the papers to be placed in the folder into three sections. Each should be labeled and three-hole-punched. Label the first divider "Books I've Read This Year." Label the second divider "Books I Want to Read" and label the last section "My Responses."

Behind the first divider, include several copies of the reproducible book log "Books I've Read in Grade ___" found in Appendix C. There's an optional form for "Abandoned Books" that can be used to help students determine why they are abandoning books and help them do a better job of choosing them.

Have students use sticky notes on the back of the second divider to post names of books they'd like to read. They can simply remove them upon finding these books. You might also include copies of the sheet "Things I Want to Read" behind the divider. To accompany this section on "Books I Want to Read," you might want to have planning sheets for kids to use for choosing books at the library. A reproducible called "My Library Plan" is available in Appendix C. Students fill out the titles of books they've heard about or seen that they'd like to read, and jot down the section of the library where they'll look for them. They can store these in the pocket in the back of the folder and take their folders with them when choosing a book.

Behind the third divider, "My Responses," place fifteen to twenty pieces of notebook paper to start the year. This is where kids will write their weekly responses to books they're reading inde-

Second divider for "What I Want to Read This Year" and following sample pages.

Third divider and notebook paper for reading responses.

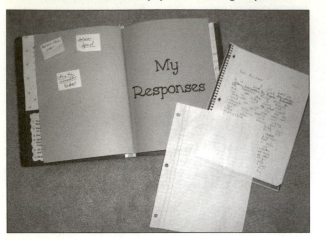

A student writes a response in his reading notebook.

pendently. You might remove the notebook paper at the end of each grading period and add more as needed. If you'd like, staple the responses together and send them home for parents along with the report card.

Response Writing as Part of Independent Reading

At first, you may have to remind students to complete their writing responses by the end of each week. Each day at the start of independent reading time, tell students that as they are reading today, they should think about their response writing. If they haven't yet completed their weekly response, today might be the day to think about their connections to and reflections about what they're reading. Remind them that they should be either reading something or writing a response to their reading during this time. Some students might need to be reminded when there are about five minutes left in independent reading time so they can stop to write a response. Of course, you should tell them that they don't have to write a response *every* day. You might also post a sample of a writing response if they need a model. Or you could staple a copy onto the inside of the back cover of their response folders.

Remind students that they might also work on their writing responses at the writing work station. Have them take their reading response folder to the station along with the book they're currently reading if that's what they choose to do while there.

Mini-Lessons for Response Writing

As you read students' written responses each week, you may see patterns begin to emerge. For example, you might see that students always use the same opening sentence. If so, do a brief mini-lesson (about ten minutes or so) to show them how to vary their leads. Either model by writing in front of them, or use a student sample reproduced on a transparency (always with that student's permission). Work together to improve the writing. If you notice that students are writing in a formulaic way, such as simply naming the book and author, followed by two connections, followed by exactly five comments, write in front of them and show them how to break up the monotony. Again, either write a response to a read-aloud together or use a student sample to demonstrate how to make the writing better. If you use a student sample, have that person write on the transparency to make the changes. Transfer ownership to help students become more independent.

You will probably want to change the format of the responses periodically to keep this routine interesting for the students. For example, if you've been working with your students on synthesis, then add that to your expectations for their responses. Be sure to model how to include synthesis in a response by writing several with your students before expecting them to do it on their own.

Another example of a new format is to create criteria to match the reading of varied genres, such as historical fiction or informational books. Make new reading response rubrics for students to use that complement the genre. See Appendix C for samples.

Yet another way to change the format is to have students change the genre of writing about their reading. Instead of writing a response letter, have them write a book blurb or advertisement. Or teach them how to write a book review (to let prospective readers know whether or not this is a book they might like to read) or an author profile (to share information about an author, how and why the author writes, and samples of this writer's work to support the information). Janet Angelillo's *Writing about Reading* (2003) includes detailed information about genres of writing about reading, including mini-lessons and samples of students' writing.

How to Solve Problems That May Arise

The writing work station works best in classrooms where students are used to writing regularly about their independent reading, as well as writing in the content areas and during writing workshop. Students who write daily learn from their teacher and peers what good writers do and become better equipped to do these things independently.

To keep your writing work station a well-organized space that inspires students to write and do their best work, the following page lists some possible problems you may encounter, with ideas for solving them.

Differentiating at This Work Station

The best way to provide differentiation at the writing station is to offer open-ended activities as well as topic choices for writing. You might have a notebook with interesting magazine photos glued onto colored paper and inserted into clear plastic sleeves. Add a possible word bank to go with each photo to get students started. This naturally provides differentiation because students can bring what they know to the task. For example, one student might write simple sentences using the word bank to describe the photo. Another student at a higher level might use some of the words to tell about an experience the photo triggered for him or her. Yet another student might create a poem or lyrics using the photo and word bank words for inspiration.

This "possible words" bank was generated with students and posted for support for second-language learners in a third-grade writing station.

Snow Words
* snowflake   * arctic
* clouds   * snowball fight
* snowstorm   * North Pole
* blizzard   * South Pole
* avalanche   * puddle
* sleet   * igloo
* slush   * icicle
* glisten

Writing Work Station

Possible Problem	Troubleshooting Ideas
Little or no writing is being done	Consider how much modeling you've done with students. Have you taught them *how* to write, or have you just assigned topics? Do you have writing charts and other supports to help them start their writing (including one on how to choose a topic)? Have you taught with these charts or just posted them? You might require students to complete at least one piece of writing at this station every other week to increase accountability.
Poor quality of writing	Discuss high-quality writing with students. Show them samples that correlate with your state testing criteria. Post these samples in the writing station to show students what you expect.
Students waste time sharpening pencils	Don't allow students to sharpen pencils during independent time. Have a can of sharpened pencils available here.
Area becomes messy	Have students help organize writing materials. Use labeled stacking trays for storing paper.
Fancy pens and other special writing materials "disappear"	Assign classroom helpers as materials managers to check this station daily to be sure all materials have been returned.
Response writing becomes dull and flat	Do more modeling of response writing. Show new ways to start the letters to give them more life. Demonstrate a variety of responses and try changing the genre of writing. Write back to students and model what you'd like to see in their writing. Change your criteria for the responses (e.g., reading nonfiction). See Appendix C for sample reading response rubrics.
Some kids are using up all the cool new supplies quickly	You might need to set limits on special supplies, such as new stationery or the amount of tape to be used at once. Placing a sign by the new material that says, "Limit 1." Or "Use 1/2-inch pieces of tape" may be helpful. Be sure to discuss and set up these rules with your class, explaining why supplies are limited. (For example, "I bought this new paper with my limited budget.")

A news article photo and a "possible words" bank are stored in a folder with a clear cover to bridge to upper-grade content areas and build writing vocabulary.

You might also provide differentiation related to editing and revising techniques. Many teachers work with small groups for both reading and writing; color-coding groups is an easy way to let particular students know your expectations at stations. If you have an editing chart, you might put colored dots beside certain skills you want particular groups of students to focus on in their writing. If your yellow group has been working on fixing up their spelling, you might put a yellow dot by that part of your editing checklist. Likewise, if your green group is working on substituting strong verbs in their writing, put a green dot beside that item on your revising chart.

Ways to Keep the Station Going Throughout the Year

Adding new touches on a regular basis will keep your writing station alive. Remember to add only one new item at a time for maximum effectiveness. Here are some ideas for keeping this station interesting:

- Change the type of paper or its color. Use white notebook paper at the start of the year, and then change to yellow or pink notebook paper. Include colored blank paper at times, too. Black paper with gel pens is a great novelty item for intermediate students.
- Add new decorative stationery periodically. Your students might enjoy using stamps, stickers, or computer graphics to create new or themed stationery. Discount stores are often great sources for inexpensive stationery, too.
- Change the writing tools. Put in new decorative pencils. Use pens with feathers or other doodads at the end. I've found pens shaped like sharks and pens that light up when you write. These writing instruments can sometimes entice struggling writers.
- Older kids often enjoy writing on clipboards. Provide these for a change. They come in all shapes and sizes.
- Provide bookmaking supplies or blank books. The Web site www.barebooks.com is a great source for blank keepsake books and other novel writing supplies.
- Add photos of your class, especially those taken with a digital camera (faster and less expensive to process). Students might even take the photos! Use these to inspire writing topics, not just for decoration.
- Add new word banks with seasonal or theme words related to science and social studies topics you're studying. Have students help you create them.
- Add new word books or dictionaries. Check out the bargain book section at large bookstores for these.
- Add colored envelopes or inexpensive greeting cards.
- Add tape and/or a stapler and teach students how to cut and paste their work to revise.
- Add a new color of pencil for editing and revising.
- Change the criteria for writing responses during independent reading time.
- Change the genre of writing about reading for the reading response folders.

How to Assess/Keep Kids Accountable

Collect student writing from this work station as well as their reading responses, and assess for skills you've been teaching. Let the class know ahead of time what you'll be looking for. You might post what you'll be grading on an index card at this station so students know exactly what's expected. For example, if you've been teaching about effective use of dialog and quotation marks, the index card might say I'll be grading:

- Effective use of dialog.
- Correct use of quotation marks.

Write back to students in their response folders if you're using them. Some teachers post a schedule for when they'll be picking up the folders; they read five or six every night. This makes reading the responses more manageable and leaves enough time for the teacher to write a short note back to each student.

Reading Response Folders Due:

Tuesday: Christi, Melissa, John, Patrick, Raul, Leah, Ricky

Wednesday: Melinda, Shauna, Lindi, Norah, Robbie, Pedro

Thursday: Denisha, Paola, Herbert, Michael,
   Sam, Brian
Friday: Adam, Tonya, Sandra, Jen, Linda,
   Maurice, Roberto

Another way to check what students are working on at the writing station is to eyeball it periodically and be sure students are actively engaged. If
you note problems, use sharing time as a forum to
discuss problems and how to solve them with your
students. Also allow students to share writing done
at the writing work station with the rest of the class
during this time. Or you might have a bulletin
board near the writing station where students can
post their finished writing for others to read. You
could include comment sheets for students to fill
out and place in each other's mailboxes for feedback. See Appendix C for a sample comment form.

How This Station Supports Student Performance on State Tests

Students who write daily with teachers who model
how to write regularly generally do well on state
writing tests. If your grade level takes the state writing test, post scoring criteria used on this test at the
writing work station. Show students what high-
quality writing looks like so they can strive for that
goal.

There is a direct link between reading and writing. Students who write well are usually avid readers. They "borrow" ideas and techniques from the
books they read and authors they know. As they
write responses during independent reading time,
they will improve their reading comprehension and
get practice analyzing and comparing texts, a skill

Fifth graders wrote these reading responses and received teacher notes back.

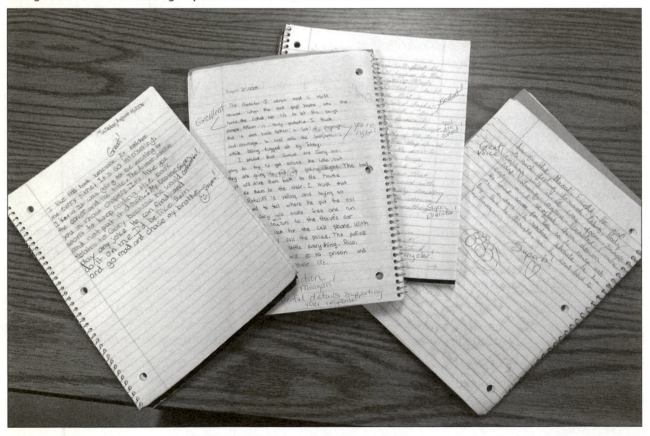

Students who will take a standardized test are reminded of specifics to include in their writing at this station and are asked to score their papers from 1 to 6 on this writing attribute-focus. The chart was generated during a writing lesson with the class.

ISAT Writing:
FOCUS   Score 1–6

• My first sentence gets the reader's attention and gives an idea of what my story will be about.

• My story stays on topic the whole time!

often required on state writing tests. One type of question on standardized reading tests, such as the national reading test known as NAEP, asks students to write responses to the test passage, as opposed to simply filling in multiple-choice answers. Some sample fourth-grade reading test questions from the NAEP include the following:

- Why did Cory think that Minnie would not survive? Use examples from the story to explain why.
- Suggest another title for the story. Use examples from the story to explain why it would be a good title.
- Use the information in this passage to describe marsupials.

Students who are used to writing responses to books read during independent reading and using text evidence to support their ideas will be better prepared to write narrative answers to reading test questions.

Be sure to include the kinds of writing practice your kids will be tested on. But don't just give them a bunch of prompts and think that will do the trick! For example, if your state tests persuasive writing, be sure to include plenty of practice in a variety of authentic ways: writing (and mailing) persuasive letters to real people, writing persuasive essays such as editorials and sending them to local papers, writing notes to request specific items. Resist the urge to be driven by prompts.

Writing at the writing work station and during independent reading adds practice time for students. Practice makes permanent! Studying authors and collaborating with peers will help students learn more about what effective writers do. The more attention you give to high-quality writing, the better the likelihood that students will increase their writing power.

Reflection and Dialogue

1. Where is your writing work station? Can a visitor to your classroom easily identify it? Is it an inviting space that encourages students to do their best writing, or is it tucked away in an obscure spot? Look at the writing work stations of several colleagues. What ideas can you borrow and use to add pizzazz to your writing station?

2. What writing supports have you provided at this station? What are students using often for help? What are they using well? What are they not using? What might you change as a result?

3. What do students choose to do when they come to the writing work station? Do you observe them mostly writing and talking about their writing? What can you do to encourage more of what you'd like to see? Are they writing mostly fiction or nonfiction? Work with them to expand their writing repertoire.

4. Where do you display student writing in your classroom? On boards, in books, on computers? Does everyone write about the same topic,

or is a variety of writing displayed? How do students help decide what will be displayed?

5. How is the writing in students' reading response folders? Is it improving, or are students writing in the same way day after day? Use response and modeling to infuse their response writing with new life. Share ideas of what you tried and how it changed student writing with a colleague.

6. Is student writing improving throughout the year? If it is, what factors contribute to this? How is your writing station supporting the growth you've seen? If student writing isn't getting better, what can you do instructionally? What can you change at the writing work station to improve writing practice? Discuss this with your grade-level team as well as across grade levels, if possible.

5

Easy-to-Set-Up Work Stations

The first four chapters of this book helped you understand how to start setting up literacy work stations in your upper-grade classroom. The first stations you'll want to establish early in the school year include both a classroom library and a writing work station, as described in detail in Chapters 3 and 4. These are necessary for building a solid foundation for reading and writing routines that will include both independent reading and response writing, which will continue throughout the year.

The easy-to-set-up work stations described in this chapter take fewer materials and less effort than others, so you might want to add some of these next. Choose the ones that best match the needs of you and your students. You might use some of them in the beginning of the year, and then substitute other, meatier work stations over time as outlined in Chapters 6–9.

Listening Work Station

Two students sit in a quiet spot listening to a CD that accompanies the social studies textbook. When they finish listening to this expository text (which the teacher marked with a sticky note), they answer the questions at the end of the chapter. At this station there is notebook paper on which to record their answers. One student writes their names at the top of the paper, and they work together to discuss and answer the questions.

A student listens to a tape of a textbook for reading support.

In another classroom down the hall, three students sport individual battery-operated listening units with headphones. They sit comfortably on pillows in various parts of the room and listen to a variety of tapes. One is listening to a chapter book; another is listening to favorite poems read aloud and recorded by a classmate; the third is listening to a selection from the basal reading series. After listening, each student will write a response in a small spiral notebook that is stored in a zippered plastic bag that holds the reading material and tape. The teacher has modeled this type of response with the large group, so the students are familiar with what is expected. Each student dates and signs his or her response after making an entry. This way others can read what their peers thought about particular selections.

A comfy chair makes the listening station inviting.

Ideas for the Work Station

The listening work station is one of the simplest to establish in the classroom. All you need is a tape recorder or CD player and some books with matching audiotapes or CDs. It is fairly easy to find commercial tapes and CDs of young adult literature read aloud. Several sources include Books on Tape from Random House available at www.school.booksontape.com and Chinaberry at www.chinaberry.com. The American Library Association lists notable children's recordings each year. Check these out at www.ala.org. You can download books on sites such as www.audible.com for a fee. Also visit eBay and amazon.com for recorded books.

You don't need a table to set up this station; it takes up too much valuable classroom space. Simply create a comfortable spot for students to sit and listen. Get student input on where they think the listening station might be placed. You might use beanbag chairs or pillows on the floor to define this area. One teacher stores the current books and tapes or CDs in zippered plastic bags in a crate placed on its side. The tape recorder or CD player sits on top. Another has a built-in counter where

kids sit and listen to recorded books on tall stools. Still others (with limited electrical outlets) use portable battery-operated players. Inexpensive models are available at many drugstores. They usually use AA batteries, which you might ask parents or community members to donate. You might also be able to get CD players donated by parents who are buying iPods and other MP3 players.

The listening station can be transformed into a recording studio to keep interest high here. Or you might add a second tape recorder so you can have both a listening station and a recording-studio station. You'll need to model how to make a tape recording, since all recorders have slightly different procedures. Write the directions together with your students and post them at this station. Some teachers have a small file box or two that contains a tape labeled for each student; give them each an address label to decorate with their name and then affix to a blank tape. Short tapes can be purchased from www.tapecenter.com. If students make their own recordings, some of these can be added to the listening station, too. Two students might read together to record the first chapter of or a favorite

Students listen to a recorded book and then use "book sticks," Popsicle sticks with generic questions written on them, to check comprehension.

scene from a book they've enjoyed from the classroom library to entice others to read that book; older students enjoy adding sound effects and reading with varied voices to represent different characters. Another option is for them to record some of their published pieces from writing workshop for their peers to hear.

Some bilingual teachers have two listening stations in their classrooms. They have one for English listening and another for listening in the second language. This both stretches work stations and gives second-language students extra opportunities to hear English being spoken.

Here are some things that you might include on the "I Can" list at this station:

I Can . . .

■ Listen to the tape or CD and follow along in the book.

■ Visualize while listening. Then I can tell my partner what I saw in my mind or do a quick sketch; compare our "mind pictures."

■ Answer questions with my partner after listening to the tape or CD.

■ Choose a reading response to do after listening.

■ Listen for new vocabulary or interesting words and use highlighter tape to mark them. Then I can write these words on list paper.

■ Listen to the way the reader used his or her voice to match the punctuation. Then I can try to read a part just like it sounded on the recording.

■ Record a piece I have written for others to listen to.

■ Read aloud and record a favorite poem or short picture book.

■ Read aloud and record the first chapter or a favorite scene from a book we like. I can read it to persuade our friends to read it, too.

■ Use a listening map to improve my comprehension. (Sample listening maps are in Appendix D.)

Troubleshooting

There are a number of problems that may arise at this station. The best way to avoid them is to model well and let students know exactly what you expect here. Get student input on how to solve problems that arise; intermediate students often come up with solutions we might not have considered as teachers.

How the Listening Work Station Supports Student Performance on State Tests

Listening to recorded reading does several things to build reading and writing skills that will be tested on state reading and writing tests. First, listening builds language; it provides all students access to on- or above-grade-level reading material. Listening to a recorded book may motivate some reluctant readers to try a piece they might not have encountered on their own. It also exposes them to new vocabulary.

Visualizing is promoted when students listen to recorded books, especially when they have a chance

Listening Work Station

Possible Problem	Troubleshooting Ideas
I don't have any electrical outlets for kids to access.	Use portable battery-operated listening units.
The tapes that accompany chapter books are long. My students don't have time to listen to them in one sitting.	Have students record their own tapes of favorite scenes from books they love; this will build your collection of shorter tapes and give students valuable fluency practice. Another idea is to use the longer tapes and let students sign up for particular books on tape. They go to the listening work station several days in a row to listen to them. Or use a tape recorder with a counter and have students record the number where they stopped listening on a log that is kept with that book. CDs that have books recorded with each chapter as a separate track might also solve this problem.
Students talk to each other with the headsets on and make a lot of noise.	Teach students to remove headsets when they want to talk with each other.
Kids are getting bored with the listening station.	Spice it up by converting it to a "recording studio." Also ask kids what would make the listening station more interesting to them. Or show them how to do buddy writing after listening. Each student writes the other about what they heard. They exchange letters, read them silently, and write back to each other.

to sketch while listening and then talk about what they listened to afterward. Another advantage of listening is that it can help students learn about text structure. They can be given listening maps, special graphic organizers on which they take notes while listening to improve their understanding of text structure. See Appendix D for samples. The understanding of text structures can also help students write in a more organized way. (Note: Students can use these same graphic organizers as they read at the classroom library or buddy reading station.)

Buddy Reading Work Station

Two students sit beside each other on the floor. Each holds a copy of the same fiction book. They are reading a chapter silently and then using discussion cards to talk about what they read. The cards relate to a reading strategy their teacher has been modeling in whole-group instruction—inference. They take turns reading the cards and then talking about what they think. For example, one

card says, "Tell something one of the characters did in this chapter and what you think was that character's motivation. Why did this character behave in this way? What would you have done in this situation?"

Another pair of students is seated in another area of the classroom doing buddy reading with two copies of the science textbook. They have looked at

Two pairs of students engage in buddy reading in this sixth-grade classroom.

the "I Can" list in the buddy reading basket and have chosen the option "I read a paragraph; you read a paragraph." They are reading the assigned chapter for science in this way and stop to discuss their reading at the end of each section. When they have finished all the assigned reading, they answer the questions in the textbook together. One is the recorder and writes their answers on notebook paper.

Ideas for the Work Station

Teachers like buddy reading because it doesn't take up much space and is easy to get started. All you need for this station is a basket (discount stores sell some that are just the right size and price!) and two copies of the same book or other short text. This is a portable station that can be taken anywhere in the classroom; you will be wise to set up predetermined places, though, so it doesn't get overcrowded in any one area of your room. You might set up two or three buddy reading stations to accommodate more pairs of students.

Buddy reading directions written with the class are posted by the buddy reading basket. A sticky note tells the pages from the social studies book kids should read together.

Figure 5.1 **How to Read Informational Text**

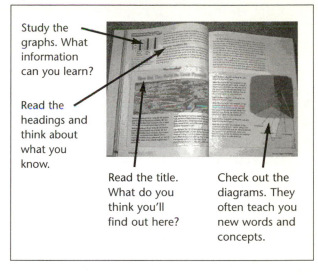

Study the graphs. What information can you learn?

Read the headings and think about what you know.

Read the title. What do you think you'll find out here?

Check out the diagrams. They often teach you new words and concepts.

You might set up different-colored buddy reading baskets for students reading at different levels or put three or four titles at different levels in one basket and code them with colored dots to help students find books at their independent reading levels. Provide sticky notes and pencils, too, so kids can mark where they finished reading for the next time.

Use a variety of texts over time, including popular chapter books, your basal reader, and social studies and science textbooks. It is wise to provide shorter text at this station so students have time to finish reading something and discuss it. Include lots of nonfiction, such as current events clipped from the newspaper, Eyewitness books, fact books such as the *Guinness Book of World Records*, and Cross-Section books. To help students read these more effectively, you might add a chart showing how to read informational text (see Figure 5.1).

To help students know exactly what is expected of them at this station, here are some possibilities for the "I Can" list:

I Can . . .

■ Read the same chapter as my buddy and discuss it when we're finished reading.

- Decide how we're going to read here (together orally; you read a page aloud, I read a page aloud; silently to a certain place).
- Read a nonfiction text together and discuss it as we read it. Then we can write a summary of what we learned as we read.
- Use the chart on how to read nonfiction text to remind us not to skip any parts.
- Write questions about what we read for the next kids who come here to read this text. We can put our questions on a sticky note and write the answers on the back.

Troubleshooting

The biggest challenge at this work station is to keep buddy reading fresh and interesting. Below are some ideas to help.

How the Buddy Reading Work Station Supports Student Performance on State Tests

Having students practice reading at this station builds both comprehension and fluency. The main

thing tested on standardized reading tests is comprehension. Having buddies to talk with about reading can increase student interest and engagement and encourage them to read more than they might on their own. When students pair up and practice reading orally, fluency can really improve as well. Improved fluency often aids comprehension. If the standardized test is timed, this can be a real boon to student performance on the test.

Spelling Work Station

Two students sit at one desk and practice their spelling words for the week. One calls out the words from a preprinted list, and the other writes them on a dry-erase board. When finished, the student who called out the words helps the writer check his or her words. They fix any errors together and talk about anything that made spelling those words tricky.

Ideas for the Work Station

A favorite activity here is to give a partner a spelling test with this week's words. Students usually enjoy this game because the spellers receive immediate

Buddy Reading Work Station

Possible Problem	Troubleshooting Ideas
Kids are getting bored with this station.	Add a novelty item to increase interest here. Put out comfy cushions to sit on while reading or add colorful clipboards to write on after reading.
Students aren't reading the same text together.	Add task cards for buddy reading with a variety of choices of how they might read here. Have students help create these. For example, they might try "I read a page; you read a page" or "We both read a chapter silently and then discuss what we read" or "We read different characters' parts aloud."
Students complain about what they must read at this station.	Have kids help choose text you'll put in the buddy reading baskets. Keep it shorter rather than long. Have them perform something they've practiced reading orally here with the class.
I usually put fiction here, but my kids need more exposure to nonfiction. How can I use that here?	Include sticky notes and the directions "Write three questions for someone to answer about what you read." Have students place the sticky notes at the end of the section read. Have them make it self-checking by writing answers on the back. Suggest that students interview each other about facts learned after reading nonfiction.

Two students play Hangman using the words from their spelling book.

Third graders practice spelling words with dry-erase boards and markers.

I Can . . .

- Give my partner a spelling test and check it together.
- Play a spelling game such as Scrabble or Hangman with my partner.
- Make an illustration of a tough word from this week's spelling list that will help me remember how to spell it.
- Create a web with my partner that shows other words linked to a word from our spelling list.
- Practice writing hard-to-spell words with a gel pen and underline the parts that are hard to remember.
- Write antonyms for any spelling words that have them (use a thesaurus if needed).
- Write synonyms for any spelling words that have them (use a thesaurus if needed).

feedback about how they spelled each word, which the brain craves. Another favorite includes using spelling games, such as crossword puzzles and word games. (Your local newspaper may carry these). Some students might even make them for the rest of the class.

This is another space-saving work station. The materials might be placed in a basket that can be carried to a student's desk or a space on the floor. Simply place this week's spelling word list and something fun to write on along with writing tools in the basket. Also include a chart of commonly misspelled words for students to work with. Note: The spelling work station may be a separate station, or you might incorporate these ideas into your word study station, which is explained in Chapter 6.

Some ideas for a possible "I Can" chart are listed below. Be sure to brainstorm these with your students so they have more ownership. Don't just type up the list.

Troubleshooting

This is a relatively easy station to set up and maintain. However, the next page has a few tips about things that may occur at the spelling work station.

Spelling Work Station

Possible Problem	Troubleshooting Ideas
Students get in arguments about who will be the teacher and who will be the student.	Design ways to make choices before students ever go to this station. You might have a chart created with students labeled "How to Decide Who Goes First." Remind students to refer to this chart, which you have posted in your classroom.
One student in the pair never gets any words wrong, whereas the other makes lots of mistakes, which leads to frustration for both parties.	Match kids up with others who have similar spelling needs. You might need to differentiate your spelling list for some students. Pair up kids who have the same list to reduce their possible frustration.
I want my students to practice content-area words, too. Should I use those words here as well?	You might have a chart listing spelling words, and another labeled "science vocabulary" or "social studies vocabulary" and/or "math words" for kids to practice.

How the Spelling Work Station Supports Student Performance on State Tests

Many states have a standardized test that evaluates how students are doing as spellers. This is often a multiple-choice test, so be sure to give kids some practice with this format at the spelling work station. This can be done by occasionally having kids create multiple-choice formats for the mock "spelling tests" they give each other. Also, working with commonly misspelled words will help students recognize when these words are spelled correctly. Some state writing tests require that students write a composition, and consider spelling as one component in the scoring. Practice at the spelling work station with commonly misspelled words and patterns studied in your grade-level spelling book can help prepare students for the spelling portion of standardized state tests.

Overhead Work Station

In a sixth-grade classroom, two students stand by the overhead and project a transparency the teacher taught with yesterday from the grammar book. They project the text onto the dry-erase board at the front of the room and fill in the blanks on the board with dry-erase markers. They are practicing using direct objects.

In a fourth-grade classroom, a pair of students is reading and reviewing with a colored transparency about their state's history from the social

Students work with transparencies the teacher previously used on the overhead for reinforcement.

studies book. The transparency is in a clear plastic sleeve to protect it; the two students read it aloud together and discuss each section after reading. They write notes in the margin about what they learned. They circle the headings and star the captions; they underline key words and use them to summarize when they finish reading. A visitor to the classroom can see exactly what their teacher modeled when he or she taught this lesson several days ago.

Ideas for the Work Station

Most intermediate teachers use an overhead daily in their teaching. This is an easy station to set up if you teach with an overhead projector. Be sure to put all materials students need for the overhead at their fingertips so they don't have to interrupt you or anyone else. You might store transparencies you have used during instruction in a three-ring binder with sections labeled appropriately: "Grammar," "Social Studies," "Reading Comprehension," "Proofreading Writing," and so forth. Put each transparency in a clear plastic sleeve for protection and ease of use. Include writing utensils in a labeled cup. Use vis-à-vis or dry-erase pens. Some teachers

have students project a transparency onto a chalkboard and students write on the board rather than the projector.

Below is a sample "I Can" list to get you started with helping kids know what to practice while at this station:

I Can . . .

- Read and discuss an overhead from the binder with my partner.
- Work with my partner to fill out a transparency.
- Proofread a piece of writing on the overhead with my partner.
- Take turns practicing cursive writing on the overhead with my partner and work together to find and circle our best handwriting.
- Use overhead manipulatives to create and solve word problems with my partner.

Troubleshooting

Some teachers are reluctant to let students use the overhead for fear they might break it. The following page has some ideas to help you avoid trouble at this station.

A three-ring notebook holds transparencies in clear plastic sleeves, sorted into categories, such as social studies, math, poetry, news articles, grammar, and handwriting.

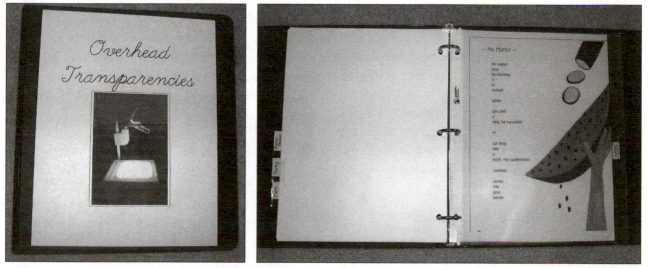

Overhead Work Station

Possible Problem	Troubleshooting Ideas
Students have trouble working together here.	Never put more than two students at this station at a time. Pair kids who get along.
Students fight over who turns the machine on and off.	Teach students that one will turn it on and the other will turn it off.
The spray bottle makes a mess with the vis-à-vis pens.	Substitute dry-erase markers for vis-à-vis pens. Or use baby wipes to clean the screen. Or have students project onto a chalkboard and write directly on the board with chalk.
I can't find the transparencies I collected and used last year.	Keep all transparencies in clear plastic sleeves in a three-ring binder labeled "Overhead Transparencies." Label each section for easy use.

How the Overhead Work Station Supports Student Performance on State Tests

An easy way for students to review content taught throughout the year is to have them practice skills formerly taught with overheads collected in a notebook over time. Some intermediate teachers also place transparencies of test prep materials at this work station closer to test time so kids can practice in the test-taking format. All skills practiced here should be related to your state standards and therefore be a support for what students need to know to do well on related tests.

Computer Work Station

This fifth-grade teacher has three computers in her classroom. One student is working at each computer during literacy work stations. They are doing a variety of tasks: one is typing a story written in writer's workshop and revising on the computer; another is using an interactive CD about the Boston Tea Party; the third is e-mailing a pen pal in another class.

Ideas for the Work Station

If you have a computer that works, you have a computer work station—no extra setup needed. Students can practice anything here that they've learned about in the computer lab. In addition, they can work with CDs, interactive computer games, and computer programs such as PowerPoint and Inspiration, as well as practice keyboarding skills. If you use a reading incentive program such as Accelerated Reader, students can work on it while at the computer work station. Upper-grade kids enjoy using WebQuests, e-mailing friends in other classes, and visiting author Web sites. They like to explore content on bookmarked Web sites and conduct research on the Internet. The possibilities for using this station are endless. In addition, you can have multiple computer stations by using every computer you have as a separate station, meaning more students can work here.

Some teachers have two "I Can" lists at this station—one that lists literacy activities they can practice and another for math activities. A sample literacy "I Can" list might look like this:

I Can . . .

- Read about an author we're studying and write facts I learned on my recording sheet.
- Do a WebQuest that's listed here.
- Use a bookmarked Web site. If it has pop-up ads, I'll write the teacher a note with the site name and stick it on the computer for her to read. Then I'll choose another Web site.

- Look up my password in the card file if I forget it.
- Use Word to type a piece from writer's workshop I want to publish.
- Save my work onto my disk from the file box.
- Choose an interactive CD from those in the CD rack.
- Take a reading comprehension test.

Troubleshooting

In some classrooms, students need help with the computers, which leads to interruption of the teacher. The list below outlines some possible problems and ideas to help solve them. An additional suggestion is to create a booklet with students that has directions on how to solve problems that may occur with the computer. Include directions on

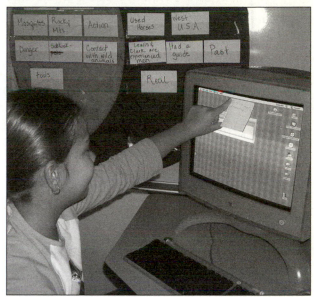

A student writes on a sticky note to record a computer problem and then does an alternate activity.

Computer Work Station

Possible Problem	Troubleshooting Ideas
The computer freezes and kids can't continue working on it.	Teach kids how to reboot the computer. If that doesn't work, have students put a sticky note on the computer telling what's wrong. Then have a backup activity for them to take to their seats.
Two of my computers work only half of the time.	See the above suggestion. If you have continual trouble, put an "out of order" sign on the computer (made by kids, of course!) and put in a work order to have it repaired. If it can't be fixed, ask for permission to get rid of it so it doesn't take up valuable classroom space.
Kids have trouble saving their work to disk.	Write directions together and post them at this station. Keep each student's labeled disk in a file box by the computer for easy access.
Kids get stuck in programs with pop-up ads.	Don't bookmark sites with pop-up ads. These are time wasters and can distract students. Teach kids what to do if they run into pop-up ads.
Students can't remember how to use bookmarked pages.	Write directions together for how to use a bookmark and post them at this station.
My students have different passwords for different programs and sometimes have trouble remembering them all.	Have a card file box with a card for each student. On the card list the student's password for any program he or she might be using.
I have only one computer. How can I have more students use it?	Double up two kids to one computer. Have one in charge of the mouse and the other in charge of the keyboard.

how to save, cut, paste, and use a password, along with shortcuts. Print a copy to keep at each computer. The key here is to create the help booklet *with* the kids so they own the information. You might also assign one or two students (in different reading groups) to be computer experts, who can help others during work stations time.

How the Computer Work Station Supports Student Performance on State Tests

Extra reading and writing practice on the computer can expand student opportunities for literacy. In addition, it can provide practice on objectives tested on state tests, especially if students occasionally practice in multiple-choice format.

Handwriting Work Station

Two desks are pulled up near a chalkboard for handwriting practice. One student stands at the board and practices writing the alphabet in cursive. The other sits at one of the desks and practices writing his name and those of his classmates on handwriting paper.

Ideas for the Work Station

The students mentioned above are in third grade and making the transition from manuscript to cursive writing. Their teacher has set up this area with pages from their handwriting workbook and a variety of writing tools, such as pens and pencils for them to use here. She has also posted a model of the entire cursive alphabet so they have it at their fingertips to use; she found it in their workbooks and laminated the page. There is also a list of students' names written in cursive. If you need a better model of cursive than you can provide in your own teacher handwriting, you might make charts using the Fonts 4 Teachers program, which includes a cursive writing font. For more information see www.fonts4teachers.com.

Clipboards are used to practice cursive writing at the handwriting work station.

The teacher mentioned in the example above has modeled how to form cursive letters during writer's workshop while writing in front of the class. She doesn't teach handwriting as a separate subject, because her time is limited and she wants enough time for writer's workshop. While she shows students how to write a personal narrative, she stops briefly to mention explicitly how she made sure that her capital R started at the top, went down, looped around, and then went down again. She refers to the large cursive alphabet posted above her chalkboard as she does this. Then she returns quickly to the piece she is writing. She chooses her comments about handwriting carefully as she thinks about which letters her students are having trouble with in cursive writing. The focus of writer's workshop is on writing a message, but the teacher realizes that handwriting can sometimes deter others from being able to read that message.

You might not use this station with every student in your classroom. Kids with easy-to-read handwriting might not be assigned to practice here. Use your management board flexibly to provide students with appropriate practice. If a child has

A third grader practices cursive using newspaper stock pages turned horizontally to provide lines.

extreme difficulty with handwriting, consult your local occupational therapist for help.

Here are some things that students might practice at the handwriting work station:

I Can . . .

- Practice writing my name in cursive.
- Practice writing the names of my friends and classmates in cursive.

- Practice writing the alphabet in cursive, using upper- and lower-case letters.
- Write the teacher a note using my best cursive writing.
- Write the principal a note using my best cursive writing.
- Write my favorite letter ten times, circle the best one, and think about why it's the best.
- Write the letter that's hardest for me to write ten times, circle the best one, and think about why it's the best.
- Practice writing cursive on the chalkboard. I can trace over it like I'm writing it with my finger and keep tracing it like that until it's erased.

Troubleshooting

Below are a few things to think about to keep the handwriting station working well.

How the Handwriting Work Station Supports Student Performance on State Tests

Most states have a writing test where students must write a composition, either about an assigned topic or in response to some reading they've done. Although handwriting isn't tested, it does often influence the reader, which in this case is the state test evaluator. Unfortunately, even a poor message

Handwriting Work Station

Possible Problem	Troubleshooting Ideas
Kids aren't practicing correct letter formation.	Be sure to have models of correct letter formation that you've taught with and referred to when writing in front of students. Include the cursive alphabet with arrows showing where to start and where to go next. You might ask a patient student with good handwriting to tutor another student here.
My kids don't like this work station. What can I do to make it more enjoyable for them?	Ask for student input. "What would you like to do here that would make it interesting to practice?" Add cool writing implements such as neon gel pens and black paper. You might need to add a ruler for them to make a baseline to avoid crooked writing.

is conceived as "higher" when it is easy to read. Teach students that handwriting is a courtesy to your reader and shows that you care about your message. For some students, the sheer act of hand-writing is difficult. Giving them additional practice might ease some of the burden once cursive writing becomes easier for them. And remember that students should be given a chance, whenever possible, to write in the way that is easiest for them to communicate their message to others—either in cursive or manuscript. Note: If your students need help with manuscript, include those materials and have them practice with manuscript rather than cursive.

Newspaper Work Station

Two third graders are working in the newspaper station writing news stories for the quarterly class paper. One is writing a want ad; she is searching for a good adventure story, preferably one set in the mountains with interesting characters. Another student is writing an article about the planets, something they are studying in science. They are writing their articles on preprinted sheets formatted for their news stories as a support. (See Appendix D for samples.) A chart is posted in the newspaper station; students have signed up on it ahead of time, noting what they want to write about so they don't duplicate articles. The teacher will help them format the newspaper by using a template in a computer program; they will type their articles on the computer while at the computer station on another day. See a sample class newspaper page in Figure 5.2.

In a fourth-grade classroom, two students are working together, reading the *Mini Pages,* a syndicated newspaper for kids. It is part of the Saturday paper that the teacher collects weekly at home and laminates. Her students choose one of the newspapers, read the articles together and then use a vis-à-vis pen to do the puzzles and answer questions on the last page. The kids enjoy the articles, and the teacher likes the simplicity of the station.

Figure 5.2 **Sample Class Newspaper Page**

Ideas for the Work Station

This work station is a great way to incorporate current events and nonfiction reading. It's a great tie-in for social studies and science. There are several ways to set it up. One way is to cut out newspaper articles of interest for your kids. Mount the headline, graphics, and article separately on three different pieces of card stock, and cut to size. Repeat this process for four to five articles. You might include one from the sports section, another from the food section, one from the front page, and another from the editorials for variety. Be sure to include articles your students will be able to read and understand on their own. Then put all the headlines in a zippered plastic bag, all the graphics in another bag, and the articles in a third bag. Have kids match them, read, and discuss them.

Students match a headline, graphics, and article, then write an inference before reading at the newspaper work station.

Another idea is to use a file folder box to collect newspaper articles. Fill it with file folders that kids label with categories such as "Community Events," "Heroes," "Political Cartoons," "Mistakes in News-

papers," "Sports," "Vocabulary Cartoons," and "Weather." On the front of each folder glue a sample of that type of article. Again, have students contribute to the files. Include colored construction paper, scissors, and glue sticks so students can affix each article to a "card" to be added to the file. You might have each kind of article glued to a certain color to make filing easier. For example, all sports stories are glued onto blue paper, which is then put in the corresponding file folder where "Sports" is written in blue letters. Include generic question cards for kids to answer about the articles. See Appendix D for samples.

A third way to set up this station is to use a commercially available newspaper for kids, such as the *Mini Pages, Time for Kids,* or *Scholastic News.* (These can be found online also.) Simply laminate the weekly newspaper, hole-punch it in the upper left-hand corner, and add a 1-inch metal book ring. Hang the newspapers on a hook and you have an instant newspaper station.

There are many things students might choose to do at the newspaper station, including some of the following that might be posted on your "I Can" list there:

A portable newspaper station made with the class includes cut-out headlines, graphics, and matching articles along with directions for the station and a sample of work kids should do there.

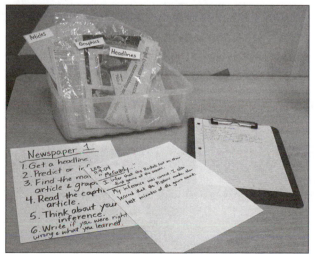

A pocket folder holds samples of what kids can do while at the newspaper station. Note: The teacher has already taught with these before placing them at this station.

I Can . . .

■ Write a news article for our class newspaper.

■ Read a newspaper written for kids.

■ Use a newspaper station task card (see Appendix D).

■ Add a news article to the appropriate folder in the news file box.

■ Read two articles from different news sources on the same topic, then compare and contrast them.

■ Read a news article with a partner. Underline facts in blue. Circle opinions in red.

Troubleshooting

Below is a table listing possible problems you might encounter at this work station, with ideas for solving them.

How the Newspaper Work Station Supports Student Performance on State Tests

Reading and writing news articles gives your students practice with one type of nonfiction used in the real world. Many state tests include articles as a genre students must be able to comprehend in the upper grades. Sometimes there are test questions about parts of a news article, such as headlines and captions. Working with features of news articles at work stations gives students lots of opportunities to become comfortable with this genre. In addition, it gives them knowledge of real-world events, which expands their background knowledge and prepares them for distinguishing between fact and opinion.

Newspaper Work Station

Possible Problem	Troubleshooting Ideas
Kids aren't reading the news articles, but are doing the recreational activities like puzzles and dot-to-dot games.	Remind students to read the newspapers first and then do the activities. If they don't do this, remove the vis-à-vis pens from this station temporarily.
I use our city's daily newspaper with my students, but it gets really messy because it's so big and has so many pages.	Try putting out selected sections each day. Ask kids which are their favorites and include just those.
My students get really silly when they come across some of the underwear ads, etc.	Again, use selected parts. Screen them before putting them into this station.
I'd like for my kids to write a newspaper, but it seems like so much work.	Model, model, model as part of your writer's workshop. Show kids how to write a news article; then have them practice at this station. Use a computer template to make this easier. Perhaps get a parent to help students, too. Also limit your class paper publication to two to three editions a year.
What do I do with all these news clippings? My kids are bringing them in faster than I can post them.	What a great problem to have! This means the students are really reading and using the newspaper at home. Ask them for solutions. One idea is to store old articles in file folders in crates. Have archivists who periodically weed these out.

Grammar Work Station

A pair of sixth graders stands at the dry-erase board. They are quizzing each other, using a grammar book. One acts as the teacher and dictates a sentence to the other, who copies it onto the board. The "teacher" then reminds the "student" to mark the simple subject and predicate. They proceed like this through several sentences until the "teacher" notices an error. He or she then shows the "student" how to mark the sentence correctly. When they are finished, they use the teacher's edition for the grammar book to correct the answers together. They discuss any the "student" got wrong and make corrections.

Ideas for the Work Station

For ages, students have loved playing teacher. That's exactly what they're doing in the example above. They practice any skill the teacher has been showing them in large-group instruction. You could set this up at a dry-erase board or your chalkboard, or you could have two kids sit together with a clipboard for this activity.

Other things that students might do at the grammar station are listed below and might be included on your "I Can" list:

I Can . . .

- Circle the helping verbs in each sentence.
- Color-code each part of speech: red nouns, blue verbs, green adjectives, purple adverbs, yellow prepositions, and so forth.
- Use word tiles to make sentences, making sure to include a noun, adjective, verb, adverb, and prepositional phrase in each. Then I can copy the sentences onto paper and mark each part of speech.
- Use Mad-Libs to practice using grammar.
- Edit a piece from writer's workshop for grammar. I can use correct editing marks.

Using colored word tiles to build sentences at the grammar work station is especially helpful for second-language learners.

Troubleshooting

The next page has a few troubleshooting ideas for the grammar work station.

How the Grammar Work Station Supports Student Performance on State Tests

Just like spelling, grammar is often on state tests. Working on grammar exercises with a partner is a good way for kids to get hands-on practice with the skills they need at their grade level. The peer element adds motivation in the upper grades. You might occasionally have students practice using a multiple-choice format here if that's how it's tested at the state level. They will even enjoy creating

Grammar Work Station

Possible Problem	Troubleshooting Ideas
My third graders aren't doing very well with using the grammar book for this activity.	Some of your third graders may be a bit immature to enjoy this; try it with them later in the year. Make sure the activities are grade-level appropriate.
Word tiles are really noisy, and the kids spend more time trying to find words than they do building sentences.	Put out fewer word tiles at a time and use them on a carpeted area. Have students sort the words into parts of speech and store each kind in a labeled zippered plastic bag. Let them make the labels. Be sure they copy their finished sentences onto paper so you can see what they did here.

multiple-choice questions for each other. Be specific about which skills you want them to practice, though. Grammar games and puzzles will add a recreational element and get students to practice what preadolescent minds often think is a dull task.

Reflection and Dialogue

Consider the following:

1. What helped you most in this chapter? Which ideas were most useful to you?

2. Which of the work stations from this chapter do you already have in your classroom? How are they working? What new ideas did you glean from this chapter? Discuss your ideas with a colleague or your team.

3. Which of the work stations in this chapter would you like to add to your classroom? Share several ideas with a colleague. (Keep in mind that this chapter includes more choices than you may want to include in your room at one time.)

4. How do you schedule students to use the computer in your classroom? How have you maximized computer time? Talk with someone about your ideas.

5. Choose a new work station from this chapter. Work with a partner or small group on ideas for establishing this station in your classrooms.

6. Choose any work station from this chapter. Make a "novelty plan" for how to keep it fresh and interesting over the next six weeks. Remember, you don't have to change everything on Fridays.

7. Ask your students for ideas on other stations they might like to have, as well as ideas for the ones suggested in this chapter. Get them to help you set up these work stations in your classroom.

8. Remember that you might choose to have some duplicate work stations in your classroom. Which ones might you duplicate so more kids can work with them? For example, computer, listening, and buddy reading could all have duplicates. Talk with a colleague about how to keep these fresh and interesting.

6

Word Study Work Station

A pair of fifth graders sits on the floor playing Scrabble. They took this game from the shelf labeled "Word Study Work Station" and got busy playing immediately because they knew exactly what to do. Their teacher played it with them in a small group previously, and now it's a favorite. They have a dictionary with them in case they need it.

In another part of the classroom, two students are working in a second word study work station. They are engaged in looking back at the chapter their teacher read aloud yesterday and choosing several words that catch their attention to investigate. They reach into the tub that holds the book *Sahara Special* by Esme Raji Codell and directions for this activity, and turn to Chapter 7, "George Gets Busted," which their teacher has bookmarked. They quietly read the first couple of pages together and jot down a few words and phrases in their word study notebooks. They choose the following: *soft rosy glow, ax, busted, accountability.* Then they stop and talk about these words and what they make them think about. They decide to sketch what each means and

Playing Scrabble builds spelling and vocabulary skills.

talk about what the words mean in this story, as well as what they might mean in other contexts.

When they are finished, they've discussed how they might try to use *soft rosy glow* in their own writing. They also have talked about multiple meanings for the word *busted*, and they've looked up *accountability* in the dictionary to clarify its meaning.

Why Have a Word Study Work Station?

In the upper grades, students need to continue to learn about phonics, spelling, and vocabulary—the components that make up word study. Instruction will look different than in primary grades, as teachers focus on word etymology, Greek and Latin roots, and deeper content-area vocabulary learning. By creating a station, or a special area in the classroom, that focuses on word study, you show students and classroom visitors that you value the study of words. Your word study station may be set up around a word wall, or you might have words posted on cards on a door, or even on the side of a file cabinet. Nonetheless, creating a niche in your room that focuses on word study says volumes to your students about paying attention to words as they read and write.

It is increasingly important to pay attention to word study as students move through the upper grades, because vocabulary greatly affects their comprehension. Many upper-grade students can decode accurately but have limited comprehension; this is often because of their lack of higher-level vocabulary. The word study station gives students extra opportunities to investigate and notice words with their peers. It can also help students reading below grade level with phonics, if they are struggling with decoding.

What Students Do in the Word Study Work Station

At the word study work station, students should be involved in a variety of word study tasks focusing on phonics, spelling, and vocabulary. They may be working with phonics patterns, frequently mis-spelled words, content-area vocabulary, and/or word orthography. Match the activities to the levels of your students. Be sure to always include activities that help children become curious about words as well as some of the other, more traditional kinds of word work that might be related to your spelling book. Here are some possibilities of what students might do while at the word study work station:

For Phonics, Spelling, and Word Analysis

■ *Sorting words.* To help students notice spelling patterns, have available individual words on cards for them to sort in a variety of ways. They might sort the words according to vowel pattern, part of speech, meaning, or prefix/suffix/root. Teach students to always sort the words, then *read* each word in the sort. In

Word sorts are kept on the teacher desk in small pocket charts. Here students sort words that end in -*um* and change to *a*, and those that end in -*us* and change to *i*.

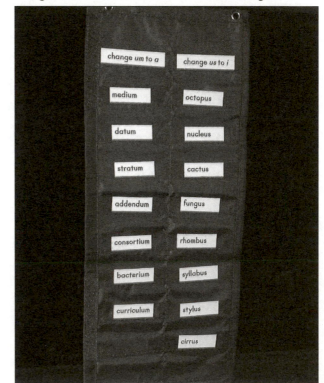

upper grades, have students sometimes *write* the sort also by copying the words sorted onto notebook paper, labeling each category at the top of the page. *All Sorts of Sorts 2* by Sheron Brown (2001) is a great resource with premade sorts geared toward upper-grade kids.

■ *Making words.* Note: This activity will work best with third graders who need help with looking at phonics patterns. Be sure to do this activity with them in a large or small group before placing it in this station for independent practice.

Working with letter tiles or cards, students make words and investigate how they change by removing or adding a letter or two at a time. For example, the teacher says, "Make the four-letter word *ride*. Then add a letter to make *ride* into *bride*. Now take away one letter and add two letters to make *stride*." Patricia Cunningham's *Making Big Words* (1994) and *Making More Big Words* (1997) are excellent resources for this activity. Have one kid read the "teacher script" for making words while the other child builds the words. They check the words together.

Or you might provide magnetic letters and a spelling list for students to practice building spelling words on a magnetic surface, such as the side of a filing cabinet, for kinesthetic practice with spelling.

■ *How many words can you make?* Another activity with making words is using a spelling list and magnetic letters or letter cards/tiles and challenging kids with "How many words can you make with the letters in one of your spelling words?" Be sure to have a dictionary on hand for checking spellings. Have kids manipulate the letters to make as many words as possible. For an extra challenge, include an egg timer. Have students record the words in their word study notebook under a section called "Word Play." Or they can just use strips of paper.

Third graders make words with letters in a pocket chart. An "I Can" list gives directions. Students record words in a word study notebook.

The "How many words can you make?" game is played with an egg timer in fifth grade.

Word study using spelling words is placed on the side of a file cabinet.

- *Playing word games.* Many educational publishers provide a variety of word games for students to play for independent practice. Commercial games, such as Boggle and Scrabble, are also favorites of this age group. Students might also create their own word study games.

- *Doing word games from the newspaper.* Most daily newspapers include some kind of word study games in the comics section. Cut these out and laminate them for kids to play with at the word study station. They can do their writing in their word study notebooks in a section labeled "Word Play." Be sure they date and name their entries.

- *Giving each other "spelling tests."* Kids love to quiz each other on their words. One reads a word from the spelling book (using this week's words or words from any lessons already studied), and the other writes the word on a dry-erase board. Students should check the words together, noting any difficult parts. Note: This should not be the only thing kids do at this station. Be sure to include other kinds of word study where kids are thinking more deeply about words.

- *Creating word webs, trees, and ladders.* These graphic organizers all help students look at relationships between words and notice patterns in spelling and meaning. To make a word web, a common word is written in the middle and related words are written around it.

  To create a word tree, kids use a drawing of a tree (either preprinted or student drawn) with a Greek or Latin root written inside the "root" part. Then students write words using that root on surrounding branches and explore how the words are connected.

  For a word ladder, students draw a ladder and write a word on each rung, starting with a two-letter word, adding or changing one letter at a time to create a new word on the ladder. For example, *at, sat, spat, splat, splats, splits, splints.* You might use a CD-ROM, the Visual Thesaurus (at www.visualthesaurus.com), as a great tool for kids to make word webs, trees, and ladders, and get to a deeper level of understanding how words are connected.

For Vocabulary and Word Investigations

- *Reading and writing ABC books.* Provide a variety of upper-grade alphabet books. These are not written to teach the alphabet, but use the alphabet as a text structure. Help students recognize how authors of ABC books choose a topic, research it thoroughly, and then organize the information around the alphabet. Students might work individually or with partners to create alphabet books around content-area topics or areas of interest.

■ *Illustrating words.* Students can investigate word meanings by illustrating words in books, on cards, or on a bulletin board display. They can even make bookmarks with new words illustrated on them and place them at the classroom library for their friends to use.

■ *Doing dictionary/thesaurus work.* Students need to learn how to use a dictionary to check the spelling, meaning, and pronunciation of words. They should also learn to use a thesaurus to help them choose better words in writing. Provide purposeful tasks for students to develop ease in using these reference books. Whenever possible, integrate purposeful dictionary practice along with a game or activity. For example, a dictionary is useful when playing Scrabble.

■ *Making books of related words, such as homophones.* Provide paper stapled together to make small blank books. On each page, students write a related homophone, illustrate it, and write the meaning or use it in a sentence to help them remember the spelling and meaning. For example, in the *Through, Threw* book, just two pages are needed. One page illustrates the meaning of *through* and the other page illustrates how *threw* is used. Students might work together to create several homophone sets in one book; have them add a table of contents and index. Then place it in the reference section of your word study work station. Students might also keep a section in their word study notebooks for recording what they're learning about homophones.

■ *Collecting words.* Make a display of small colorful construction paper jars with a student's name on each. Demonstrate how to collect new words while reading, write them on small sticky notes, and add them to the individual word jars. These are like personal word banks where students are encouraged to keep track of new words they come across.

Sixth graders play Concentration with vocabulary words and definitions and use a dictionary for checking questionable words.

Figure 6.1 **Word Web**

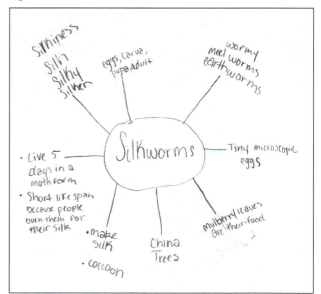

Students write new words found during their reading on small sticky notes and post them on their individual word jars.

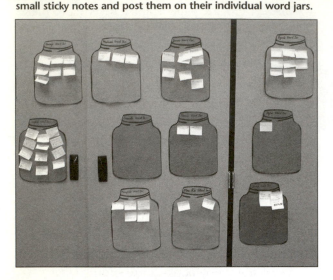

Two boys play Perquackey, building as many words as possible with letter cubes before the timer runs out, in the word study station.

- *Making crossword puzzles with content-area words or interesting words from read-aloud.* A great tool to help kids make their own crossword puzzles is available at www.puzzlemaker.com. Another is Matchword from www.wrightgroup.com. Be sure students are using important words from content-area study or interesting words you're teaching them to pay attention to from read-aloud. The purpose of this activity is to get kids to notice words and begin to "own" them.

- *Playing word study games to develop vocabulary.* Many commercial games are available that preadolescents love. Try Pictionary, Jr., Cranium Cadoo, Upwords, A to Z Game, Password, and Word Sense. Scattergories and Guesstures are two more games that are best for ages twelve and up.

- *Using short text to pay attention to new words.* Use informational text such as *Time for Kids* (go to www.timeforkids.com for printable articles), fact cards (like those at http://yahooligans. yahoo.com.content/animals), and field guide pages. Have students read and take notice of new and interesting words. For example, while reading a field guide on insects, they might jot

down *daddy longlegs, numerous,* and *widespread.* They discuss these words using the context of the card and may even consult a dictionary. They do a quick sketch of a daddy longlegs to help them remember these words. During sharing time, they might share their new words with the class.

- *Use quotations to think about words and their meanings.* Copy quotes that might be of interest to your students on individual cards. Or

Quotation cards build vocabulary and promote deeper thinking strategies.

provide a book of quotes for kids to use to copy onto their own cards. *Incredible Quotations* by Jacqueline Sweeney (1997) is a good source. Have students read and discuss the most important words and ideas. You might have available a few question cards to prompt deeper thinking, such as What do you think this quote means? What does it remind you of in your own life? What do you think is the most important word in this quote and why?

How to Set Up the Word Study Work Station

You may have a permanent space set up for word study and/or use portable word study stations. Start with a space in your classroom where you can display special words to focus student attention on them; use a bulletin board, a wall, a door, or even the side of a file cabinet that everyone can see. This can become your word wall, and you might set up your word study work station nearby. You might also hang quotes about words around this station to inspire kids to be "word collectors." For example, try these:

■ "Artists develop a love for the feel of their tools, the smell and texture of clay, wood, or

paint. Writers are no different. Writers love words."—Ralph Fletcher
■ "Words. I seek words, I chase after them."—Cynthia Rylant
■ "Read like a wolf eats."—Gary Paulsen
■ "I was a wordful child. My family says I talked before I walked."—George Ella Lyon

You will probably need some low shelves for storing word study materials, such as board games, dictionaries, and a few dry-erase boards and markers. Some teachers put word study activities in clear plastic shoe boxes, placing the items needed for each game or activity in a container. You might also set up a magnetic space, like the front of your teacher desk or the side of a file cabinet, to use for sorting or making words. Some teachers fasten a pocket chart to a bulletin board or the front of their teacher desk for sorting and investigating words.

Using a Word Wall in Grades 3–6

Many teachers have word walls in their classrooms because of a building or district mandate, but they're

A portable word study station holds word study games. Students choose to play Scrabble, or add their spelling book and build spelling words on the Scrabble board, as pictured.

Shelves for storing games and materials, plus display space under a window, create a cozy word study nook in a third-grade classroom.

not sure which words to put there or exactly what to do with it. As I have investigated word walls in upper grades, I've considered using them somewhat differently from primary grades. In kindergarten through second-grade classrooms, children are beginning to look more closely at print; however, in grades 3 through 6 our emphasis should change slightly to have kids become more involved as word investigators. This means they should look at word origins, related words, and visual patterns of related words. In upper grades, we move toward looking more at word meanings as well as how words are spelled.

Think about what purpose(s) you'd like your word wall(s) to serve. Talk with students about these and ask for their input on the best place(s) in the classroom to display the words. You might have one or more word walls in your upper-grade classroom. Choose what works for you. As you teach, refer to your word walls. Tell students that you expect any words on these walls to be spelled correctly and hold them accountable for it. Here are four different kinds of word walls to consider:

1. Mini-High-Frequency-Word Wall—By the upper grades, there are usually too many high-frequency words to display in large print like teachers do in kindergarten through grade 2. So, you might have a mini-word wall to save wall space while still focusing on words that are commonly misspelled in the upper grades. Simply display a chart or poster of commonly misspelled words. (Often this kind of chart is included in your spelling book or reading series.) Post this chart along with a note telling students to always spell these words correctly in their writing; display it where students can see it (perhaps in the writing work station) as a visual reminder to always check these words! Be sure students have individual copies to keep in their writing folders or their planners, and remind them to use the chart often.

A mini-high-frequency-word wall is displayed to remind kids to spell these commonly misspelled words correctly. The words are listed in students' planners.

Consider giving each student a personal word wall kept in the back of a word study notebook. Another option is to glue the reproducible sheets in Appendix E onto the inside pages of a file folder, and have students record words they have trouble spelling in the space that matches the first letter of each word. Expect students to spell these high-frequency words correctly in all writing they do. Make them accountable by taking off points for misspelling these words in the work you grade.

2. Interesting-Words Wall—The purpose of this word wall is to help students notice and wonder about words. You might use a bulletin board for this display of words. You have options on how to arrange the words. Get kids' input on this; for example, words might be displayed by part of speech or written under the title of the read-aloud book they came from. Write the words on sticky notes or index cards as students notice new words in large-group instruction. Encourage students to use words from this wall in their daily conversation and in their writing. Reward them for trying out these words by giving them compliments and/or extra points.

The class adds words that got their attention during read-aloud and shared reading to their interesting-words wall. The goal is to use these words in both speaking and writing.

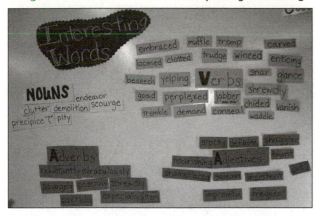

This content-area word wall uses science words.

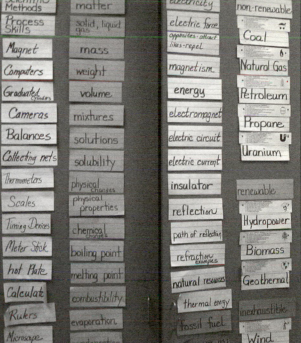

3. Content-Area Word Wall—Paying attention to technical vocabulary is critical to comprehension of informational text. Students encounter many new words as they read in social studies, science, and math. You might keep a chart of new words related to your current unit of study posted on a board where all students can view it. If you teach all subjects, have a separate chart for each subject. Again, you might want to display these charts on a bulletin board. Each time you encounter an important new content-area word, add it to the chart. You might chart it as a word web or simply in a list. Refer to these words frequently as you teach in the content areas. If you have a pocket chart, you might make games using the content-area words. Have students copy individual words onto index cards with the definitions on the opposite sides. Play games with the words on the wall, such as "I'm thinking of a word that . . ." or Hangman. The student must both spell the word and give its definition.

   At the end of a unit of study, simply remove the chart from the bulletin board and add a blank piece of chart paper, labeled with the topic of the new unit. Laminate your old charts and either hang them on clip-on skirt hangers or bind them together to make a Big Book by hole-punching them in the left-hand margin and joining them with 1-inch book rings. Kids can use these for review or reference.

4. Homophones Chart—Intermediate students commonly misuse words that sound the same but have different spellings. Have students create a class chart that shows how to spell them. For example, write *their, there,* and *they're* under one another with a box around them; then have a student draw a sketch to show the meaning of each. In Max Brand's book, *Word Savvy* (2004), he suggests that students compose a sentence with homophones and post that on the homophone chart for quick reference. See his book for excellent examples of upper-grade word walls. After you set up the word wall(s), be sure to teach with them. Refer frequently to words on the wall as you write with students, and expect them to spell these words correctly.

This homophones chart was started in third grade.

Homophones Chart

- to
- two
- too
→ We are going to read two books, too.

- way
- weigh
→ Which way do I go?
→ I weigh 65 pounds.

- through
- threw
→ We walked through the park.
→ He threw the ball.

- buy
- by
→ I must buy some food.
→ This book is by my favorite author.

For example, as you model how to write a lab report in science, refer to science words from the content-area word wall, thinking aloud about how to spell each technical vocabulary word and reflecting briefly on what that word means or why you used it there. As you model how to write a persuasive piece, choose appropriate words from the interesting-words wall and reflect on why you chose those particular words. As you confer with students during writing workshop and notice that they've misspelled homophones, direct their attention back to the homophones chart on the wall and have them correct errors and tell why they are making those particular corrections.

Using Word Study Notebooks

Some upper-grade teachers have students keep their own word study notebooks for recording what

they're learning about words. You might use a composition book divided with sticky notes into several sections, including "Interesting Words," "Word Play," "Spelling Patterns," and "Content-Area Words." If you want the class to use this notebook for recording what they've done at a word study work station, have them use the appropriate section, as noted in directions posted with that station.

Use the notebooks during large-group instruction so kids can record what they're noticing about interesting new words, spelling patterns, and how words work. Keep your own notebook, too, as a model. As you read aloud, have students sit with their notebooks and listen for and record interesting words in that section. They will enjoy using colored pencils, markers, and clipboards while doing this. If you're studying or reading about content-area information, have them do the same in the "Content-Area Words" section. Likewise, encourage students to record new words found in their independent reading in the "Interesting Words" section. You might also include sections for special kinds of words you're studying as a class, such as "Homophones" or "Multiple Meaning Words." Be sure students use this notebook at the word study work station for recording their work there. Remind them to take it with them to the writing work station, too, so they can use what they're learning

A word study notebook is filled with all kinds of words found while reading that can be used during writing.

Interesting Words.
from: The Battle for the Castle
- redefine
- inevitable
- barreled
- shrimps (little)
- reservoir
- glared

about words in their writing. You might view the video *A Day of Words* (2005) to see word study notebooks in use in an upper-grade classroom.

Materials

Materials you could have in the word study work station include the following. Remember that you shouldn't put out *all* these materials at once. This is a menu of choices to consider throughout the school year:

- Word sort materials—words written on small individual cards that can be sorted in a small pocket chart or with magnetic tape on the back that can be adhered to a magnetic surface (Sheron Brown's *All Sorts of Sorts 2* has premade sorts for intermediate students.)
- Magnetic surface for word sorts and making words (side of file cabinet or front of teacher desk or large cookie sheets)
- Student word study notebooks
- Magnetic letters or letter cards (sorted and organized by letter in a labeled tackle box)
- Egg timers or quiet kitchen timers
- Directions for making words activities (If you use these with third graders, Patricia Cunningham's *Making Big Words* and *Making More Big Words* are excellent resources and will save you teacher time.)
- Task cards for working with word wall words (may be made by students)
- Word wall(s)
- Commercially made word games, such as Boggle, Jr., Scrabble, Pictionary, Jr. and homophone, synonym, or antonym games
- Word cards or tiles (for sentence building)
- Small dry-erase boards, markers, and erasers
- Word jumbles and other word games from the newspaper
- Upper-grade alphabet books, such as Jerry Pallotta's *The Extinct Alphabet Book* or *U.S. Navy Alphabet Book.*

- Blank books and pencils for making ABC and other word study kinds of books
- Blank paper and colored pencils for sketching and illustrating words
- Variety of dictionaries and thesauri
- Word-jar cutouts
- Sticky notes
- CD-ROMs for making word study games, such as Puzzlemaker or Matchword
- Short informational text such as field guides, *Time for Kids,* and animal fact cards
- Books of quotations, such as *Incredible Quotations* by Jacqueline Sweeney

How to Introduce the Word Study Work Station

The best way to introduce the word study work station is to begin with large-group teaching of word study routines. You might begin with an easy activity, such as word sorting or matching vocabulary words with their meanings. Another possibility is setting up and showing students how to use the word wall; or you might help students set up individual word study notebooks to introduce this station.

Students' independent practice will go most smoothly if you take time to teach one of the lessons for modeling in the next section. Gather kids near you on the floor, show them the materials you want them to use, and get their input on how to use them. Then write directions together for the activity, have two students model for the class, and make adjustments to your directions as necessary.

In one classroom, I introduced the word study station with a simple prefix, root, and suffix game. All prefixes were written in brown ink on index cards; all roots were written in black, and the suffixes were green. I added a card to label each category and used the matching color to help students remember the terms. Then I asked students what they thought we might do with the cards. They suggested a Concentration game. We placed the cards

A prefix-root-suffix Concentration game with directions and scorecard was made with students.

facedown in three columns, labeling each with the category card showing. Then one student turned over a card in each column. We decided they'd get two points if they could use two cards to make a word and three points if they used all three cards to make a word. We agreed that the words had to be real ones, which meant we needed a dictionary for checking. We stored each kind of card in a snack-size zippered plastic bag labeled with the type of part (prefix, root, suffix). We put the cards, our directions, a dictionary, and a clipboard with a score sheet in a plastic shoe box and labeled it "Word Study Work Station 1." We had plans to add another word study station with commercial games in it, which would become Word Study Work Station 2.

What the Teacher Needs to Model

It is important to carefully model the use of word study materials before placing them at this station so students know exactly what is expected of them. Upper-grade teachers often assume that older kids should simply be able to read directions and work with materials independently—without taking the time to teach students word study routines they want practiced at this station. Time invested in teaching will pay off in high-quality practice time for students (and fewer interruptions for teachers). Here are some possibilities for what you might model across the year:

For Phonics, Spelling, and Word Analysis

How to sort words.

This routine can best be taught in a whole-class setting. The procedures include

1. Sort the words.
2. Read the sorts.
3. Write the sorts.
4. Reflect on the sort and add other words to it.

You might model this on the overhead or in a pocket chart. Write words on cards ahead of time, according to a pattern you're studying, such as words that end in *–ent* or *–ant*. Use those endings as headings, and sort the words with the students according to the patterns. Then read the words with the kids; show them how to copy the words onto a page in their word study notebooks (if you use them) or a piece of notebook paper. Finally, discuss what they noticed about the pattern (words that end in *–ent* or *–ant*). For example, more words end in *–ent* than *–ant*. If the word has two syllables, it ends in *–ent* or *–ant*; if the word has more than two syllables, it ends in *–ent*.

How to do a speed sort.

Once students know how to do word sorts, challenge them to do speed sorts. Provide a timer or stopwatch and show them how to use it to record how long it takes to do a particular sort. Encourage them to try to beat their own times. In word sorting, they are looking at spelling and phonics patterns; fluency and automatic processing are the goals of speed sorting. Another bonus of speed sorts is that the more often students work with a group of words, the more opportunities they have to see and remember those spelling patterns.

How to make a word web, tree, or ladder.

Model how to make word webs before expecting your students to create them in response to words they find in their reading. Do the same with word trees and ladders. For example, to model word webs, start with an interesting word or a content-area vocabulary term, such as *stitching*. Write the word inside an oval with spokes coming out from it. Use the web to record related words; group them together at the end of each spoke in a meaningful way. See Figure 6.1 for an example. Follow similar procedures for demonstrating word trees and ladders. See Figures 6.2 and 6.3 for examples.

How to give a "spelling test."

Students love to quiz each other on their words. Make a note at this station for kids to bring a spelling book when they work here. Have two students model for the rest of the class how to take turns giving a word from the book (from a lesson already taught) while the other writes the word on a dry-erase board. Suggest that the spelling child underline parts that look tricky. Then have them check the words together, noting any difficult patterns and fixing up the mistakes. Do not let them

Figure 6.2 **Word Tree**

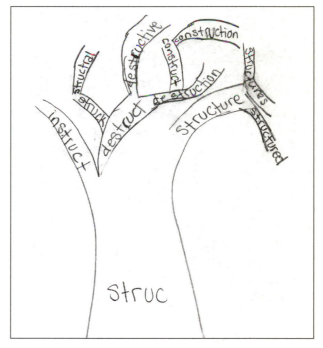

Figure 6.3 **Word Ladder**

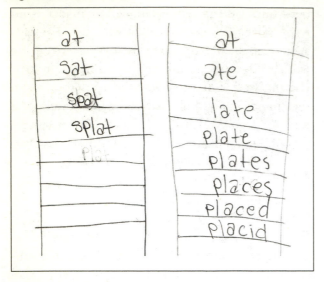

spell the words orally; insist that they write the words on a board. Spelling is a visual skill in the upper grades, and students will benefit most by writing and seeing correct spellings.

For Vocabulary and Word Investigations

How to create an ABC book.

Read aloud several alphabet books that are geared to upper-grade students, such as *Q Is for Quark: A Science Alphabet Book* by David M. Schwartz or *D Is for Doufu: An Alphabet Book of Chinese Culture* by Maywan Shen Krach. Discuss what the author had to do before writing to create this book. For example, in this book the writer might have listed the letters of the alphabet and brainstormed a word that starts with each; the author also had to look for facts about that particular topic. Write a class alphabet book related to a content area of study. For example, if you're studying the Civil War, it might begin with a list like this:

A—Abraham Lincoln
B—Bravery
C—Civil War

Model how to use your social studies textbook or an index from a book about the Civil War to find words that fit each letter. Then assign a letter and matching word to each student to research, write about, and illustrate. Compile all in a class book. Use this as a model for students to write their own ABC books. You might use the planning sheet in Appendix E.

Place other ABC books in this station, being sure to include some by Jerry Pallotta. Kids might also enjoy visiting his Web site at www.alphabetman. com to learn about how this author writes his alphabet books. A few other good ABC book titles include *The Graphic Alphabet* by David Pelletier, *Z Was Zapped* by Chris Van Allsburg, *L Is for Last Frontier: An Alaska Alphabet Book* by Carol Crane, and *D Is for Democracy* by Elissa Grodin.

How to use a dictionary/thesaurus.

Model how to use a dictionary as you read aloud to students and come across new and interesting words. Show them how to look up a word's meaning or pronunciation. Also model how to use a dictionary to check the spelling of words while you're writing with the class. Another resource to model with during writing is the thesaurus; demonstrate how to find another word to replace an overused one. The more you use these language tools, the more likely your students will be to use them. Provide a variety of dictionaries, thesauri, and other word study books; include foreign language dictionaries if you have bilingual students. Provide dictionaries at word study stations where kids will use them for authentic purposes. For example, place one with a Scrabble game or with multiple-meaning books they are making. Teach students how to find a word quickly in a dictionary by thinking aloud while looking up a word. Say, "Charades starts with *c*. That's in the beginning of the dictionary so I'll turn there fast. Ch . . . that's close to the start of the *c* words, and there'll be a lot of them since I've read many ch words. Ca, ce, ch . . . a . . . that's in the beginning. I found it!" Repeat this often so students will have models of how to find words fast. This will encourage their dictionary and thesaurus use, too, if they can find what they need quickly.

How to play word games.
Show students how to play commercial word games such as Scrabble, Boggle, Wordthief, A to Z Game, and Upwords. If a student in your class already knows how to play one of these games, ask him or her to teach others in a small group. If the game is new to the whole class, model how to play it in a large-group setting. Go over the directions, show a few sample moves, and have a couple of students model it for everyone. (This is a good way to work through the kinks.) If the directions are complex, you might rewrite them as a class in simple terms so everyone agrees on how it will be played in your classroom.

Another source of word study activities is to make card games with your students using spelling or vocabulary words. For example, give students vocabulary cards that have the definition on one side and the word on the other. Have them invent games to play. In one fifth-grade classroom I visited, two girls were both copying definitions onto a dry-

Two girls copy social studies vocabulary and definitions on a dry-erase board to help them remember new words—just one way they choose to work with the words.

erase board. When finished, they asked each other to identify the vocabulary word. I asked them why they had copied the definitions, and they explained that it helped them remember. They said that sometimes they just used the cards as flash cards and named the word on the back. Favorite games kids can make include Concentration (matching definitions and vocabulary words) or Go Fish (matching definition, vocabulary word, sentence using that word, and illustration). Students can help make these games. For example, they can make four cards in a set for Go Fish using content-area vocabulary or words from the novels you are reading.

How to Solve Problems That May Arise

Because there are many materials (and often multiple pieces) for the word study work station, management may be challenging from time to time. Listed on the next page are some things you'll want to consider to keep this station working well.

Differentiating at This Work Station

Because students are often at different levels in their spelling, this is a work station where differentiation is crucial. You may have students who still rely primarily on sound spellings; others are having trouble remembering when to double syllables or drop the *e* when adding endings; others are working on more sophisticated word study as they learn about word derivatives and think about Greek and Latin roots. Observe students to see which ones need practice with what. Then plan accordingly for appropriate word study for them.

You might use color-coded baskets or shelves (tape a colored strip of construction paper on the edge of a shelf) for different levels of materials. Or you can place colored dots on materials to match the word study level. For example, syllable work activities might be in blue baskets or have blue dots

Word Study Work Station

Possible Problem	Troubleshooting Ideas
Kids are goofing around and not using materials appropriately.	You may need to reteach how to use the materials. Or you may simply need to send students back to their seats to do something less enjoyable. Clear expectations and consistent follow-up often get rid of poor behavior at work stations.
Why can't my students just read the directions for the board game and play it independently?	Don't assume that all upper-grade students can read and follow board game directions. It's more effective to play the game with them first, usually in a small group; or go over the directions and play through a few moves with the rest of the class watching. That way you can work through possible areas of dispute with them. Once you have played the game together, put it in the word study station for independent practice.
Students are playing a word study game, but they are having trouble making words or finding matches.	First, check how many cards are in the activity. You might need to limit the number of cards in a Concentration game or matching game, so students can be successful. Try playing the game with students in a small group if they're having difficulty. Work through any snafus, and then let them play on their own.
What do I do with all these word study materials and charts?	Get students to help you organize them! Create a system that works for your class. For example, have students help you decide where to store things; have them make labels for where to keep everything. You might bind charts into a Big Book using a hole punch and 1-inch metal book rings.

on them. Prefix and suffix materials might be stored on a red shelf or in a red basket. Assign students to the color that best matches what they need to practice.

Using different colored baskets for word study materials at a variety of levels helps with differentiation at the word study station.

An excellent resource for leveled word study activities is *Words Their Way* by Donald Bear et al. (2004). This book describes various spelling stages and appropriate activities for each stage. Many games for word study follow-up and practice can be taught and then used independently at this work station.

Ways to Keep This Station Going Throughout the Year

To make this station effective all year, be careful to keep it uncluttered. It is easy to keep adding materials and run out of room. If you find this area getting too crowded, consider breaking up this station into several portable stations (with materials stored in different clear plastic shoe boxes); or designate two different places in the classroom for word study, such as a vocabulary station (possibly at a pocket chart hung on a bulletin board) and a spelling station (on the side of a file cabinet).

In addition, you'll want to keep this station interesting by adding novelty throughout the year. Here are some ideas to get you started:

- Change the words on the interesting-words wall as you see most students using them and spelling them correctly.
- Change the words on the content-area word wall as you begin a new unit of study. Let students add illustrative borders to add interest and promote ownership.
- Add new word study games over time. Remove those that students aren't using as frequently and reintroduce them later in the year.
- Change the words for sorting.
- Replace the small dry-erase boards with small chalkboards. Or substitute a black dry-erase board for a white one. Office supply stores sell black marker boards and neon-colored markers for writing on them.
- Add new dictionaries or thesauri throughout the year. Introduce students to a variety of these resource materials.
- Let students design their own task cards to use at the word study station, particularly related to your word wall(s).

How to Assess/Keep Kids Accountable

How will you know if students are benefiting from using this station? The best place to look is in their independent reading and writing. Students who are practicing appropriately will be able to decode more and more challenging words as well as extract deeper meaning from what they read. In addition, you'll notice improved spelling of the patterns they've been studying with you. Listen to individuals read, and confer with them during independent reading time; likewise, look at the spellings they use in their writing and confer with them about improvements you notice during independent writing time.

Expect students to spell word wall words correctly and let them know how you will mark off on work with these words misspelled. This should hold true both in language arts and in content-area classes. If you don't see improvement in students' reading, writing, and spelling, look closely at your word study instruction. Is your teaching targeting exactly what each student needs?

One way to keep students accountable at this work station is by having them use their word study notebooks. Periodically, collect them and assign a grade. You might look at them once every week or two. Let students know exactly what you expect them to have completed. For example, have them complete a specific type of sort, or request that they collect five to ten new words each week and try using them in their daily reading and writing.

Have students share what they're learning at this station during the "sharing time" following independent work time. Be specific in having them report what they learned and noticed about words during independent work time that day (including independent reading, small group with the teacher, and/or literacy stations).

How This Station Supports Student Achievement on State Tests

Being able to decode words automatically and accurately improves fluency and affects reading comprehension. Therefore, students who have difficulty with phonics patterns should practice them so they can learn to decode with increasing automaticity. Literacy work stations are highly motivating for most students, and practicing phonics in a gamelike manner with the support of a peer can influence students more effectively than giving them stacks of phonics worksheets.

However, decoding alone won't improve reading scores. Upper-grade students need to understand vocabulary to improve their comprehension, and comprehension is the focus of standardized reading tests. Practice at the word study work station can help students pay attention to new words and their meanings (and old words and their multiple meanings). Word study at this station also encourages students to use dictionaries and thesauri and to think about words in both their reading and writing.

Students who love words and are on the lookout for new and interesting ones will use them in their writing, which will certainly boost performance on state writing tests. Celebrate students' experimentation with new words and interesting phrases in their writing during individual conferences and sharing time. In addition, spelling is often evaluated on state writing tests. Students must take a multiple-choice test and recognize correct spellings (an editing type of test) and/or be expected to spell most words correctly on tests that sample student writing (usually from a prompt or piece of text). As students practice spelling words correctly, remind them that spelling is a courtesy that helps the reader understand the message. Working with a partner to practice spelling and vocabulary highly motivates students to practice. And practice makes permanent.

Reflection and Dialogue

Consider the following:

1. Do you have a word wall? What is its purpose? How are you teaching with it? How are students using it? What effect is it having on students' decoding, spelling, and vocabulary development? Share your thoughts with a colleague and work together to get the full use of this teaching tool. Use ideas from this chapter on upper-grade word walls.

2. How have you and your students organized your word study work station? Can students easily get to the materials they need? Are they returning materials to the proper place? Take a "field trip" to another teacher's classroom to see his or her word study station. Share your ideas and observations with each other.

3. Periodically observe students to see if they are doing the activities you assigned them. Pay close attention to students who need the most practice with phonics, spelling, and vocabulary to see if they are doing what they should.

4. Do you have several activities for students to choose from at this station? How have you differentiated them? Share your ideas with a colleague.

5. What new word study activities can you introduce to the group as a whole? In a small-group setting?

6. Are you bogged down in paperwork generated from this station? If so, determine which types of written work best demonstrate what students are learning here. Get rid of extraneous tasks you may have instituted in the name of "accountability." Perhaps you could begin to have students use word study notebooks as described in this chapter. For more information on word study notebooks, see *Words Their Way* by Donald Bear et al. or *Word Savvy* by Max Brand.

7. Look at the activities you have placed in the word study station. Plan for a balance of practice geared toward phonics, spelling, *and* vocabulary. Get a colleague to help you critique your word study station with this balance in mind; then do the same for him or her. Work together to brainstorm ideas to address all three aspects of word study. Try to use materials you already have, such as resources that come with your textbooks.

Poetry Work Station

Poems are posted all around the poetry work station. The students have written some; others are photocopied from books. A basket is filled with poetry books. Today two students at this station are reading poems together and responding to them. They have chosen two poems and are reading and answering open-ended questions that are listed on cards on a ring. First they read aloud the two poems so they can hear and feel the language:

That Mountain Far Away
by Tewa
My home over there, my home over there,
My home over there, now I remember it!
And when I see that mountain far away,
Why, then I weep. Alas! What can I do? . . .
My home over there, now I remember it.

Untitled
by Papago
There was a mountain, over its black roots [the
    deer]

jumped in and in front of it danced, and
    behind a grey
mountain it stood.
(Whipple 1994)

Then one of the students, Lizbeth, reads from a card, "Which words feel important? Highlight them. Read the poem again and emphasize these." She and her partner take small pieces of highlighter tape and talk about which words they think are most important. They decide to cover *there, mountain, now, far away, weep, I,* and *remember* in the first poem. In the second one, they highlight *was, black, jumped,* and *danced.* They read the poems again, and suddenly they come to life. The words have more meaning.

Maurice reads the next card: "What does the poem make you feel?" He replies immediately, "The first one made me sad. I could feel that this person's home and mountain had been taken away."

Lizbeth chimes in, "Yeah, it's kind of like what we were reading about in social studies class about

103

Students use highlighter tape to remind them to emphasize important words when they read a poem.

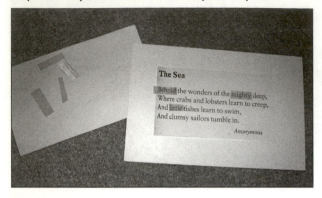

A chart on "How to Copy a Poem" reminds kids what to consider when copying favorite poems into their poetry anthologies.

when the Native Americans lost their land. Who wrote this, anyway?"

Maurice answers, "Tewa. Let's look that up on the Internet." They walk over to the computer and log on to a search engine. Soon they find out that the Tewa, a Pueblo tribe, inhabited the Southwest, which confirms their thinking. They look at the second poem and predict that this also might be written by a Native American tribe. They look up Papago and find that they are correct. It's another Southwest tribe known as the desert people.

Lizbeth moves on to the next question on a card and reads it. "Does the poem remind you of anything in your own life?" She tells Maurice that it reminds her of her grandma, who talks about life in her former country before she moved to the United States. Lizbeth thinks she might talk more about this with her grandma and perhaps write a poem about it the next time she comes to this station.

Maurice reads the last card: "What pictures do you see in your mind?" He tells Lizbeth that he can see an old, weathered man with a sad face who is thinking about when he was forced to leave his former land. He says there is a photo of a Native American in a classroom library book, *Eyewitness: Wild West,* a book he recently browsed. He walks quietly to the library to show the photo to his partner. She agrees that it is a clear picture of what the poem is describing. They decide to look for more poems by Native Americans in the basket of poetry

books in this station to see if they have a similar feeling.

In third grade, down the hall, students are also working at the poetry work station in their classroom. Their teacher has shown them how to copy a favorite poem, line by line, onto notebook paper. Because younger writers are often not as familiar with poetry layout, there is a model of a poem with tips for how to copy a poem posted in the poetry station. Each student will place his or her notebook pages of favorite poems in a 1-inch, three-ring binder that becomes a personal poetry anthology and may be read during independent reading time.

Why Have a Poetry Work Station?

Exploring poetry gives students a chance to think deeply about things that really matter to them. It can help them slow down and notice both the world around them and the world inside them. As Charles Simic says, "A poem is someone else's snapshot in which you see yourself."

The poetry work station can give preadolescents opportunities to imagine and develop creativity; it can also help them create mental images, which improves reading comprehension. Poetry gives kids a chance to read smaller bits more thoughtfully and compose meaningful pieces without the threat of so many words (especially for struggling students or students learning English as a second language). Poetry teaches students to listen . . . to words and rhythm and the music of language as well as to the voices within their hearts and souls. Poetry gives students opportunities to play with language and try new words in interesting and enjoyable ways. It can improve reading fluency as students have fewer words and shorter lines of text to read at a time. Most kids enjoy poetry. They delight in funny poems by Jack Prelutsky and Shel Silverstein, they are awestruck by the simplicity of everyday objects in Valerie Worth's poems, and they love the lilting language of David McCord. Poetry offers a break in the hectic world we inhabit; give children the chance to linger with language in the poetry work station.

What Students Do in the Poetry Work Station

Throughout the year, many of the activities in the poetry work station will remain the same. What changes are the forms, the reading levels, the sophistication of the poems, and students' responses to them. As intermediate classes study new content-area material, poetry that supports that subject matter may be added. As you present new forms of poetry, you will have students focus on them in both their reading and writing. Here are some possibilities of what students might do at the poetry work station. As students are introduced to new activities, they may be posted on the "I Can" list.

Third graders read new poetry books and reread poems from charts used in shared reading.

- *Reading poems.* Students may choose to read poems from a variety of poetry books placed in this station. Change or add books to the collection throughout the year to keep it interesting. Explain to students that you want them to read silently to find poems, but that you'd also like them to read poetry aloud (with quiet voices) so they can *hear* and *feel* the language. Poetry is best when read aloud. Set purposes for what you'd like students to look and listen for in the poems. Task cards for the poetry work station are included in Appendix G. Use them to help focus students' reading of poems.

  Because kids sometimes feel intimidated by poetry anthologies, you might try a "poetry pass" periodically (as recommended by Franki Sibberson). Have students sit in a large circle, and hand a poetry anthology to every student, or to pairs if you don't have as many books. Be sure each student has a pencil and his or her reading folder to make notes in the section called "Books I'd Like to Read" about anthologies that look interesting. Give kids a minute or two to browse the book they are holding, then signal them to pass it clockwise to the

A "Poetry Pass" gives kids a chance to preview poetry anthologies before reading them at the poetry station.

next student(s). Continue in this way until the books have been passed all around the circle.

■ *Writing poems.* Students are often successful in writing when they are allowed to write poems, especially at the start of the year. Teach students how to write their own poems and let them compose and display their poems.

■ *Submitting poems online or entering poetry contests.* There are several Web sites that post student poetry. Check out the Web for current sites and submission guidelines. There are also numerous poetry contests that may be held locally as well as nationally. Post rules for these contests at the poetry station and let students create their own entries.

■ *Performing poems.* Let students work with partners or alone to choose favorite poems and dramatize them. They can practice at this station and then perform the poems during sharing time after independent work time.

■ *Copying poems for personal poetry anthologies.* This is good handwriting practice, especially for students making the transition to cursive writing. However, it is also an opportunity for students to search for favorite poems and copy them into their personal poetry anthologies for personal reading and reflection. (I still have

one I created in high school that has meaning for me today!)

■ *Illustrating poems.* Poetry can help students create mental images as they read short amounts of text. Have students read poems, think about the pictures in their minds, then illustrate them. They can copy favorite poems and illustrate them in their personal poetry anthologies. Or they might draw an image on an index card and place it in a library pocket at the back of a poetry book; they can write the page number of the poem it matches for others to see.

■ *Comparing poems.* Show students how to use a Venn diagram to compare ideas in two poems. It's easiest if you preselect several poems about the same topic by putting matching colored flags on those pages in a poetry book.

■ *Responding to poems.* Teach students how to think about poetry as you read poems during both read-aloud and shared reading. Help students connect to poems by choosing poems you love and sharing your personal links to them. Use the "Poetry Task Cards" in Appendix F.

■ *Harvesting words to use in their own writing.* As you read aloud poems to your class, have

Poems flagged in a poetry book can be compared using a Venn diagram.

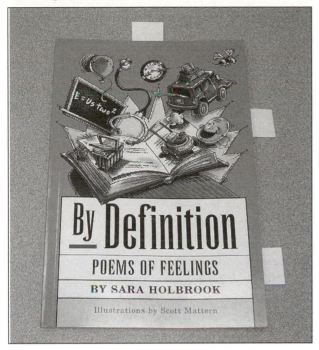

Students list "interesting words" on the back pages of their poetry anthologies.

> Interesting Words:
> 1. declared
> 2. observe
> 3. gorgeous
> 4. dear old trout
> 5. dismay
> 6. Good gracious
> 7. wandering bears

them keep their ears open for interesting words. You might keep a chart labeled "Interesting Words" that students can use when they're writing. Encourage them to do the same as they're reading poetry. They might have a section in their personal poetry anthologies or word study notebooks for favorite words and phrases they've found. Or you could show them how to use a highlighter pen to mark special words in their own anthologies that they can use when writing.

■ *Studying poetry craft.* Guide students toward understanding how poems are crafted, including the study of poetry structure (such as line breaks and stanzas), poetry tools (such as alliteration, rhyming, rhythm patterns, repetition, and personification), and interesting word choices.

■ *Learning about poets.* Create a poet study monthly or every grading period. Include information about the poet as well as sample

poems. Bookmark the poet's Web page if one is available for students to explore at the computer. Here are some to get you started:

Arnold Adoff	Myra Cohn Livingston
Aileen Fisher	Eve Merriam
Betsy Franco	Lilian Moore
Robert Frost	Naomi Shihab Nye
Nikki Giovanni	Christina Rosetti
Lee Bennett Hopkins	Carl Sandburg
Langston Hughes	Shel Silverstein
Paul B. Janeczko	Valerie Worth
Karla Kuskin	

■ *Making poems with a magnetic poetry kit.* Provide a commercially produced magnetic poetry kit or make your own with your computer and magnetic paper, available where office supplies are sold. Check out www.magneticpoetry.com for information.

■ *Memorizing favorite poems.* Challenge students to memorize a poem of their choice once every six to nine weeks. Let them practice at the poetry station. Some may enjoy adding simple props and dramatizing the poems. Some intermediate teachers host a "poetry café" several times a year during which students perform their memorized poems; they invite friends and family to their performance.

Magnetic poetry kits are available commercially and are easy to set up on a file cabinet. Kids can organize words by parts of speech jotted on sticky notes.

tape to identify a particular type of word and then read the poem aloud, emphasizing those words. Have them tell if the poem took on a different meaning when read that way. You might have them use poetry bookmarks to record their words. (See Appendix F.)

- *Exploring metaphors, similes, personification, alliteration, onomatopoeia, assonance, and other aspects of grammar.* As you study each of these terms, have students collect examples of them from poems. You might have them label sections in the backs of their poetry anthologies and search for poems that represent those terms to be copied there. They can then use these to help them write their poetry.

- *Reading poetry cards.* In *Still Learning to Read* (2003), Sibberson and Szymusiak suggest the use of laminated poetry cards that have a poem on one side, and a note saying "If you like this poem, you might like . . ." on the other to help students move from favorite poets to similar writers or whole anthologies.

Here are some of my favorite anthologies that give background information about poets and contain some of their poems.

A Jar of Tiny Stars: Poems by NCTE Award-Winning Poets edited by Bernice E. Cullinan
This collection has a section for each of ten poets (who were chosen by children as favorites), including a picture of and a quotation by each, followed by several poems by that writer. Some of the poets are David McCord, Aileen Fisher, and Arnold Adoff.

The Place My Words Are Looking For edited by Paul B. Janeczko
This anthology is peppered with poems by a wide assortment of poets. Photos of the poets along with a piece telling about that writer's thoughts about poetry follow many of the poems. Poets range from Jack Prelutsky to William Cole to Gwendolyn Brooks.

- *Finding poems to match people, places, and things.* Have students search for poems that can be displayed around the classroom and/or around the school. Georgia Heard calls this the Living Anthology Project. Work with students to gather poems that might be read around the school where people wait, such as the water fountain, the front office, the nurse's room, and the cafeteria line. They might also find poems that match their personalities or that remind them of a friend that they can share with that person. If you display found objects from nature in your poetry or your science station, students might find poems to match those, too.

- *Learning about parts of speech.* Because poems are short, they are excellent for examining parts of speech. Have students read poems and look for different types of words: interesting nouns, strong verbs, descriptive adjectives, and expressive adverbs. They might use highlighter

Poetry for Young People: Robert Frost edited by Gary D. Schmidt
Other recommended books in this series are about Carl Sandburg, Edgar Allen Poe, and Edward Lear. There are also books in the series about American poems and animal poems. They are beautifully illustrated and include a biography about the poet at the beginning of the book.

I Heard a Bluebird Sing: Children Select Their Favorite Poems by Aileen Fisher, selected by Bernice Cullinan
Information about Aileen Fisher, an award-winning NCTE poet, is included along with short personal statements and forty-one of this author's poems selected by children.

A Child's Introduction to Poetry by Michael Driscoll
This book includes a CD with poems read aloud. Part I covers a variety of poems from limericks to haiku to ballads and sonnets. Part II gives information on poets from Homer to Maya Angelou in chronological order. Poems by each writer are included. A nice feature is the vocabulary boxes called "Words for the Wise" that bring attention to unusual vocabulary in the poems.

Opening Days: Sports Poems selected by Lee Bennett Hopkins
This one appeals to kids who love sports but may not be too interested in reading and writing. A wide variety of sports by an assortment of poets is included.

How to Set Up the Poetry Work Station

You don't need much space for a poetry station. It is helpful to have a bulletin board or a bit of wall space on which to display poems with a small

A space-saving poetry station on a countertop contains poetry baskets, paper, and cool pens, with cinquain and haiku samples in the background.

table in front of it on which you place materials. But if you don't have a board, you can simply display poems in clear acrylic picture frames placed on the table, or attach poems to a trifold science project board that can be folded up and stored when not in use. Label your poetry station and add a sign that says, "Observe the world around you AND look within." (Let kids design and decorate this.) Post this in your poetry station to remind students where they can get ideas for poems.

One teacher I know used her teacher desk placed beside a low metal filing cabinet for a poetry station. She posted poems on the front of her desk, placed a magnetic poetry kit on the front of the filing cabinet, and provided index cards attached with magnets on the side of the cabinet for students to display poems they created. You could place a tub of poetry books there (under your teacher desk) along with a container holding two clipboards, writing materials, and clean paper (for copying and/or illustrating poems). And you could place natural objects either on the edge of the teacher's desk or in another clear plastic container or attractive open basket.

If you can't find any other space, make a portable poetry work station. Just be sure to place materials in a neat, organized container or two, preferably clear plastic or an open basket so you can

This poetry station uses the front of the teacher's desk and a file cabinet.

be sure it stays orderly. Make sure to provide a place where poetry is displayed so student work can be shown and encouraged. You might use that wasted space under the chalkboard ledge and place your containers there, so students can just sit there to work using clipboards. Or have a poetry corner out in the hallway on a wall with poems (written by kids and poets studied) to display and share with other classrooms and visitors.

Materials

Start with a collection of favorite poetry books. You might want to start with some listed in Figure 7.1.

Students build poems using a magnetic poetry kit. Student poems are displayed on the other side of the file cabinet for peers to read.

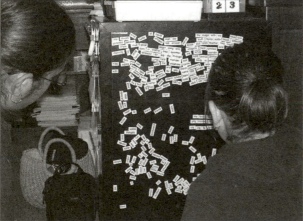

Figure 7.1 **Some Favorite Poetry Books**

The Random House Book of Poetry for Children selected by Jack Prelutsky
This has been one of my favorite anthologies for years. It includes 572 poems and is arranged by topics of interest to kids, such as "Nature Is . . .," "The Four Seasons," "Me I Am!," and "I'm Hungry!" This book is indexed by the names of poets as well as by subject, which makes it a useful tool for teachers and students.

The Dream Keeper and Other Poems by Langston Hughes
Originally written in 1932 by a Harlem Renaissance poet, this book is still fresh and pertinent for today's students.

Talking Like the Rain: A Read-to-Me Book of Poems compiled by Dorothy Kennedy and X. J. Kennedy
More than 100 poems with beautiful watercolors introduce students in K–5 to a wide variety of poems and poets.

The Pig in the Spigot by Richard Wilbur
These wordplay poems contain words within words. Cleverly written.

Good Books, Good Times! compiled by Lee Bennett Hopkins
This collection of poems celebrates books and reading.

All the Small Poems and Fourteen More by Valerie Worth
Each page contains one poem written sparsely and beautifully about a common object such as a cow, zinnias, and a clock.

- Poetry charts (taught with in shared reading)
- Jump-rope rhymes and tongue twisters
- Magnetic poetry kit (available commercially, or can be teacher made)
- Poet study information
- Highlighter tape, precut and stuck to index cards, and/or highlighter pens
- Paper (for copying poems or writing your own)
- Pencils, markers, gel pens, crayons
- Magazine pictures (to inspire writing)
- Natural objects (to inspire writing)
- Notebook of student poems written by the class
- Rhyming dictionary and thesaurus
- Class-made charts about poetry craft (highlighting poetry terms, such as alliteration, simile, personification, etc.)
- Task cards, bookmarks, and sticky notes for reading and thinking about poetry
- Poems displayed in acrylic frames or on a bulletin board
- Blank note cards and envelopes (for copying special poems to give as gifts)

How to Introduce the Poetry Work Station

Introduce the poetry station during read-aloud. Tell students you are going to place some of the poetry books and poems you've been reading into the poetry work station. Show the materials you already have set up there, including paper and pens for copying poems and markers for illustrating favorite poems. Model how to copy a poem onto a card, being sure to match the line breaks as determined by the poet. Talk with students about searching for poems they like and copying them onto pages of a spiral notebook you've provided for them as a personal poetry anthology.

Hand out the notebooks to kids and let them spend a few minutes cutting out words and images from old magazines to decorate their new poetry

Read aloud from these daily; it takes only a minute or two. Remind the students that these poems can be found in the poetry work station and that they might begin copying favorites for their personal poetry anthologies. Over the course of the year, add more poems and related activities as they tie into content-area themes and lessons you've taught in a whole-group setting. Here are some things you might add during the year:

- Favorite poetry books (might have some sorted by favorite poets)

"Borrow" a basket of poetry books from your classroom library (or the school library) to get your poetry station started. Model how to read a poem during short read-aloud moments throughout the day. Connect to content areas to save time.

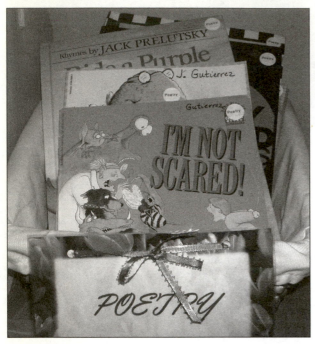

This sample "I Can" list was brainstormed in a third-grade classroom.

books. Have them add a label that says "My Personal Poetry Anthology by ____." Place these notebooks in a crate and store them in the poetry station.

Students help the teacher come up with what they can do at the poetry work station.

The following day take a few minutes to meet with the class and visit the poetry work station once more. Brainstorm an "I Can" list with them. It might look something like this to start:

I Can . . .

- Find poems that I really like.
- Read poems and think about how they make me feel.
- Copy favorite poems into my personal poetry anthology.
- Add words or images to the cover of my poetry anthology.
- Begin to collect words I like from poems I read (put on the back page of my anthology).

How to Choose Poems for the Poetry Work Station

Finding poems that students enjoy and connect to is key to a successful poetry work station. For ease in starting, many teachers choose humorous poems

Figure 7.2 **Humorous Poetry Books**

> *If You're Not Here, Please Raise Your Hand: Poems about School* by Kalli Dakos
>
> *When the Teacher Isn't Looking: And Other Funny School Poems* by Ken Nesbitt
>
> *A Light in the Attic* by Shel Silverstein
>
> *Where the Sidewalk Ends* by Shel Silverstein
>
> *A Pizza the Size of the Sun* by Jack Prelutsky
>
> *The Butterfly Jar* by Jeff Moss

that kids have loved for years, such as those by Prelutsky and Silverstein. See suggestions in Figure 7.2. Choose poems that you like, too, especially for read-aloud and shared reading; you set the tone of the poetry station with your enthusiasm and interest. Ask students to be on the lookout for poetry they enjoy, and have them add it to the station; they might search in the school or public library as well as in bookstores. The Internet is another source for poetry.

You might find out if any poets live nearby and invite them to visit your classroom to share their writing with students. A good source to use for this is www.onlinepoetryclassroom.org/what/map.cfm. It displays a U.S. map to click on and locate local poets.

What the Teacher Needs to Model

The poetry work station will be most successful if you model the following routines over time. Many models, not just one, will help students perform at their best. Model first; then repeat the activity with the students, either in large or small groups, to be sure they understand before moving the activity to the station. Here are some things you'll need to model:

How to read a poem.

The best way to model this is to read poetry aloud, thinking aloud and showing students how to savor the words. Some teachers begin with humorous

poetry, because it touches kids instantly. But you'll want to read a wide variety of poetry, so students don't think of it as just being funny. Let them see that poetry can be comforting, thought-provoking, tender, and inspirational as well. Read each poem aloud twice. First read it and have students listen quietly. Ask them to think about images that come to mind, or their connections to the poem. Have them share with partners, and then with the class. Read the poem a second time and ask students what they notice this time. They might hear rhyming words or alliteration, or something they didn't hear the first time. Here's what you may say to the students as you model how to read a poem. Be sure to include these same suggestions on the "I Can" list you later create with them:

- Read the poem aloud. What do you see in your mind? What does the poem remind you of? Talk about this with your partner.
- Read the poem aloud again. What did you notice this time? Which words did you like? Discuss this with your partner.

How to write a poem.

Many teachers avoid writing poetry with students, because they don't like poetry themselves or don't feel comfortable writing poems with kids. Actually, poetry can be one of the easiest types of writing to do, if you let go of the idea that poems always have to rhyme. You can use students' poems as models if you don't want to write in front of your students. Regie Routman's *Kids' Poems for Grades 3–4* (2000) walks you through the process, step-by-step, of how to write poems with kids. She provides wonderful poems written by students in your grade level to use as models.

Another resource to help you write poetry with kids is *Awakening the Heart* by Georgia Heard (1998). She includes a chapter titled "Writing Poetry" that gives you lots of ideas for writing poems with students of all ages. There is an appendix of student poems to share with your class, too.

In *Conversations with a Poet: Inviting Poetry into K–12 Classrooms* (2005), Betsy Franco shows teachers how to write poetry with kids using a variety of forms. She shows you how to write list poems, riddles, free verse, limericks, odes, and ballads, among others. There is a whole chapter on how to demonstrate writing poems in front of the class.

How to submit a poem for a contest or online publication.

Be on the lookout for poetry contests; some may be sponsored locally or nationally. Numerous Web sites and several magazines publish student poetry. Check online for current information on poetry publishing and contests, but read the fine print to be sure no costs are involved. Go over rules and specific formats for submission so students have a better chance of having their poems published. Provide forms at the poetry work station. You might even display some kids' poetry that has been published. Encourage your students to keep trying if they get rejected; this is part of the publication process!

How to respond to poetry.

Show students a variety of ways to respond to poems. They might talk about poems, collect poems, illustrate them, or act them out. Model how to do each of these things; then allow students to choose the response that appeals to them. Include samples of different kinds of student responses in the work station. For example, you might include a personal poetry anthology from last year or an illustrated poem or photos of students acting out poems.

How to perform poetry.

This is a great outlet for your students who have boundless energy and can't ever seem to sit still. Again, your reading aloud of poetry sets the stage. Show students how to enunciate and project every word, pausing for emphasis on important words and phrases. Have the class suggest motions that

Fifth graders read and perform poetry in their Poetry Café.

might accompany certain poems you've read aloud or used in shared reading. Occasionally, bring a prop or two to add to the performance of a poem. Remind students that they can practice performing a poem at the poetry work station, but that they must do so quietly so they don't disturb others who are working. Give them opportunities to sign up to perform poems on a monthly "poetry performance day" (such as the Poetry Café) or during sharing time after independent work time.

How to copy a poem line by line.

As students learn about new poetry forms, they may need specific directions to help them copy poems from books. Show them how to copy line by line, placing line breaks exactly where the poet did. Provide wider paper for those who need it; if students are using computers to copy poems, show them how to use landscape format or how to reset the margins or change the font size to better accommodate the space. Post directions at the poetry station as a support.

How to compare poems.

Show students how to choose two poems and compare them; they may be about a similar theme or by the same poet or of the same form. Compare some during shared reading, displaying them either on charts or transparencies or by giving each student

Poetry bookmarks can be used to record interesting words and phrases and can come in handy for marking favorite poems for others to read.

copies of the two poems. Walk through the process and think aloud. You might use a Venn diagram to show how they are the same and different; then place Venn diagrams at the station for students to use. Once they can successfully compare poems using this graphic organizer, show them how to write an analytical piece comparing and contrasting the poems.

How to find interesting words and record them.
Model this during read-aloud and shared reading. Keep a chart of interesting words found in poems. Display the chart and remind students to do the same while reading poetry. They might use the back pages of their poetry notebooks to record these words. Encourage them to use some of them in their writing.

How to look at the structure of poems.
Look at all kinds of poems with students throughout the year. Investigate poetry structure, including where and why the poet uses line breaks and stanzas. Point out places where the poet uses alliteration, rhyming, rhythm patterns, repetition, personification, and other literary devices. You might use a highlighter pen or highlighter tape to point out these features as you study them. Challenge students to look for the same features while at the poetry work station, and encourage them to use them while writing, too.

Studying a variety of poetry forms will aid in this process. An interesting source of ideas for poetry forms is *Fly with Poetry* by Avis Harley (2000). It includes a sample of twenty-six kinds of poems, one form for each letter of the alphabet.

How to use a magnetic poetry kit.

Show students how to manipulate the words to create new poems each time. Make some poems with them; have a student copy one onto an index card and post it by the magnetic poetry kit to encourage others to give it a try. This is a great activity for kids who don't like to write or take risks as writers; the only "writing" that must be done is copying the final poem.

How to memorize a poem.

The secret of memorization is practice, practice, practice! It's especially helpful to read a poem aloud over and over again. Show students how to take a stanza at a time and picture something to help them remember it. Challenge yourself to memorize a poem or two during the year, and show students the process. It's best not to assign a particular poem; students will generally be more successful if you let them choose the poem they want to memorize.

How to use a poetry bookmark.

These are provided in Appendix F and can be used to help students record certain kinds of words (such as strong verbs or particularly descriptive adjectives) you've asked them to look for in their reading of poetry. Show students how to fill out the bookmark while you do shared reading of a poem, so they will know exactly what you expect of them while at the poetry work station.

How to Solve Problems That May Arise

The poetry work station will thrive in a classroom where the teacher reads and writes poetry with the class. Including poetry in your day takes just a few minutes because it's short text, but it takes a conscious effort to include it.

To keep your poetry station an interesting, inspiring spot, below are some possible problems you may encounter, with ideas for solving them.

Poetry Work Station

Possible Problem	Troubleshooting Ideas
Kids appear to be bored.	Teacher modeling should improve this. Add some fresh new poetry titles to this station after you've read aloud a few poems from them first to generate interest. Ask kids what else they'd like to do at this station and add it to the "I Can" list.
Some students just don't like poetry.	Find out what those students *are* interested in, and search for poems about those topics to include here. Challenge them to help you in your search. Let them pick poems you'll read aloud next.
Students are having trouble copying poems and including the correct line breaks.	Provide a sample of a poem from a book and the same poem copied by a student. Make notes of what the student had to pay attention to while copying the poem. Check to see if the paper is too narrow to match a student's handwriting; if so, provide wider paper with lines so the poem will fit better.
This station is getting too cluttered because of all the poems kids are writing and the objects they're bringing in to write about.	Limit the number of poems you display here and change them more frequently. Give a student the job of poetry curator. This student keeps the station from getting dull or too messy by examining weekly what's there and what could be changed. You might have a clear plastic shoe box in which to place found natural objects to use for writing poems; have a similar box in which to keep the poetry books used here. Place paper in stacking plastic trays and writing tools in labeled containers.

Differentiating at This Work Station

Be sure to provide poems at a variety of reading levels for your students so that all students can read independently. If you have resource or Title I students, you might place colored dots on some of the books that have easier poems in them as a support. Let students buddy read at this station to provide scaffolding for those who need it; buddy reading here may also boost fluency. Lots of kids like reading poems for two voices. See Figure 7.3 for suggested titles.

Teaching with poems in shared reading will also help your students be more successful at the poetry station because you're reading poems together. For more information on shared reading in upper grades, see Janet Allen's *On the Same Page* (2002). Reading aloud poems will provide good models of how to read poetry, which can bolster kids' success at this station.

Opportunities to write poetry provide differentiation. Students can write at their own levels without intimidation, because there's not a "correct" product. Showing students how to write free verse, acrostics, and list poems allows them to write wherever their skill level is. You may be surprised by what some of your struggling students can do as poets; likewise, writing poems gives your advanced students ways to go deeper in their thinking.

Ways to Keep This Station Going Throughout the Year

Adding new touches on a regular basis will keep the poetry work station alive. Remember to add only one new item at a time to keep things novel. Here are some ideas for keeping this station interesting:

- Change the poetry books periodically. Don't put every book you own in the station to start;

Figure 7.3 **Poems for Two Voices**

Joyful Noise: Poems for Two Voices; I Am Phoenix: Poems for Two Voices by Paul Fleischman

Big Talk: Poems for Four Voices by Paul Fleischman

Math Talk: Mathematical Ideas in Poems for Two Voices by Theoni Pappas

then you can add novelty as needed. Read several poems from the new poetry book before adding it to the station to generate interest.

- Write poems with your class and add them to the station.

- Add magazine pictures to help spark ideas for writing poems.

- Display natural objects to provide inspiration for writing poems.

- Teach a new poetry form to generate interest here. Try haiku or list poems or acrostics or ballads. You might introduce a new form every grading period.

- Add a new medium for illustrating poems, such as glitter crayons (available at discount stores).

- Study a new poet and add information and poems by this writer to the station.

- Use poems when teaching in the content areas. See Figure 7.4 for some suggested poetry books.

- Add poems with interesting formats and themes that appeal to preadolescents, such as those in Figure 7.5.

- Highlight a student's "Pick of the Week" (or every other week) on a poster in the poetry station. Three-hole-punch the posters on the left-hand margin and fasten them together with 1-inch metal book rings to create a large anthology of favorite poems of classmates. Students could add a cover and a table of contents page to the front.

Figure 7.4 **Books with Content-Area Connections**

Mathematickles! by Betsy Franco
These poems are written in the form of math equations and are an interesting mix of mathematical thinking and wordplay.

Messages to Ground Zero: Children Respond to September 11, 2001 collected by Shelley Harwayne
Written by children in New York City and from across the country, these letters and poems are poignant examples of voices ringing loudly in response to an event that changed everyone's life.

Celebrating America: A Collection of Poems and Images of the American Spirit compiled by Laura Whipple
Fine art provided by The Art Institute of Chicago is presented alongside poems by American poets about historic and cultural events in our country. I often use this book when teaching upper-grade students in social studies.

Weather: Poems for All Seasons selected by Lee Bennett Hopkins
Written for kids in grades 2–4, this book has poems about all kinds of weather. Perfect for a science unit of study about this topic.

Flicker Flash by Joan Bransfield Graham
These twenty-three concrete or shape poems focus on the properties of light.

Figure 7.5 **Poetry Books with Interesting Formats and Appealing Themes**

Love Letters by Arnold Adoff
This book contains love letters and valentines written to everyone from teachers to dogs and cats. It includes a variety of interesting formats for kids.

Pieces: A Year in Poems & Quilts by Anna Grossnickle Hines
The illustrations in this poetry book are photos of quilts. Each quilt has a theme, and a poem to accompany it through the seasons.

I Never Said I Wasn't Difficult by Sara Holbrook
This poetry collection was written by a mom for her daughters to record their joys and trials of growing up. Preadolescents will connect with the theme of the book.

Heartsongs by Mattie J. T. Stepanek
Written by an eleven-year-old boy who had muscular dystrophy, these poems will touch readers deeply.

Ten-Second Rainshowers: Poems by Young People edited by Sandford Lyne
Free-verse poems written by 130 children are included in this book, a great model for student writing.

How to Assess/Keep Kids Accountable

This is an easy station to assess, because students will usually have some type of product for you to see here. Periodically collect students' poetry anthologies and assign a grade on handwriting (if you need one) or the quality of the completed work. If you have students look for certain kinds of words and collect them on poetry bookmarks or write comparisons of poems, you can grade some of these products. Be sensitive to how you grade poems written here; remember that poems are very personal expressions. Create criteria together as a class that relate to what you've been studying, and use them when grading student poems. If you have students memorize poems, you can assign grades on completion of these assignments. Another way to gauge how students are doing at this station is to "eyeball" it and see if they are actively engaged (versus playing around). Inviting them to share a favorite poem or something they learned at this station during sharing time is also a way to keep students accountable here.

How This Station Supports Student Achievement on State Tests

Although most state reading and writing tests don't include poetry as a tested genre, it is still valuable to explore with students, because it provides them with opportunities to read and write additional text they might never have experienced otherwise. Exploring poetry gives children a chance to play with words, which builds vocabulary and helps them learn about language structure—items that are included on state achievement tests. Reading poetry helps provide reading fluency practice. By reading and performing poems, students have opportunities to read with improved expression and fluidity; they learn to pause at line breaks and punctuation, which adds meaning to the reading of poetry (and can even change the meaning if ignored or changed). Reading fluency and reading comprehension (tested on state achievement tests) are directly linked. Reading and writing poems helps students improve reading comprehension, especially as they learn about creating mental images.

As students write poems, they learn about word choice, which can improve other kinds of writing as well. Poetry improves students' observational skills, which can influence what they're doing both as writers and as scientists, so there may even be spillover into science. Examining poems about content-area material may help some students who have trouble retaining information about science, social studies, and math, areas all of which are tested on state achievement tests.

Reflection and Dialogue

Consider the following:

1. Observe several groups of students in the poetry work station. What do they spend most of their time doing? Which activities do they enjoy most? Least? Talk with them about what they are learning in this station. Share your findings with a colleague.

2. Do you enjoy reading poetry to your students? Teaching with poetry? Writing poetry? How is this reflected in what you see happening at the poetry work station?

3. What kinds of poems do your students seem to like best? Who are their favorite poets? Find more poems related to their interests to build enthusiasm for this station. Find poems related to content-area studies, such as social studies and science. Work with your colleagues to collect poems for students at your grade level.

4. Build a poetry resource notebook. Divide it into sections labeled by topic, such as alliteration, personification, parts of speech, Civil War, geography, nature, back to school, and so on. Strive to include more poetry in the content areas to improve student retention of information and deeper understanding of concepts taught.

Content–Area Work Stations

This class of upper-grade students is learning about Latin America. They are working at a variety of literacy work stations, including several focused on social studies. Two students work at the geography station, using several atlases and a variety of maps to examine the landforms of several countries they have chosen. The teacher has posted the following scenario there on a card along with a blank physical map of Latin America. The card reads "Look at the physical features on this blank map of Latin America. Label the countries and guess where you think the major cities are. Make a red pencil mark to show where you think those cities are. Your only clues are the physical features. Then look at the atlases and maps provided in this station. With a blue pencil, mark the major cities and label them. Were your guesses correct? What do you notice about where they are? What natural resources are they near? Why do you think these cities are where they are? Write a paragraph on the back of your map explaining your ideas." Students work in pairs to do this activity. They use one map and wonder together as they pinpoint where they think major cities are. They help each other read and interpret the maps, and then write a paragraph together. They put this piece in a basket on the teacher's desk when they are finished.

Another pair of students works at the culture station. Their teacher has gathered a variety of books about Latin American countries written for kids; he has chosen books at different reading levels so all students can be successful at this station. Each student has chosen a country and scans the texts to take notes about traditions and celebrations, religion, music, ethnic groups, and so forth on a chart the teacher made earlier with the class. They have been learning how to take notes, so that's the focus at this station.

A third social studies station centers around history. There is a long time line with Velcro on it under the chalkboard. As a class, the students are helping their teacher make a time line of important historical events from Latin America. Dates are attached under the time line with Velcro. Above are

Sixth graders take notes about the culture of a Latin American country at this social studies work station.

empty Velcro tabs; stapled nearby is a zippered plastic bag filled with index cards noting historical facts (on the back of each is the matching date). Two students work together to assemble the time line; they review important historical events and occasionally consult their social studies textbooks to check on a date. They add a new event by making a card to add to the time line. In another week or so, students will use this station to review for an upcoming social studies test. There are also question cards to promote deeper thinking here, with questions such as "What would change if one of the events on the time line was removed? Take one major event away and explain what might have happened in history as a result. Discuss and then write about it in your social studies notebook."

Why Have Content-Area Work Stations?

Many teachers of grades 3 through 6 tell me they don't have adequate time to teach social studies or science. Content-area work stations provide time for extra reading and writing practice integrated with social studies and science. These work best when linked directly to content-area instruction. For example, when the teacher creates or teaches

with a graphic organizer during social studies or science, this same tool can then be used to gather information independently at the content-area work station.

Content-area stations can also provide opportunities for students to engage in inquiry. Students might peruse books on a content-area topic of study, such as volcanoes, and begin to formulate questions about things they wonder about. These questions can be posted at the station on a chart for others to begin to investigate as well. Note-taking and other research skills can be practiced at this station, as students explore textbooks, atlases, brochures, newspapers, almanacs, and other informational text available here.

What Students Do in Content-Area Work Stations

At content-area work stations, students should be involved in a variety of tasks focusing on science, social studies, or both. They may be working with materials from their content-area textbooks, information related to district and state content standards, and/or inquiry and investigations (such as science experiments or research). Here are some possibilities of what students might do while at content-area work stations. Also refer to other chapters in this book, which note many additional content-area applications.

Science or Social Studies Ideas

■ *Reading and writing about historic figures, scientists, and inventors.* Provide books and other information about important people in science and social studies; be sure to have material at a variety of reading levels to make this accessible to all students. See suggested biography series under the materials list in this chapter. Encourage kids to read about these people and their lives. You might also post related Web sites here. For example, on the cover of a

This tub of books about scientists, historic figures, and inventors is available for students to use for research and writing their own biographies. A chart noting characteristics of biographies, written with students, reminds them what to include.

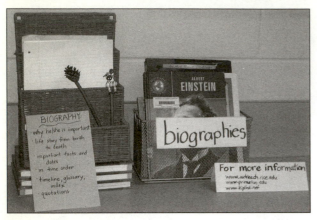

Content-area vocabulary cards were made by students for a Concentration game at the science station.

biography, post a sticky note with a related Web site. Or post a chart of Web sites by the computers.

As students write their own picture books or brochures about favorite historic figures, display those works here as well. Encourage students to write analytically by comparing people and explaining how they may have influenced each other.

- *Taking notes about a topic of study.* Many students find it difficult to master this skill and can practice at the content station. The key is not to expect students to do a report every time they gather information. Instead, provide charts and simple graphic organizers where they can gather small bits of information. Mini-research will make this process less threatening.

- *Engaging in inquiry projects.* Students should have opportunities to choose questions about things they're interested in learning more about in social studies and science. Each unit you study will prompt questions that students might want to search for answers to. Lead them through the inquiry process as a class before asking them to do this on their own at

stations. Having the support of a partner can be very helpful for some students before they do independent research.

- *Writing authentic nonfiction about topics being studied.* Students will enjoy writing nonfiction and reading nonfiction written by their peers. Provide many samples of these first. You could post a list of kinds of writing they might do at this station, including some of the following: informational picture books, feature articles, biographies, poems, diaries and journal entries, logs, letters, essays, historical fiction, brochures, field guides, postcards, and dictionaries.

- *Reviewing and working with content-area vocabulary.* Students can make flash cards to use for practicing content-area vocabulary. These can be used to play Concentration or a matching game. You can also create a vocabulary chart that goes with your unit of study for students to practice using the words on it. Have students create a decorative border around the chart that depicts ideas and vocabulary from this unit. Read Chapter 6 for additional ideas on word study related to content-area learning.

- *Using quiz cards.* Have students make quiz cards about the topic of study. They can do this simply by using index cards, writing the question on one side and the answer on the other. Model how to write higher-level thinking questions as well as factual ones.

Kids decorated a water cycle vocabulary chart with a border.

Fifth graders add captions and details to their mural about the water cycle as they come to the science station. Students build onto the mural, using science texts and information learned throughout the unit of study.

■ *Making a mural.* Place a piece of posterboard here, or cover a bulletin board with blank paper. Students make a mural with cutout paper glued onto this, adding details of what they studied in this unit. They add captions, labels, and details. This can serve as great review for a test. On sticky notes, have them write inferential questions about the mural, such as Why do you think____? What can you tell about ____ from ____?

■ *Doing a quick write about a topic studied.* Provide a three-minute egg timer for timing the writing. Post the topic for kids to write about (or put the topics on slips of paper for students to draw from a container), and then have them write all they can about this topic for three or six minutes. When they are finished, have them read their writing together and see what they know. This is a great way to help them review materials already studied. And it's a good way to have them practice writing in the content areas, too.

■ *Buddy reading of textbook pages.* Make copies of several pages from the textbook and laminate them. Have students read together and mark important ideas with one color, important facts with another, new words with a third. Have them answer end-of-the-section questions together in their social studies or science notebooks. Or have them just read and discuss a chapter from your science or social studies book and jot down important words on sticky notes. Or have them create a mind map about the chapter as they read and discuss.

■ *Buddy reading of related texts (to social studies and science).* Provide books and articles related to what you're currently studying in science and social studies. For example, have two copies of Jean Fritz's *Shh! We're Writing the Constitution* (1998) available in a basket when you're studying the Revolutionary War. Add a

Students buddy read *Shh! We're Writing the Constitution* and refer to the social studies textbook to answer a question.

Buddy readers record their social studies connections and new words found. They consult the dictionary for clarification of a word's meaning.

chart where kids add their connections to what they've read in the social studies book as well as a place to record new vocabulary words. (See Appendix G for a reproducible to place on a clipboard.) Likewise, add two copies of a Bailey School Kids book about a field trip to a geology park titled *Mrs. Jeeper's Monster Class Trip (Adventures of the Bailey School Kids Super Special)* by Debbie Dadey and Marcia Thornton Jones (2001) as your students study rocks and minerals in science.

■ *Listening to social studies or science tapes.* Use commercial tapes that come with your content-area materials provided by the publisher. If you don't have any, or if yours aren't of good quality, have readers from your class make the tapes. (Upper-grade teachers have told me on occasion that students find the tapes that accompany their series too slow or boring.) You might have students use one of the listening maps for informational text found in Appendix D.

■ *Using paired text.* Find an informational text that matches a poem or fiction piece. Or challenge your students to do this. Then have stu-

dents read the two pieces together and compare and contrast them. They might use a Venn diagram to take notes and then write a paragraph or two comparing the pieces. Let them work with a partner for support. Commercial materials are available for this, including Pacific Learning's *Double Take* series, the *Pair It Books* from Steck Vaughn, and Wright Group's *Take Two* books.

Social Studies Ideas

■ *Exploring geography.* Use atlases and maps that come with your social studies textbook. Have students answer questions about the maps related to your unit of study. Most teachers' guides or resource books have these kinds of questions already formulated. Add a gamelike component to the station by writing questions on cards and having kids work with partners to answer them.

■ *Investigating culture.* Students can do mini-research projects by reading books about cultures you are studying as part of your social studies curriculum or simply cultures they are interested in. They can practice using an index, scanning, taking notes, filling out charts, and comparing and contrasting. Have

This portable geography work station uses atlases and materials from a social studies textbook series.

them record the information found on a graphic organizer created by the class. A reproducible sheet can be found in Appendix G.

■ *Working with historical data.* Much study of history centers around dates, facts, and figures. Information can be provided at this station in the form of tables, graphs, and charts. Some may be provided by your social studies textbook and related resource information. Students may create graphics representing historical data. They might make time lines or other physical representations of information being studied. They should also answer higher-level questions about the data, such as identifying contributions of individuals and changes in society resulting from significant historical events.

Science Ideas

■ *Using scientific inquiry methods to investigate.* Set up easy-to-do science experiments for students to do with a partner. Include simple directions and the supplies needed. Some science series have short experiments in the textbook, such as the "Quick Lab" component in McGraw Hill Science. You can teach with these labs in large groups, and then have the same or similar experiments set up for kids to try again with buddies at this station. This will give

them more hands-on experience. You might also include books with simple experiments in them, such as *47 Easy-to-Do Classic Science Experiments* by Asterie B. and Eugene F. Provenzo (1989) or *The Ben Franklin Book of Easy and Incredible Experiments: A Franklin Institute Science Museum Book* by the Franklin Institute Science Museum (1995). *Janice VanCleave's Biology for Every Kid: 101 Easy Experiments That Really Work* (1990) is another excellent resource for kids. Janice VanCleave has similar books about chemistry, earth science, and physics as well. *Creepy Crawlies and the Scientific Method: More Than 100 Hands-On Science Experiments for Children* by Sally Stenhouse Kneidel (1993) is another book you might place at the science work station.

■ *Using scientific tools to conduct science inquiry.* As students are conducting science experiments, they will need to learn to use scientific tools such as: hand lenses, goggles, beakers, a compass, a ruler, a stopwatch, measuring cups and spoons, thermometers, a spring scale, and so on. Introduce these, one at a time, in large-group instruction, and then provide them for student use during independent work station time. You might write directions together as a class for how to use each piece of equipment and place this information on a card beside the tool to remind students how to use each one.

■ *Examining scientific data.* Provide charts and graphs that show data related to a unit of science study. These are often in your science textbook or can be found on the Internet; you can even collect your own data as a class to use. For example, provide a chart that compares smoking now and in the past. Have students make up questions about the chart for their classmates. Have them write each question on a card. (Make it self-checking by having the same student write the correct answer on the back.) Number the cards and have students record their answers on a sheet of paper.

Tell them ahead of time how many you expect them to answer, such as ten. When they finish, have them check their papers. If you want to check these yourself, have students put them in their literacy work stations folders that you collect once a week. Teach students how to include charts and graphs in the nonfiction writing they are doing, too.

■ *Studying scientific systems.* Just as you had students examine data, have them study diagrams. Again, most science books have numerous visuals related to systems, such as life cycles, the solar system, ecosystems, and circuits. Have students choose a diagram related to your unit of study (that you have provided at this station). Ask them to write about the conclusions they draw from reading and studying this diagram. Have them tell what might happen if a part of the system is removed. You might also have them write questions for each other about the diagram as suggested in the previous section. Students might also create diagrams to represent information they have read about.

■ *Exploring earth science concepts.* Students love studying topics such as rocks and minerals, water, and weather. As you study each, provide simple science experiments, as well as related charts and diagrams, and follow activities

The human body is the subject of this science work station. These books contain many diagrams for students to read.

listed above. Also be sure to include collections, such as real rocks, related news articles, and books written on their level that they can use for researching their own questions.

■ *Exploring physical science concepts.* Upper-grade students enjoy learning about how things work as they study matter, energy, simple machines, electricity, and magnets. Again, place objects related to your unit of study at this station for kids to explore. Include simple

Simple physical science experiments are set up for students to do at the science work station.

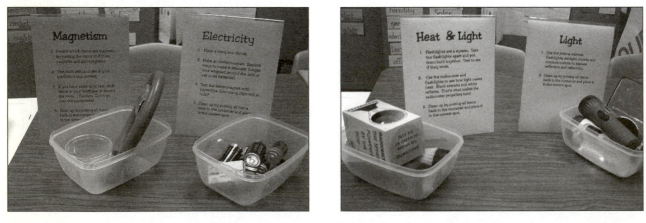

experiments from your textbook series, as well as those you find in other resource books. Provide books written on their level that they can use to conduct research.

■ *Exploring life science concepts.* Favorite units of study in science often focus on animals and plants. Your upper-grade students will be learning how organisms are classified and investigating their characteristics, which will provide lots of opportunity for them to examine charts, graphs, and diagrams. They will also have chances to compare and contrast a variety of animals and plants. After teaching students how to read these graphics, encourage them to create their own as they read and report on living things.

How to Set Up Content-Area Work Stations

First, determine what kind of station you'd like to set up. You might choose to have a social studies station centered around maps and globes; you might want to establish a permanent inquiry sta-

tion; or you might want a portable science station with materials in a container that move to a student desk. There are advantages to each kind.

If you set up a social studies station near a bulletin board, you can staple maps and geography-related news stories there. This can help students stay interested in the world around them. You might place a globe on a table under the bulletin board and place social studies activities in zippered plastic bags here. Also put a tub of books related to the unit you're currently studying.

If you choose to have an inquiry station, you might use a science trifold board on which students can post their topics and questions; likewise, you can display charts on note taking and finding information fast here. Books for research can be kept in clear plastic shoe boxes or baskets, labeled appropriately, and can be changed as your social studies and science units change. Kinds of nonfiction writing might be listed here, with samples to give students models. For example, if you've studied how to write informational picture books, poems, and field guides, these might be listed with a class-made sample hanging beside each one.

Social studies stations are set up by wall displays, with a large map on one and maps and diagrams on the other.

A science station is set up by a chart about electricity called "New Things I Learned, Connections, and Questions." Kids write information on sticky notes and add to the chart as they read here. This same information could be stored on a trifold project board to save space.

Some teachers prefer to just have portable stations in clear plastic boxes that students take to their desks or to the floor. These save space but limit the amount of materials students can use at once. You might choose to have several content-area stations and make some portable and some stationary.

Whatever you choose, try to create an environment that celebrates the content areas. Use your walls, floors, and tables to display charts, books, artifacts, and research materials that encourage curiosity about the world. Be sure to display student work prominently, too. If you have a classroom pet, this area can be a nice springboard for a content-area station. Provide books about this kind of animal, and display informational charts about it, as well as student questions and observations of your pet. Likewise, if you collect plants, set up the same

kind of display around them; add labels noting genus and species, and provide detailed information about their care. Your display will model for students how to care and be inquisitive about the world around them.

Materials

Think about what you want students to practice before placing materials in content-area work stations. The following is a possible list of materials to be used over time, sorted by category:

Geography Work Station

- Atlases and maps
- Questions about geography (may be from textbook) written on cards

This content-area station is built around a class pet.

- Blank maps
- Map pencils

Culture Work Station

- Social studies textbook
- Other books about the states/regions/countries being studied (variety of text written on students' reading levels)
- Index cards for note taking
- Graphic organizers for note taking (may be created with students)
- Chart on how to take notes and use an index (may be written with students)

History Work Station

- Social studies time line(s)
- Tables, graphs, and charts with historical information depicted
- Children's books on and pictures of historic figures
  David Adler's *A Picture Book of . . .* biographies
  Childhood of Famous Americans series

Cornerstone of Freedom series
Real-Life Reader Biographies
Photo-Illustrated Biographies
- Trade books about historical period being studied (variety of text written on students' reading levels)
- Bookmarked Web sites listed for reference

Science Work Station

- Directions for easy-to-do science experiments (from science textbook and/or library books)
- Scientific tools, such as hand lenses, goggles, beakers, compasses, rulers, stopwatches, measuring cups and spoons, thermometers, and spring scales (put out only what relates to the experiments currently being done)
- Simple directions for how to use each scientific tool written on an index card and posted by each one (may be written with students)
- Charts, graphs, and diagrams depicting scientific data and/or information related to a science topic of study
- Cards or sentence strips on which students write questions about scientific data for peers to answer
- Teacher-made questions about graphic information for students to answer
- Collections and artifacts related to a science topic of study (rocks and minerals, electric circuit board, etc.)
- Trade books written at a variety of reading levels about a science topic of study
- News articles related to science topics being studied

Inquiry Work Station

- Tubs of books about content-area topics being studied
- Chart with student-generated questions of interest related to content-area topics being studied (might be displayed on trifold science project board)

- Graphic organizers and index cards for note taking
- Large file box holding file folders for individual students with notes stored in each
- Laptop computer and bookmarked Web sites (or list of suggested Web sites to use)
- Class-made chart with reminders and examples of how to take notes and how to document sources
- Class-made chart with ideas for organizing information. Include photos and samples of file folders with notes, lists of topics, outlines, question/answer format, and so on.
- List of ways to report on information gathered (picture book, poem, brochure, poster, essay, news article, etc.)
- Sample projects and reports done by students

Content-Area Vocabulary Work Station

- Vocabulary card sets made by students with index cards (word on one side and definition on other side of one card, and picture on the other card)
- Content-area word chart made by the class with chart paper
- Dictionaries (specialized ones are available, such as the *Scholastic Science Dictionary* by Melvin Berger)
- Dry-erase boards and markers (for quizzing each other on words)
- News articles about current events laminated so kids can circle specialized vocabulary with vis-à-vis markers

Test Practice Work Station

Note: This station works well as a portable one with the following materials stored in a clear plastic tub.

- Brown envelopes or zippered plastic bags with testlike items inside (laminated reproducible sheets from textbook series written in standardized test format)
- Vis-à-vis marker (for marking answers) in one color; red for checking

A test practice station gives kids opportunities to practice working with content-area information in a reading test format. Laminate commercial materials and provide vis-à-vis pens and an answer sheet.

- Answer key (to make this station self-checking)
- Social studies or science book for reference
- Class-made chart on test-taking strategies

How to Introduce Content-Area Work Stations

Choose an activity in either social studies or science and introduce it to the students to begin this work station. For example, if you decide to start with vocabulary words, provide a list of words along with index cards and colored pencils. Include their related textbook and a dictionary, too. Show them a sample pair of cards; one says *omnivore* on one side and *animal that eats meat and plants* on the other side; the other card has a picture of a bear with an ear of corn and a piece of meat and a caption that says *I choose both.* Write directions together for this station. They might look something like this:

1. Choose a word from the list.
2. Create a pair of cards to show what it means.
3. On one card write the word on one side and the meaning on the other side. Use a dictio-

nary or the glossary from your textbook for help.

4   On the other card draw a picture or diagram and caption to show what the word means. Make it self-correcting by putting a small matching symbol on the back.

5. Put a check mark on the list beside the word you chose so no one else does that one.

6. Put your finished cards in the zippered plastic bag provided.

This will probably be enough for students to get started. Once about fifteen card sets are finished, they can be placed in an envelope for kids to use for matching. At that point, add another set of directions for how to play games with the cards. Let the students help you come up with games and directions. Play the games together to make sure they understand the rules, and then place them in the station for independent use.

Directions were made with students for using content-area vocabulary cards, also made by students.

Or bring in an article from the newspaper or the Internet about a current event. Use this as a springboard for inquiry or further reading. For example, one upper-grade teacher logged on to www.timeforkids.com and displayed an article called "Back to School After the Tsunami" on her monitor for the class to read with her. As they read together, they discussed what it would be like to try to return to normal after a huge disaster in which many students had lost their families. They read about aftershocks, and some students decided they wanted to read and learn more about them. The class decided to add this word to their content-area word chart.

As they read about how UNICEF is helping children affected by the tsunami, they wanted to learn more about how they could help. The teacher clicked on another section titled "Find out how you can help tsunami victims." The class read this together and decided to donate to UNICEF by saving their snack money. They began a chart showing how much they had collected and what it could buy. The news article said that five dollars could pay for an emergency health kit, so they chose to chart money saved by five-dollar increments to see what they could provide. This lesson sparked interest in current events, reading informational text, and how to help others around the world. The teacher then bookmarked the page on the computer and told kids they could read more about it when they went to the content-area station. She also placed books about earthquakes, volcanoes, floods, and tsunamis at the station for further inquiry. The chart for money collected was also placed in the station.

What the Teacher Needs to Model

You'll be modeling much of what you want students to practice at work stations during large-group instruction in science and social studies. For example, as you're teaching a science lesson on how to use lab equipment, you can create a card with the class for how to use that piece independently, and then place it at the science work station as a reminder. As you read information related to social studies content, you might use a transparency of a graphic organizer for note taking that will later be placed at the social studies station. Be sure to make the connection between what you're modeling and what kids will be using for independent work. You might say something like this: "Pay attention to how I'm showing you how to take notes on these cards. I'm going to put this example and some blank cards at the inquiry station for you to use on your own after we've done some together." Listed below are some of the routines you'll want to model explicitly to help students work more effectively at the science and social studies work stations:

How to formulate questions for inquiry.

Model this as you read in your science or social studies textbooks and/or related materials. Show how to ask questions that move beyond simple yes or no answers. Point out good inquiry questions used as headings in books you read to and with the class. Post questions you and the students have on a chart in the inquiry work station if you choose to have one. Place related books and teach the following lessons so students can begin to answer their questions. Several excellent resources for teaching this process are *Nonfiction Matters* by Stephanie Harvey (1998) and *Investigate Nonfiction* by Donald Graves (1989).

How to take notes.

The best way to model this is to demonstrate on the overhead or a chart. You might read aloud a page from informational text and show kids simultaneously how you'd jot down notes on the overhead. Think aloud and show how you decide what to write down. Also make explicit how you don't copy sentences but write just a few words. You'll have to do this multiple times before expecting most students to do this on their own.

How-to-take-notes chart made with the class.

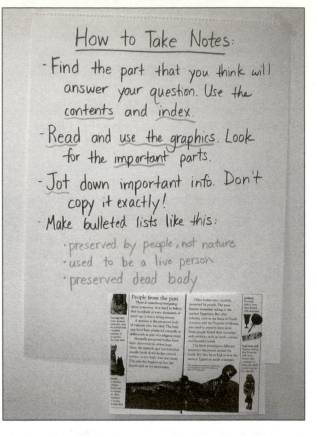

How to use an index, scan, and find information fast.

Again, do this as you work with the content-area textbook and related materials in class. Think aloud as you do this with your students. Post a reminder of how to do it at stations that require students to take notes.

How to organize notes and use them for writing.

File folders are great places for keeping notes. You might have each student label a file folder with the topic being studied and his or her name on the front. Inside have them divide the folder into sections, one for each related question they'd like to answer. Place a library pocket below each question; students can put related notes on cards and put them in the matching pocket for easy organization and storage. Model how to do this with the class by

File folder used for note taking.

Teach students how to record data when doing experiments at the science station.

making several class folders before moving this task to the work station for independent use. Also show your kids how to take notes and write with them to create a project, such as a report, picture book, or brochure. See below for ideas.

How to write authentic nonfiction.

Introduce your class to many forms of nonfiction, such as informational picture books, poems, brochures, biographies, logs, and diary entries. Provide samples of these and include them at the station, so students can see examples made by their peers. Always write one together first, being sure to point out features of that kind of text.

How to read and interpret graphic information (data, charts, graphs, diagrams, etc.).

Model this during science and social studies class while reading textbooks and related informational text. Teach kids to read graphic information carefully and not skip this while reading. Steve Moline's book, *I See What You Mean* (1996), is a great resource for ideas on helping students work with visual information.

How to play content-related games.

It's a good idea to play games with students before putting them out for independent use, so you can be sure all students will be successful. It also helps

head off potential problems from the start. Either try the games in a small group first, or model how to get started with a couple of kids while the class gathers around and gives feedback. This will work for content-area vocabulary games, using quiz cards, and putting together time lines.

How to make a mural.

Start the mural with the class gathered around. Jot down a possible list of what could be put on it, including content-area words, captions, labels, details, dates, facts, and so forth. Make the list as specific as you think it needs to be to lend support.

How to do a quick write.

Do some of these in class first before you ask kids to do them independently at this station. You might post a sample or two at the station. Brainstorm a possible list of topics related to your content area, too, to provide here.

How to buddy read.

Have a pair of students briefly demonstrate how to read with a partner. Let them take turns reading aloud, or give them the option to read a part silently and then discuss it. Write directions for buddy reading with them. Also see the buddy reading section in Chapter 5.

How to use the tape recorder (or CD player or computer).

Review this with students before sending them off to this station. You might even write directions with them on how to use a piece of equipment to be sure it will be used properly. See computer work station and listening work station ideas in Chapter 5.

How to use paired text.

Model how to read a fiction and nonfiction piece about the same topic and how to use a Venn diagram to compare the two. Do plenty of these as a whole class, modeling on the overhead or a chart, before asking students to do this on their own. Post a sample chart at this work station.

How to do a science experiment.

Do experiments with the whole class before releasing students to do them with partners at the science station. Be sure you have provided all materials needed as well as simple directions, so students know exactly what to do there. Write directions and rules for using this station together so kids know what you expect.

How to use lab equipment.

Likewise, be sure that students know how to use lab equipment and that they are careful with it. If you have doubts about safety or behavior, don't put

Scientific-method charts illustrated by fifth graders provide a backdrop for the science station.

those materials out for independent use. Make students responsible for their own behavior here by teaching well the first time and setting clear expectations for independent use. If you've written note cards on how to use each piece of equipment together while using it, display them here as a reminder.

How to Solve Problems That May Arise

Most upper-grade students enjoy working at content-area work stations, because they are related to the world around them. They will enjoy doing inquiry and searching for answers to their own questions if you carefully scaffold this experience for them. The next page has a few ways to help your students get maximum benefit from these stations.

Differentiating at This Work Station

Be sure to provide informational texts at a variety of reading levels for your students so that all students can be successful at this station. This is especially important, because your science and social studies textbooks might be difficult for your students to read. Use tapes that go with your textbook at the listening station to support students reading below grade level. Buddy reading of the textbook, as well as related informational text, can also help lower-level readers.

Likewise, be sure to make available higher-level texts for those reading above grade level. Give these students additional opportunities for inquiry projects on topics of interest. Gifted and talented students often perform better when given choices as well as good instruction.

Teaching students how to read informational text in shared reading will help them be more successful at the content-area station because most of the reading here will be nonfiction. Kids need to learn to read the titles, headings, captions, graphics,

Content-Area Work Stations

Possible Problem	Troubleshooting Ideas
Kids don't like to take notes. How can I make this more fun and interesting?	Model with them multiple times until they feel more comfortable. Provide books that are easy enough to read so that students don't get easily frustrated. Note taking is a challenging skill and takes lots of practice, so make it easy at first. Provide colored folders and neon-colored index cards to make the procedure more fun. And don't grade *everything* they do!
Students are just doing the bare minimum to get by at the station. How can I get them to go deeper in their thinking?	Discuss this problem with the class. Get their input on how to study topics related to your content-area objectives. They will generally put more effort into something of high interest. Include current events related to the topics being studied so students see relevance in today's world. Post higher-level thinking questions and response samples at this station for them to use as models. Have them write their responses and turn them in so you can see how they're doing. Share their best with the class during sharing time.
My students can't do science experiments on their own. They get too loud and make too much of a mess.	Definitely have students work on science experiments with partners only (not in groups of three to five). This should help reduce noise. Control messiness by putting out materials and experiments that are neater in nature; avoid liquids, soil, and things that must be mixed if kids have trouble managing their behavior.

and bold words along with the regular text on a page. This might be a station where you partner students of different reading levels so they can work together to gather and share information.

A fourth-grade teacher models how to read informational text using a Big Book in shared reading.

As students write their own informational texts at this station, differentiation is instantly provided. They can write at their own levels, bringing to the task what they know and can best produce. Posting a sample or model helps students know what their work could look like. Allowing students to present information in a variety of formats helps them do their best; in this way a student who excels in art might present facts graphically, and a child who has trouble writing can create a poem (which takes fewer words).

Ways to Keep This Station Going Throughout the Year

To keep this station interesting to students, you'll have to update it periodically. This is easy to do since the content areas you study will change throughout the year. Gradually add new activities as you teach with them. Here are some ideas to keep this station meaningful and motivating to your class:

- Read and post news articles related to your area of study frequently. Kids are interested in the world around them, and current news will help them understand the importance of studying this topic. Invite them to bring in related news stories, too, and add them to your display.

- Change the informational text as your units of study change. Be sure to provide a wide variety of text, including children's books, reference books, magazine articles, information printed from the Internet, field guides, brochures, and fact cards. Encourage students to be on the lookout for materials they come across in the library, at home, or in bookstores that they can share with the class.

- Include artifacts and "real stuff" at the station to provide interest. Again, invite students to add to this display. Invite people to your class who can share firsthand knowledge of the content area being studied. Interview these folks, take their photos, and add the information to your station as a resource.

- Read aloud a bit from informational text daily, and then show students where they can find this material in the classroom library or at the content-area work station.

- Write informational text with your class regularly and post it in the work station for students to use as models.

Teach kids how to read nonfiction text. Display charts generated with students in the content-area station.

- Vary materials for writing and note taking in this station. Periodically add special pens, neon-colored note cards, and clipboards to spark interest.

- Study an author of informational text to give kids a model and get them revved up about reading and writing nonfiction. Here are some good nonfiction authors to study:

George Ancona	Jill Krementz
Isaac Asimov	Kathryn Lasky
Rhoda Blumberg	Patricia Lauber
Joanna Cole	David McCaulay
Russell Freedman	Jim Murphy

News articles and artifacts added to science stations create interest.

Jean Fritz	Dorothy Hinshaw
Jean Craighead George	Patent
Gail Gibbons	Laurence Pringle
Jim Haskins	Seymour Simon
Steven Jenkins	Diane Stanley

How to Assess/Keep Kids Accountable

Much of what students do at the content-area work station will involve writing, so you will have some instant accountability here. For example, if kids are reading and taking tests, you can have a recording sheet where they record their scores. Because they're working with partners (and you can control who those partners are), they should keep each other in balance. You don't have to assign a grade to go with these scores; just use them to assess how students are learning the information here.

Sometimes students will be producing notes and/or products at this station. If you like, you might create a rubric with your class so they know what you expect. You can grade these activities. At other times, children will be playing games or prac-

ticing reading. You will not be able to collect a "product" from these activities, but you can be sure students are doing what they need to be by "eye-balling" the station at this time. You can also periodically have students tell or write about what they did during sharing time after independent time. The true test is how students perform on evaluative tasks. You will still be giving tests regularly, and you will be able to see how students are learning the information they are working with. You should also see improvement in reading and understanding informational texts when you work with students in small groups if they are practicing working with these kinds of materials at the content-area work station.

How This Station Supports Student Achievement on State Tests

Many states are instituting standardized tests in social studies and science, as well as reading, writing, and math. Practicing with content-area information at work stations gives students additional

Content-area vocabulary is displayed in a pocket chart and on a cabinet.

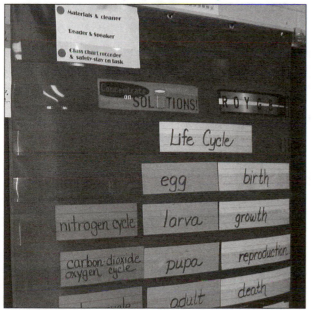

opportunities to learn this material with the support of a partner. It is increasingly important to expose students to as much reading in the content area as possible in upper grades, both to improve their understanding of science and social studies content and to increase background knowledge, which improves reading comprehension, particularly inference.

Teachers often tell me their kids have trouble with content-area vocabulary. This work station is a place where they can work with these specialized words, which often are interesting to kids but need to be applied to something meaningful for them to "stick." Looking them up in a dictionary and writing the definition in a notebook is not enough for most students to remember the words. Teaching with them in large-group instruction, highlighting them on a class-made chart, playing games with them, and paying attention to them at the content-area work station ensure multiple uses in meaningful contexts, which help students own them.

In addition, most state reading tests include both fiction and nonfiction passages. Practicing reading informational text with a partner at this station gives kids more exposure to nonfiction. In some states students are asked to read and answer questions about paired passages with both a fiction and nonfiction piece about the same topic. This station provides for practice with that task, too.

Reflection and Dialogue

Consider the following:

1. What are you teaching in science and social studies that you could easily transfer to a work station for practice? Look through your resources, including your textbook and teachers' editions, accompanying resource books with reproducible sheets and test-taking materials, atlases, and content-related information to see what you already have that you can use for work stations. Work with a partner at your grade level and share resources and ideas.

2. Visit Web sites to get ideas for hands-on social studies and science lessons that could be taught and placed at this work station. For example, check out www.historyalive.com and www.nationalgeographic.com as well as www.timeforkids. com and www.pbskid.org/zoom/. These Web sites can also be bookmarked for kids to use at the computer station.

3. Do you have a class pet or plants in your room? Do you have an interesting collection you could display? Perhaps you have a bulletin board with maps and current events. If so, build your content-area work station around this area. Add informational text about your pet, plants, or collection. Include posters, diagrams, books, and other items to spark interest in this subject. Or post questions about the world that could be answered by looking at the maps or news articles. Encourage kids to add to the information there. Have them read and write about this topic and post their work there to get this station started.

4. Start to gather short texts related to the topics you'll be studying in science and/or social studies this year. Keep a resource notebook or file. Organize it by units, such as Energy or Civil Rights Movement. At the front of each section, keep a list of content-related words you want kids to learn. Then add news articles, magazine pieces, related poems, plays, reader's theater scripts, Internet printouts, diagrams and charts, science experiments written for kids, and copies of interesting pages you might use for shared or buddy reading. You might also list titles of books to use for read-aloud. Divide the work by sharing with your team and building resources together.

5. Observe students at the content-area work stations. Which activities are they most engaged in? What's not working as well? Work with your class to strengthen what they're doing for practice so it is meaningful and helping them grasp concepts being studied.

Drama Work Station

Two students have a reader's theater script about a story set during the Civil War. They are reading it with fluency and expression, and are simultaneously building background knowledge for the social studies unit they are studying. They have written each character's name on a separate index card and chosen cards so they each have an equal number of parts. For the next twenty minutes they read the play dramatically and then switch parts. When they are finished, they do a self-evaluation of how their dramatic reading went, using question cards to prompt their discussion.

One student begins, "I liked being the soldier. I think I used a very strong voice and could convince others of my cause. I had trouble reading some of the names. Next time I'll read silently before we read aloud."

The other adds, "I thought I made the spy character come alive the best. I moved my eyes back and forth when no one was looking and sounded innocent when talking to the enemy. To improve, I want to reread and work on the captain's part. I need to sound like I'm in charge."

Students use a reader's theater script related to social studies content at the drama station.

Because the teacher has taught them these routines (how to read a script fluently, how to create and share character cards, and how to self-evaluate), students are working successfully and independently.

139

In another classroom, two students are working with dramatization. They choose a book they have both read that they think their classmates will enjoy. Then they read the opening scene together and discuss how to dramatize it. They select *Help! I'm Trapped in Obedience School* by Todd Strasser (1995). After they finish reading the first chapter, they make notes about characters and actions they'll need to include. Their notes look like this:

Characters

■ Dad—serious, then angry
■ Jessica—setting table
■ Mom—upset, dramatic
■ Lance the Labrador retriever—chewing on everything, including tonight's dinner

They then act out Dad coming home from work, loosening his tie, sitting down, sniffing the air for dinner and smiling, and asking if anyone knows where his new soft leather loafers are. He spies the coffee table with a chewed-up leg and calls Mom into the living room, and the action heightens as the dog gnaws on the lamb they were supposed to have for dinner.

Because there are only two students here, they decide to play multiple parts. One will be the dad. The other will pretend to be Jessica, then the mom coming in from the kitchen. They don't act out the dog's part but look his way and talk to him so that you can imagine he is really there. They decide that because dogs don't talk, they don't need to act out his part.

During sharing time after independent work, they ask if they can do their dramatization for the class. The class enjoys their three-minute scene, and several ask if they can read *Help! I'm Trapped in Obedience School*. The teacher hands it to one of the students, who usually has trouble with book selection. She suggests that they create a signup sheet to post in the library for others who might want to read the book next.

Why Have a Drama Work Station?

Most teachers don't plan for teaching with drama, because they must cover so many objectives to meet district and state mandates that there's simply no time for it. In addition, it is scary for some teachers to think about letting eight- to twelve-year-olds loose to act things out. They worry that noise and rambunctious behavior might result.

However, there are many benefits to teaching with drama. Interpreting texts and improvising with words, phrases, and stories give kids chances to use their bodies and minds in a positive way. Many teachers are losing the battle to keep kids sitting still at their desks all day, so why not channel some of that physicality in a positive way? Dramatic activities can improve student engagement, which has been shown to increase motivation and learning. Drama also develops creativity. Current brain research has proved that movement even helps students remember.

Drama can also be used to improve reading fluency and comprehension. As students do dramatic readings of stories and scripts, they become the characters; they practice reading until they sound and act like the characters, using inference to interpret. Jeff Wilhelm, best known for his book *You Gotta BE the Book* (1996) uses Patricia Enciso's (1990) research focusing on symbolic story representation in which students created cutouts symbolizing characters, objects of importance, themes, and even the reader himself. Kids then used these to dramatize the story events and talk about their reading.

Including drama in the classroom can help students build confidence and positive social attitudes—both attributes upper-grade teachers can appreciate. Drama builds teamwork and collaboration; it provides healthy channels for expression of emotions (for which preadolescents need an outlet). Vocabulary can be built through the dramatization of words and phrases.

What Students Do in the Drama Work Station

Students can do a variety of things in the drama work station. These activities should be related to your reading and writing curriculum and/or to the content areas. Students are not doing formal plays or puppet shows for an audience at this station. Instead, they are inventing and enacting dramatic situations for themselves, to enhance their understanding. Occasionally, you may have students share their improvisations and dramatizations with the class, but this is not necessary on a daily basis.

Ideas are grouped by categories below to help you with planning. Please note that some will fit in more than one category.

Oral Reading Practice

- *Reading reader's theater scripts.* These are available commercially as well as on the Internet. Upper-grade students can also be taught how to write reader's theater scripts using classroom library books, stories from their basal readers, and science and social studies textbooks. (See Appendix H for a list of resources for reader's theater and plays for grades 3–6.)
- *Doing "Stress the Highlighted Word(s)."* Write a sentence that a character might say in a dramatization on a sheet of paper. Write it sev-

eral times, highlighting a different word or words each time. Students take turns reading it, with the emphasis changing each time as they stress the highlighted word(s). Have them write the interpretation beside the sentence after they read it dramatically. See Appendix H for a sample.

- *Playing "Guess the Emotion."* Copy quotes from read-aloud books portraying interesting characters and including dialogue onto large index cards. (Or have kids do this.) On the back of each card, write the emotion the reader should convey. Students take turns dramatically reading these excerpts while the partner guesses the emotion.
- *Working with mood.* Have students dramatize fairy tales and stories that evoke a sense of mystery, emphasizing mood. Use poems that depict mood by their descriptive words. Also use pictures that evoke particular moods as springboards for dramatization. Have questions provided, such as "What is the mood? What do you feel as you read this piece or look at this picture? What makes you feel that way? Show feeling as you read the piece aloud and dramatize it, or act out what is happening

"Stress the Highlighted Word" cards.

Name		Date

Read each sentence below, putting the emphasis on the highlighted word. Then write how the meaning changed in the box beside it.

I don't want to know what happened here.	
I don't want to know what happened here.	
I don't want to know what happened here.	
I don't want to know what happened here.	
I don't want to know what happened here.	
I don't want to know what happened here.	
I don't want to know what happened here.	

Front and back of "Guess the Emotion" cards.

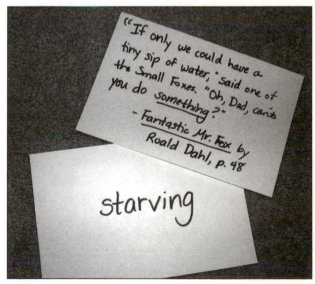

"If only we could have a tiny sip of water," said one of the Small Foxes. "Oh, Dad, can't you do something?"
— *Fantastic Mr. Fox* by Roald Dahl, p. 48

starving

in the picture." See Appendix H for question cards related to mood and character that students might use.

- *Working with dialogue, plot, and conflict.* Choose stories with several characters and expressive dialogue. Short stories or chapters from fiction are excellent for this. Students pick one, read it, and discuss it with a partner. They might fill out a graphic organizer with notes about dialogue, plot, and conflict to help them pay close attention to these features. (See Appendix H for a sample.) Then have them read it dramatically, concentrating on the things noted on their story map.

Writing Practice

- *Writing character sketches.* Have students write paragraphs describing characters that might be included in a play. Consider tying this to your content-area units by having them develop a character who may have lived during colonial times, for example. Have them include physical descriptions and social and psychological information about the character. Several students might put their characters together to write a short script. See Figure 9.1 for a student-written sample.
- *Writing reader's theater scripts.* Teach students how to take a familiar piece of fiction or nonfiction and rewrite it into a reader's theater script. This will take modeling, but can be an excellent activity for students needing higher-level, more challenging work.
- *Using drama as rehearsal for writing.* Students might take a topic they are writing about and dramatize it before writing to help them organize, visualize, and articulate their ideas. For example, a child who wants to write about a camping trip might enact the story for a partner before writing it down. He may show how scared he was in the middle of the night when he heard scratching outside the tent and then

Figure 9.1 **Character Sketch Written by a Fifth Grader**

> **Character Sketch**
>
> Mr. Krupp from *Captain Underpants* by Dav Pilkey:
>
> Mr. Krupp is a tall, yet fat person with a short ugly wig. His eyes are somewhat beady. He has a very large mouth and a mostly bald head. His skinny arms have giant hands and fingers. His thick legs stand on average sized feet.

tell how his dad bravely took a flashlight to search and discovered raccoons by the trash can.

- *Producing a one-minute sound bite.* Using content-area information, have students work together to produce a news script for a one- or two-minute sound bite. For example, during a science study of volcanoes, students might synthesize what they've learned by creating a brief news report on a volcanic eruption. They will be able to integrate content-area vocabulary into the script as well. Show students how to use the planning sheet in Appendix H to help them focus their broadcast.

Students produce a one-minute sound bite related to content-area information.

Dramatizing

- *Working with characterization.* Provide poems or other short text for students to read and then discuss conceptions of the character. For example, have them read poems such as "The Dragon of Grindly Grun" from Shel Silverstein's *A Light in the Attic* (1981). Have questions provided as a stimulus for thinking about the character, such as What is this character really like? How would you describe this character? Do you think he/she always acted this way? If not, what may have had this character act like this? What kinds of problems might this character have had in the past? In the future? They might use the card in Appendix H. Then have them read the poem aloud and dramatize it.

- *Adding motions to poems read.* Have students choose and read a poem, then add motions to aid in comprehension. Prompt with questions on cards or a chart generated by your students, including What do you see in your mind? What are you feeling? What is moving? to help them use their visual imagery.

- *Dramatizing stories.* Kids love to act out stories. Begin with familiar ones to give them practice. Again, include stories from your basal reader as well as picture books or even chapters from a favorite book.

- *Dramatizing informational text.* Provide nonfiction books, magazines, and newspaper articles for students to dramatize. Show them how to read a bit and then act it out.

- *Enacting science and social studies content to better comprehend and remember it.* Ask students to translate information read in social studies or science with their physical bodies. For example, they might act out the life cycle of the butterfly by curling up like a cocoon and gradually emerging into a butterfly that unfurls its wings and spreads them majestically.

- *Dramatizing an opening scene from a book and using it to get others to read that book.* Have stu-

A student enacts information learned by reading about Albert Einstein.

dents take the first scene from a favorite book and act it out with the idea of persuading others to read the book. Then have them do their dramatization for the class. Be sure they show the book, too.

- *Pantomiming a word or phrase.* This is a great vocabulary-building activity. Provide vocabulary words and idiomatic expressions on index cards. Have students take turns choosing a card and then acting it out while the other

Kids play charades with vocabulary cards.

person guesses it. Use vocabulary gleaned from read-aloud texts (placed on your interesting-words wall) or from content-area study. Idioms and homophones are also good for pan-tomime.

■ *Acting out a word or phrase in different contexts.* Encourage students to use a dictionary to look up multiple meanings of a word and act out each one in a different context.

Improvising

■ *Doing improvisations of fables and proverbs to develop inference skills.* Fables and quotes or proverbs are wonderful for improvisation because they don't have many characters, and they require the students to go beyond the surface to act out character feelings and deeper meanings. Arnold Lobel's *Fables* (1980) is just right for upper-grade readers to interpret dra-matically. Cards with proverbs and quotes can also be provided here.

■ *Using "conflict lines" to spur improvisations and develop oral language and problem-solving skills.* Conflict lines can be written on cards to start

improvisations. Students must use thought and language to act them out. These might say something like the following:

Where do you think they could possibly be?
I can't *believe* she actually did that!
This looks too dangerous!
That isn't what I said at all.
How in the world did this happen?

■ *Doing plot extensions with familiar stories.* Have students read a story and think about what might have happened before and afterward. Then have them do an improvisation based upon their ideas. It might be helpful for them to use a graphic organizer to jot down ideas of what could have happened before and after the story. See Appendix H for a sample organizer.

■ *Doing character additions based on familiar sto-ries.* Using a familiar story, such as a folk or fairy tale, have students list the characters. (You might use Jon Scieszka's funny takes on

An "improv bag" and its contents.

Students improvise with a conflict card reading "This is too dangerous!"

classic stories, *The Stinky Cheese Man* [1992]. His humor appeals greatly to tweens.) Then have students brainstorm several additional characters that could be in that story. Have them think of how the story would change if these characters were part of the story. Let them do an improvisation using one of these new characters. For example, how would *Little Red Riding Hood* change if the wolf had a sister looking for him? What kind of character would the wolf's sister be? Why would she be looking for him?

■ *Using artifacts and objects for improvisations.* Provide a bag with two or three objects in it to get students thinking. For example, try an apple, a magic wand, and a baseball mitt. Let kids create their own "improv bags" at home and bring them in to add to this station. Check these before using them!

Evaluating

■ *Self-evaluating the dramatic work.* You might have a list of questions for kids to consider after a dramatization. Teach them to think critically about their work and how they might improve it next time.

How to Set Up the Drama Work Station

You don't need a puppet theater or props to set up a drama station. You can simply put the materials in a plastic tub and make it a portable one. Label the container with a "Drama Station" sign and add materials to it as you go.

Of course, if you want students to use puppets or props, you may add these over time. But they are not necessary. Remember that this is a *drama* station where students work with the process of acting out stories and information, rather than a *theater* station where children perform for an audience.

A portable drama station contains scripts, character cards, markers, and directions written with students.

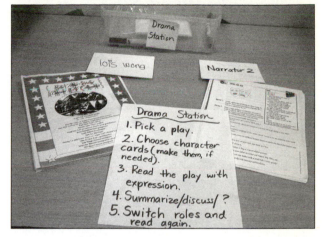

Materials

Simple materials will be needed for this station, and might include the following:

For Oral Reading Practice

■ Reader's theater scripts and mini-plays (see Appendix H for a list of suggested resources, including Internet sites)

■ Sentences that can be read in a variety of ways for "Stress the Highlighted Word" (see Appendix H for a sample)

■ Story excerpts copied onto index cards with the accompanying emotion for the reader to convey written on the back

■ Poems with descriptive words

For Writing Practice

■ Sample character sketches, written with the class

■ Directions for how to write a reader's theater script (written with your class)

■ News script sheet for short sound bites (see Appendix H)

For Dramatizing

■ Poems and short text with vivid characters and lots of action words

- Fairy tales and stories that evoke a sense of mystery (for studying mood)
- Graphic organizers related to dialogue, plot, and conflict (see Appendix H)
- Mood and character cards (see Appendix H)
- Informational text to dramatize (use short text)
- Social studies or science book with ideas of what to dramatize
- Vocabulary words on cards for pantomiming (including content-area words, idioms, and homophones)

For Improvising

- Fables, quotes, and proverbs for improvisation
- Conflict lines written on cards
- Familiar stories (for plot extensions)
- Graphic organizer for plot extensions (see Appendix H)
- Artifacts and objects in bags for improvisation (three or four objects per bag)

For Evaluating

- List of self-evaluation questions generated with the class (see Appendix H for a sample)

How to Introduce the Drama Work Station

Setting up a drama station requires thoughtful planning, lots of modeling, and clear expectations. This station will work best if the teacher engages students in informal drama periodically during the week, integrating it into language arts and content-area instruction. For example, some teachers already use role playing and simulations in social studies and science. While studying simple machines, you might have students pretend they must move a heavy piece of furniture to the third-floor apartment in an old building with no elevator. Together you brainstorm solutions, such as using a pulley, and then act this out briefly.

Likewise, in social studies during a study about a river community, you and your class might dra-

This graphic organizer helps students improvise what may have happened before and after a piece read.

matize being on a paddle-wheel boat on the Mississippi. You pretend to listen to the band playing and the engine throbbing; you talk about the barges and other boats as you pass them on the river. You stop to talk to people who live there and tell about the great floods that affect this area and how rich the land is as a result of the silt that is distributed.

Incorporating drama in the classroom brings teaching to life. It can enrich students' understanding of concepts and vocabulary. Here's one way you might introduce the drama station to your students. Read aloud a picture book or the first chapter of a new novel to your students. Ask them to think about what may have happened before the story, as well as what might happen as a sequel. After reading, chart their ideas on a large copy of a graphic organizer like the one pictured. Then work together to do improvisations of their ideas. You might have them work with partners, or have half the class act out what they think happened before the story and the other half act out what may have happened after it. Or you might do the improvisation together as a class to give more support.

A good book to use for this is *Going West* by Jean Van Leeuwen (1992). It relates well to upper-grade social studies content, too. In the "before the story" segment, students may act out Papa and Mama having a deep discussion of the benefits and drawbacks of moving their family west in the 1800s. Part of the improvisation includes thinking about where this family originates (somewhere in the eastern United States, possibly West Virginia, because the book mentions leaving the town, the woods, and the hills) and where they travel to (maybe Nebraska, because the book mentions prairie, snow, Indians, and farming). This promotes lots of discussion and even research skills, such as looking up a map of the Oregon Trail and looking at the map's physical features. In the "after the story" improvisations, kids may act out a scene from the next year, when Papa buys a piano for Mama after a successful harvest. This activity involves comprehension, inference and research skills, and higher-level thinking.

After introducing this activity to the class, you might put other books in the drama station along with the graphic organizer used above, and have students do improvisations of what they think happened before or after the story. This activity will work best if you start with familiar books and stories.

Another way to introduce the drama station is to choose any item from the suggestions in the section called "What Students Do in the Drama Work Station" and model it with the class before moving it into this station for independent practice.

What the Teacher Needs to Model

The drama station will need lots of modeling to ensure success as students work independently here. Modeling and setting clear expectations are critical at this station. Here are some of the things you'll want to model over time:

How to read a script.
Start with enough copies of a short reader's theater script for the whole class. Assign parts so everyone has something to read. If more than one student

has the same part, have them read that part chorally. Point out that they don't need to read the stage directions or the name of who is talking. Encourage expressive, fluent reading. You might take the part of the narrator to model this.

How to play games.
You'll want to demonstrate with the whole class how to play Stress the Highlighted Word and Guess the Emotion. Have all materials available and give everyone a chance to try these together. The directions are simple; you might even write the directions with your class and include them with the game. This saves teacher time and builds student ownership.

How to use question cards and graphic organizers for dramatization and dramatic reading.
Again, as a class work with some of the same cards and graphic organizers you'll want your students to use on their own. Do a few together so students understand the process before releasing them to work on these during independent time.

How to write a character sketch.
Use a character from something you're reading as a class, and write a character sketch together. Do this several times with familiar characters before asking kids to write them on their own. Post a sample at this station for students to use as a model.

How to write a reader's theater script.
Take a familiar story such as Goldilocks and the Three Bears and rewrite it as a class in reader's theater format. You might do this on the overhead. When finished, place this script in the drama station for kids to practice reading, as well as to provide a model of how to write a script. Your more accomplished writers may want to try writing reader's theater scripts for the class.

How to produce a news script for a one-minute sound bite.
Model this activity in science or social studies. This is another great activity to encourage your higher

readers to synthesize. It's great for your struggling writers, too, because they don't have to use many words. Take something you're studying and create a sound bite together. Model writing it on the overhead, complete with cross-outs, as writing shorter pieces often requires a bit of editing. Use the form in Appendix H if you'd like. Place the model with the directions for writing a sound bite script at the station. Write these directions with your kids, too.

How to dramatize stories and informational text.

Incorporate brief dramatizations into your weekly teaching of social studies, science, reading, and vocabulary. Take teachable moments for students to all dramatize the meaning of a new word or a concept being studied.

How to pantomime.

Likewise, have students take turns acting out their spelling words, idioms you come across during read-aloud, and new content-area vocabulary. Remind them that pantomime involves the body only. No sounds or words allowed!

How to do character additions and plot extensions.

Integrate these into read-aloud occasionally. Use the examples provided in the section on "How to Introduce the Drama Work Station." You might use the graphic organizer in Appendix H to model how to plan.

How to improvise.

Include this technique in your weekly teaching also. Take opportunities to improvise to build background knowledge for a book you're going to be reading or a concept you're teaching in the content areas. Serve as the facilitator while practicing this with your class. This will improve what students can and will do at the drama station.

How to do self-evaluation.

Post questions at the station for kids to consider when thinking about how they did and how they might improve their work. (See Appendix H for a sample self-evaluation form for students to use.) The questions might include the following:

- Which were the best parts of our dramatization?
- What did we do to make the story or information clear?
- Which parts could be improved? How could we do that?
- Which characters were most believable? What made them come alive?
- How did the dialogue sound? What made it interesting?
- What did we do today that worked well that we want to do again?
- What could we do to make it better next time?

How to Solve Problems That May Arise

Most problems that arise at the drama station relate to behavior. Listed on the next page are some things to plan for ahead of time to make this station work

Limit the number of puppets in this station if you choose to add them for dramatization.

Drama Work Station

Possible Problem	Troubleshooting Ideas
Students are playing around here instead of working properly with the materials.	Consider how much modeling you've done with students. Have you taught them *how* to dramatize and improvise? Or have you put out materials and expected kids to be able to do this right away? You might need to do more work as a whole class before placing some of these tasks here for independent practice.
Kids are fooling around when I want them to read.	Be sure the reading materials are on the students' independent reading levels and are of high interest. Try changing the reading material with student input.
I've put out props, but kids are playing around with them instead of using them for improvisation.	Are *all* kids fooling around, or just some of them? Let students who can handle it use these materials. Have something else for others to do. Perhaps some students won't be assigned to this station until their behavior shows that they can manage it.
I put puppets out for kids to use here, but they're just messing around with them.	Remove the puppets. Try them again once you've modeled exactly what you want students to do with them. Or try putting out just a few at a time related to stories you want them to reenact. Remember that it's not necessary to provide props at this station.

as smoothly as possible and provide maximum instructional benefits.

Differentiating at This Work Station

This is a work station where all students can be successful, especially with the support of a stronger reader in the partnering. Children who normally might not excel at reading may be very good at dramatizing and improvising. I've found that students who learn kinesthetically really enjoy and benefit from the activities at this station.

The use of varied reading materials can provide something for everyone to read. You'll notice the use of familiar fairy and folk tales, and even single sentences to read, which can give even your lowest readers a chance to be successful. The beauty of the work at this station is the opportunity for deeper thinking.

Look for reader's theater scripts and mini-plays written on a variety of reading levels to provide differentiation. Benchmark Education has a series called Reader's Theater with a variety of parts writ-

ten at different reading levels within the same script. Fountas and Pinnell guided reading levels are provided for each part to help the teacher choose appropriately.

Ways to Keep This Station Going Throughout the Year

Variety is the key to keeping the drama work station interesting. Change the tasks and reading materials as you see interest and motivation beginning to wane. Get student input on what they are enjoying at this station and add more of that. Here are some ideas to keep this station going throughout the year:

- Change the reader's theater scripts periodically.
- Relate the reader's theater scripts and mini-plays to content-area topics of study whenever possible. This will keep the activity fresh and relevant.
- Write a reader's theater script together sometimes.

- Teach kids how to write reader's theater and include their scripts. (These are easiest to read if typed on a computer.)
- Change partners at this station occasionally. It's enjoyable to read and think together with someone new.
- Use new graphic organizers that you've introduced to the whole class.
- Bring in improvisations related to what you're studying in science and social studies.
- Use news articles focusing on current events for dramatization and improvisation.
- Change the poems, fairy and folk tales, informational text, and other pieces students are reading once everyone has had a chance to work with them (probably about once every three to four weeks). Don't put out too much at once and your materials will "last" a longer time.
- Strive to have a balance of activities that focus on some oral reading, some writing, some dramatizing, and some improvising rather than having too many of one kind.
- Change the color of paper the reader's theater scripts are written on.
- Use a different color or shape of card stock for vocabulary and/or question cards for novelty.

How to Assess/Keep Kids Accountable

This can be a challenging station to keep an eye on. You have to trust that your students are learning through drama and that you have established a strong enough community of learners that they will take responsibility for their learning. If you have doubts about this, it is quite likely that the children will not do well with this station. Success comes from shared ownership of the classroom and the routines established there. When you use informal drama in your teaching, you are a facilitator—releasing control to students to think and act for themselves.

Nonetheless, you need to be sure students are doing what you expect at this station. There are several ways to do this. Be sure you have directions posted for expectations at this station. Write them with your students and tape them to the inside lid or the side of the container you're using. Shared expectations brainstormed with your class might look something like this:

At the Drama Station, I Will . . .

- Stay on topic and think about the piece we are reading and discussing.
- Control my body to dramatize and show emotions of characters, not play around.
- Use materials properly and respect my partner.
- Work collaboratively with my partner.
- Strive to think more deeply and learn something I didn't know before working here today.

Clearly defining parameters can help students be successful at this station. If kids are fooling around, remove them immediately and send them back to their seats to do something less desirable such as seatwork. Don't tolerate poor behavior, and don't close down the station just because one or two students can't handle it.

Although the goal of work at this station is not production or performing for an audience, periodically students might like to show the class what they did here. Sharing time is a great venue for this.

Occasionally, walk around the class during work stations time and observe what students are doing, especially at the drama station. You might get a small group started with reading a book at your small-group table and then walk around for a few minutes, checking on what the rest of the class is doing.

Also be sure to glance in the direction of the drama station frequently. You'll be able to tell immediately if students are on-task. You can also have students write answers to some of the questions on the cards at this station from time to time to more closely see what they are doing here.

How This Station Supports Student Achievement on State Tests

It's hard to imagine a state test ever requiring students to dramatize a reading passage, but students who are visualizing vividly will have better comprehension, especially involving inference skills. Students who are used to thinking deeply will usually apply those same skills to reading and thinking on a standardized test if they are motivated.

As demonstrated in this chapter, upper-grade students can use drama to improve their reading fluency and comprehension, which are tested on state tests. Drama can also help students retain content-area information and vocabulary, which may improve student performance on science and social studies, as well as reading tests.

Reflection and Dialogue

1. Do students enjoy using the reader's theater scripts and mini-plays provided? Are they reading with greater fluency and expression throughout the day as a result of extra practice?

2. Observe students at the drama station. What do they choose to do most often? What do they do the least? What do you need to add or change to improve the effectiveness of this station?

3. Plan to do dramatization and improvisation briefly with students at least once a week as part of your large-group instruction. Remember that these should not take lots of instructional time. You are not producing a play for an audience. Model activities you'd like students to practice at this station, using ideas from this chapter.

4. Take a piece from a familiar book or story and write a reader's theater script together with your class to model the process. Watch them dig into reading this at the station on their own.

5. Watch student behavior at this station. Are kids behaving cooperatively here? If so, what have you done to foster those behaviors? If there are problems, what do you notice specifically? Is it the pairing of students, the reading level of the materials, or the need for more modeling and direction? Problem-solve with a colleague and/or with the students themselves.

6. With a teammate, plan how to integrate materials from your reading curriculum, social studies, and science into this station.

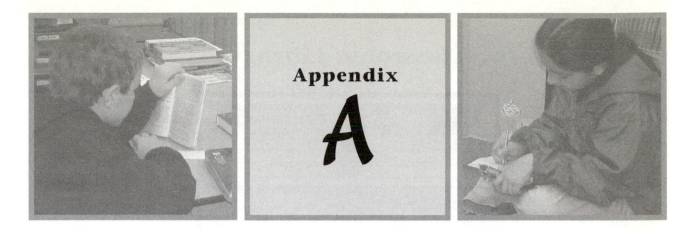

Icons and Management Tools for Work Stations

Spanish translations of the icons are available for printing at www.stenhouse.com/0395.asp.

Classroom Library

Writing Work Station

Drama Work Station

Poetry Work Station

Word Study Work Station

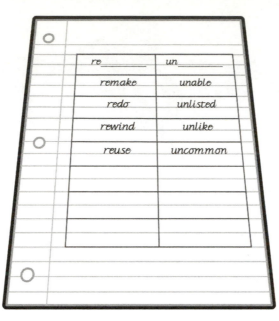

re_____	un_____
remake	unable
redo	unlisted
rewind	unlike
reuse	uncommon

Science Work Station

Social Studies Work Station

Listening Work Station

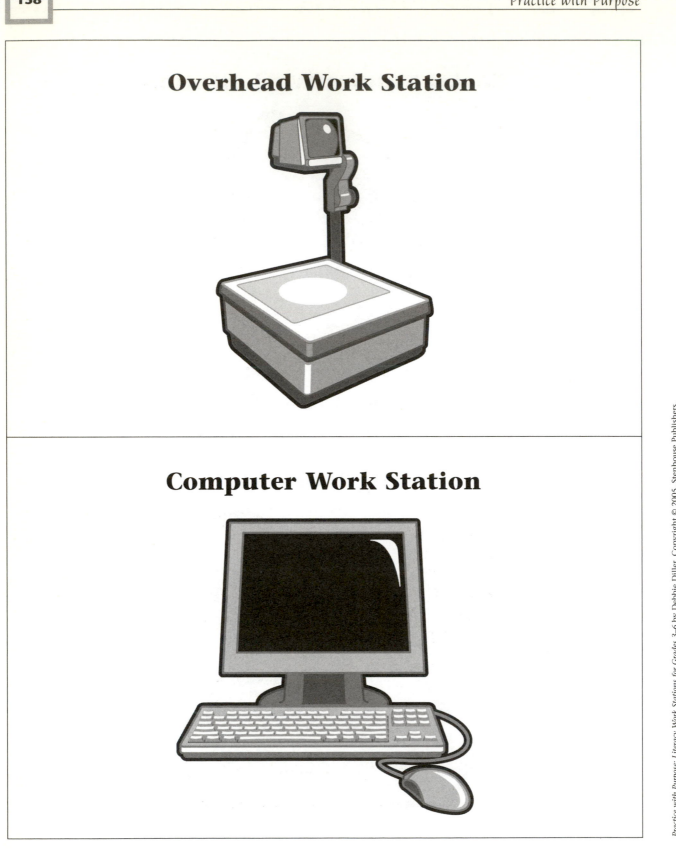

Overhead Work Station

Computer Work Station

Practice with Purpose: Literacy Work Stations for Grades 3–6 by Debbie Diller. Copyright © 2005. Stenhouse Publishers.

Newspaper Work Station

Spelling Work Station

List

1. meeting
2. treats
3. keeper
4. leaped
5. street

meeting

treats

Handwriting Work Station

$$\textit{Aa Bb Cc Dd Ee Ff}$$

$$\textit{Gg Hh Ii Jj Kk}$$

$$\textit{Ll Mm Nn Oo Pp}$$

$$\textit{Qq Rr Ss Tt Uu}$$

$$\textit{Vv Ww Xx Yy Zz}$$

$$\textit{1 2 3 4 5 6 7 8 9 10}$$

Vocabulary Work Station

Practice with Purpose: Literacy Work Stations for Grades 3–6 by Debbie Diller. Copyright © 2005. Stenhouse Publishers.

Games Work Station

Grammar Work Station

Buddy Reading Work Station

Spanish Titles for Work Station Icons

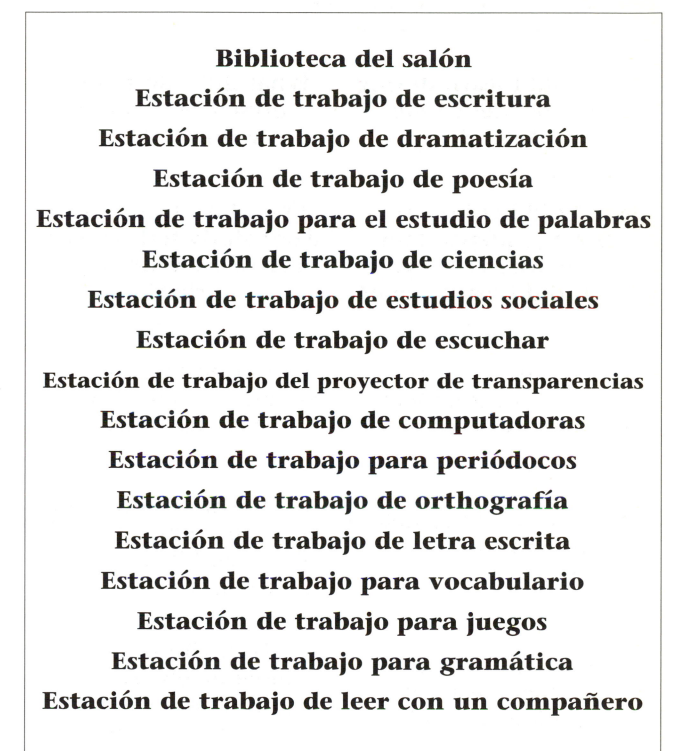

Biblioteca del salón

Estación de trabajo de escritura

Estación de trabajo de dramatización

Estación de trabajo de poesía

Estación de trabajo para el estudio de palabras

Estación de trabajo de ciencias

Estación de trabajo de estudios sociales

Estación de trabajo de escuchar

Estación de trabajo del proyector de transparencias

Estación de trabajo de computadoras

Estación de trabajo para periódocos

Estación de trabajo de orthografía

Estación de trabajo de letra escrita

Estación de trabajo para vocabulario

Estación de trabajo para juegos

Estación de trabajo para gramática

Estación de trabajo de leer con un compañero

Work Stations Sharing Time Cards

Cut apart and place on a ring to use during sharing time.

What did I learn during independent time today?	What did I do to help myself be a better writer today?
What did I enjoy doing during independent time today? Why? What did I learn there?	What did I learn about word study today? New words? New strategy I tried?
What didn't I like during independent time today? Why not?	What do I think we should change at work stations? Why?
What did I do to help myself be a better reader today?	What else would I like to do at work stations? What and how would that help me to learn?
How did I solve a problem at work stations today?	How did I help someone else solve a problem at literacy work stations?

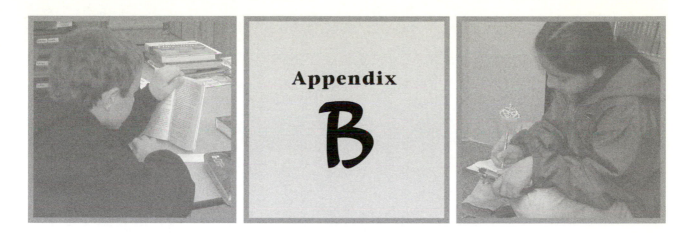

Resources for Comprehension, Fluency, Phonics, and Vocabulary

Appendix
B

Literacy Work Stations That Build Comprehension

Work Stations That Build Comprehension	What Students Do Here That Supports Comprehension	How This Station Supports Comprehension
Independent Reading Time and Response Writing	■ Read self-selected books that are just right for the reader for extended periods of time ■ Interact with text read by writing personal responses	Students need independent-level text so they can practice comprehending more easily. Students who practice reading and thinking for extended periods of time develop reading stamina (needed on standardized reading tests). Response writing encourages interaction with text and helps kids think about their reading.
Classroom Library	■ Choose just-right books for independent reading ■ Talk about books read with others ■ Recommend books to each other ■ Use graphic organizers/questions for discussion	Organizing books by categories in the classroom library can help students better select just-right books for independent reading. It also can help them think about genre and what to expect while reading (if combined with good instruction). Graphic organizers can also help kids understand how texts are organized. Talking about books with others can deepen understanding if students are taught to ask higher-level questions as part of those discussions.
Listening Work Station	■ Listen and think about the story or information ■ Talk with others about the story or information ■ Interact with the text by writing personal responses ■ Use graphic organizers to help them understand text structure	Listening comprehension is an easier task than reading comprehension. Listening to a book frees up the brain to think about the text, rather than having to decode every bit. Adding responses to listening helps kids interact with what they've heard, which improves comprehension (especially if the teacher has taught students how to think deeply about text).
Newspaper Work Station	■ Read and respond to news articles that are of high interest and may motivate students uninterested in other kinds of "school reading"	News articles can be of high interest to students. Many times kids have background knowledge about items in the newspaper, especially if they have heard about this same news on TV. Talking about news with each other and responding to it encourages thinking, which improves comprehension.
Word Study Work Station	■ Read text and pay attention to new words by highlighting them, listing them, and exploring their meanings ■ Play vocabulary-related games to learn new word meanings	If you know what words mean, you have a greater likelihood of making meaning of the whole text. This separates comprehenders from decoders. Kids play with words and their meanings at this station to help them pay attention to new words and try to figure out what these words mean.
Buddy Reading Work Station	■ Read a bit at a time together and talk about it ■ Help each other as they read, especially to figure out the meaning when comprehension breaks down	Buddy reading promotes social interaction. When kids share the reading, it makes the task easier and frees up the brain to better comprehend. Reading a bit at a time and then talking about it helps readers monitor and fix their comprehension.

Literacy Work Stations That Build Comprehension (*continued*)

Poetry Work Station	■ Read poems and think about the pictures in their minds	Visualizing is an important comprehension strategy. Reading poems encourages this, because of the visual imagery used in poems. Poems also give students practice with short text, which does not demand as much reading stamina and may free up the brain to think more deeply.
Drama Work Station	■ Act out what they read to demonstrate understanding	If you can dramatize what you've read, you're demonstrating understanding. It helps passive readers become more active.
Content-Area Work Station	■ Read, discuss, and write about what they learned as they read nonfiction text. ■ Use graphic organizers to record what they learned as they read	Some students will choose to read only fiction. Working at this station gives them an opportunity to comprehend nonfiction as well. Reading and understanding nonfiction requires thinking a bit differently than reading fiction. Students can use graphic organizers to help them think about how nonfiction is structured.
Overhead Work Station	■ Read a piece of text together and discuss it	Reading with a partner and discussing it can help students better understand what they read.

Comprehension Research References

Duffy, G. G., and L. R. Roehler. 1989. "Why Strategy Instruction Is So Difficult and What We Need to Do About It." In C. B. McCormick et al., *Cognitive Strategy Research: From Basic Research to Educational Applications.* New York: Springer-Verlag.

Pressley, M. 1998. *Reading Instruction That Works: The Case for Balanced Teaching.* New York: Guilford Press.

Stevens, R. J., R. Slavin, and A. Farnish. 1991. "The Effects of Cooperative Learning and Instruction in Reading Comprehension Strategies on Main Idea Identification." *Journal of Educational Psychology* 83 (1): 8–16.

Literacy Work Stations That Build Fluency

Work Stations That Build Fluency	What Students Do Here That Supports Fluency	How This Station Supports Fluency
Independent Reading and Response Writing	■ Silently read a self-selected book with fluency so they can stick with a book for an extended period of time ■ Share a favorite part with a buddy after reading (oral reading that is read so it sounds interesting to another) ■ Write about/respond to what was read with fluency	Giving readers opportunities to read for a sustained period of time helps them practice reading fluently if they are reading material at their independent reading level. Sharing favorite parts gives them chances to read orally, which can build reading fluency. Writing about what they read helps develop writing fluency. We write with more facility about what we know than about what we don't know.
Listening Work Station	■ Listen to a fluent reader read with good expression, pacing, and phrasing as a model on a recording ■ Choose a favorite part to read aloud to a buddy afterward	Listening to a fluent reader on a recording provides a model for students who are learning to read more fluently. Oral reading of favorite parts gives students opportunities to practice reading fluently to an audience.
Recording Studio (converted listening work station)	■ Read fluently and record it ■ Listen back to their reading and reflect upon their fluency	Listening to one's own reading and doing self-reflection can make students more aware of their fluency and improvements they are making over time.
Buddy Reading Work Station	■ Read orally or silently with a partner	Oral reading practice, combined with instruction on how to read fluently, can improve reading fluency.
Drama Work Station	■ Read orally in reader's theater	As students use expression, their phasing and intonation generally improve.
Poetry Work Station	■ Read poems orally and listen to them for interesting words and parts that paint a picture	See above.
Word Study Work Station	■ Look for patterns through word sorts ■ Pay attention to new words and what they mean to help students read around those words so meaning doesn't break down	Working with patterns in words can help students learn how to decode longer words. The more easily they can decode, the more fluent they will become as readers, especially when combined with instruction and practice in fluency.
Overhead Work Station	■ Read or write together ■ Practice cursive handwriting	Reading orally or composing with a buddy can promote fluency as students read or write together for real purposes and audiences. Working with partners can also provide models for fluency. Learning to write cursive well can improve writing fluency, because students won't have to spend as much energy thinking about how to form letters.

Literacy Work Stations That Build Fluency *(continued)*

| Computer Work Station | ■ Type writing pieces on the computer
■ Use computer programs designed to promote fluency | Students who have good keyboarding skills can often write more fluently at the computer. Computer programs designed to promote fluency can provide immediate feedback to students about their fluency. |

Fluency Research References

Allington, Richard. 1983. "Fluency: The Neglected Reading Goal." *The Reading Teacher* 36: 556–561.

Fuchs, L. S., D. Fuchs, C. Hamlett, et al. 2001. "Oral Reading Fluency as an Indicator of Reading Competence: A Theoretical, Empirical, and Historical Analysis." *Scientific Studies of Reading* 5 (3): 239–256.

Rasinski, T. V., and J. V. Hoffman. 2003. "Theory and Research into Practice: Oral Reading in the School Literacy Curriculum." *Reading Research Quarterly* 38: 510–523.

Literacy Work Stations That Build Phonics

Work Stations That Build Phonics	What Students Do Here That Supports Phonics	How This Station Supports Phonics
Writing Work Station	■ Use what they understand about phonics to spell words correctly as they write messages for others to read ■ Apply phonics lessons to their spelling	Spelling and phonics are closely related. Students' spelling provides a "window" into what they understand about how words work. Their spelling errors may offer insight into what they need to practice in phonics.
Spelling Work Station	■ Practice writing high frequency words ■ Work with spelling patterns that directly relate to phonics patterns being studied	See above.
Word Study Work Station	■ Do word sorts, which help students focus on phonics patterns	Phonics study focuses on patterns of letters that represent particular sounds in English. As students practice working with these patterns, they should begin to apply them more readily to their reading and writing with guidance from their teacher.
Poetry Work Station	■ Look for words with various patterns related to phonics lessons being taught	See above.
Computer Work Station	■ Use computer programs related to upper-level word study	See above.

Phonics Research References

Adams, M. 1999. *Beginning to Read: Thinking and Learning About Print.* Cambridge, MA: MIT Press.

Freppon, P.A. 1991. "Children's Concepts of the Nature and Purpose of Reading in Different Instructional Settings." *Journal of Reading Behavior* 23 (2): 139–163.

Stahl, S. A., A. M. Duffy-Hester, and K. A. Stahl. 1998. "Everything You Wanted to Know About Phonics (but Were Afraid to Ask)." *Reading Research Quarterly* 33: 338–355.

Literacy Work Stations That Build Vocabulary

Work Stations That Build Vocabulary	What Students Do Here That Supports Vocabulary	How This Station Supports Vocabulary
Classroom Library and Independent Reading	■ Read a wide variety of text and encounter many new words in their reading ■ Make note of new words they are learning as they read	The more students read, the more vocabulary they are exposed to. Helping them choose books that are "just right" can expand their vocabulary if they are taught how to pay attention to new words and figure out their meanings.
Response Writing and the Writing Work Station	■ Use new words from reading in their writing ■ Try out interesting words in their writing	Students who apply new vocabulary in their writing will "own" those words and continue to grow in vocabulary development.
Listening Work Station	■ Listen for new words and figure out what these mean	As students pay attention to new words and their meanings, they learn more vocabulary, especially if given opportunities to use these new words repeatedly.
Buddy Reading Work Station	■ Notice new words and think about their meanings ■ Use a dictionary to look up word meanings, as needed	See above.
Newspaper Work Station	■ Jot down new words or familiar words with new meanings	Reading in a variety of genres exposes students to new words across the curriculum and can also expand content-area vocabulary.
Drama Work Station	■ Pay attention to new words and how words are used as they read dramatically ■ Play charades and act out vocabulary words	See above.
Poetry Work Station	■ Read poems aloud and note interesting words and phrases	See above.
Word Study Work Station	■ Study words and their origins and relationships ■ Explore new and interesting words	The highest level of word study is to have students look at the interrelationship and origins of words. This can improve both vocabulary and spelling.
Content-Area Work Station	■ Jot down new words as they read in content areas ■ Study content-area vocabulary together	Reading in the content areas exposes students to new vocabulary. Many textbooks and informational texts note new words with bold print and/or italics. Teaching students how to stop, pay attention to these words, and figure out their meanings can help them develop this new vocabulary.

Vocabulary Research References

Beck, I. L., M. G. McKeown, and L. Kucan. 2002. *Bringing Words to Life.* New York: Guilford Press.

Blachowicz, C. L. Z., and P. Fisher. 2000. "Vocabulary Instruction." In M. Kamil, P. Mosenthal, P. Pearson, and R. Barr, eds., *Handbook of Reading Research: Vol. 3:* 503-523. Mahwah, NJ: Erlbaum.

Nagy, W. E. 1998. *Teaching Vocabulary to Improve Reading Comprehension.* Urbana, IL: ERIC Clearinghouse on Reading and Communication Skills.

Comprehension Bookmarks

_____'s

Bookmark

My Connections:

_____'s

Bookmark

My Questions:

_____'s

Bookmark

What I'm
Visualizing:

Comprehension Bookmarks

_____'s

Bookmark

Interesting Words:

_____'s

Bookmark

Interesting Facts:

New Words:

_____'s

Bookmark

What I'm Inferring:

Some Recommended Web Sites of Children's Book Authors for Grades 3–6

Author	Sample Title	Web Site
David Adler	Cam Jansen series	www.davidaadler.com
Avi	*Poppy*	www.avi-writer.com
Judy Blume	*Freckle Juice*	www.judyblume.com
Betsy Byars	*The Summer of the Swans*	www.betsybyars.com
Louise Borden	*The Greatest Skating Race*	www.louiseborden.com
Debbie Dadey and Marcia Jones	The Bailey School Kids books	www.baileykids.com
Paul Fleischman	*The Whipping Boy*	www.paulfleischman.net
Jean Fritz	*What's the Big Idea, Ben Franklin?*	www.waldsfe.org/Authors/ fritz.htm
Gail Gibbons	*Mummies, Pyramids, and Pharaohs*	www.gailgibbons.com
Jean Craighead George	*Julie of the Wolves*	www.jeancraigheadgeorge.com
Will Hobbs	*River Thunder*	www.willhobbsauthor.com
Brian Jacques	*Redwall*	www.redwall.org
Paul Janeczko	*That Sweet Diamond: Baseball Poems*	www.pauljaneczko.com
Kathleen Krull	*A Woman for President*	www.kathleenkrull.com
Jane Kurtz	*Bicycle Madness*	www.janekurtz.com
Jerry Palotta	*Read a Zillion Books*	www.alphabetman.com
Mary Pope Osborne	Magic Tree House books	www.marypopeosborne.com
Katherine Paterson	*Bridge to Teribithia*	www.teribithia.com
Gary Paulsen	*Hatchet*	www.garypaulsen.com
Dav Pilkey	*Captain Underpants*	www.pilkey.com
Patricia Polacco	*Thank You, Mr. Falker*	www.patriciapolacco.com
Allen Say	*Home of the Brave*	www.houghtonmifflinbooks.com/ authors/allensay/
Shel Silverstein	*A Light in the Attic*	www.shelsilverstein.com
Seymour Simon	*Earth: Our Planet in Space*	www.seymoursimon.com
Diane Stanley	*The Last Princess*	www.dianestanley.com
William Steig	*Shrek*	www.williamsteig.com
Jane Yolen	*Dinosaur Dances*	www.janeyolen.com
Colin Thompson	*How to Live Forever*	www.colinthompson.com
Chris Van Allsburg	*The Polar Express*	www.eduplace.com/author/
Elizabeth Winthrop	*The Castle in the Attic*	www.elizabethwinthrop.com

Practice with Purpose: Literacy Work Stations for Grades 3–6 by Debbie Diller. Copyright © 2005. Stenhouse Publishers.

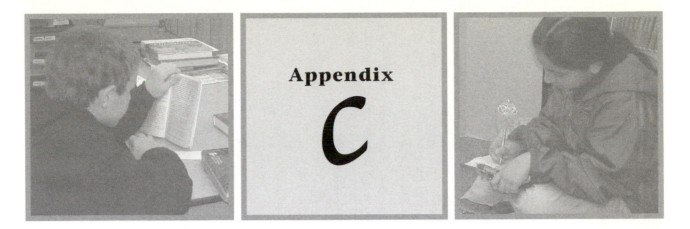

Resources for Response Writing and the Writing Work Station

Literacy Work Stations That Build Writing

Work Stations That Build Writing	What Students Do Here That Supports Writing	How This Station Supports Writing
Independent Reading and the Classroom Library	■ Write book reviews and notes to others about books they've read ■ Learn about authors and their craft	As students write to their peers, they have an increased sense of audience, which may strengthen their writing. Studying authors and their craft can give students insight into how to improve their writing.
Response Writing and the Writing Work Station	■ Respond in writing to books read and get feedback ■ Investigate a variety of writing genres at the writing station	Increased opportunities to write, coupled with good writing instruction, will help students improve in their writing. Giving students choices about what they will write and the genre they will use may increase motivation.
Listening Work Station	■ Listen to stories, which may give them ideas for their own stories ■ Respond in writing to books on tape	The more stories students hear, the more they learn about story construction. This, combined with good instruction on story structure, can help students write better stories. Response writing is another opportunity to practice writing about something students know.
Word Study Work Station	■ Explore new and interesting words that may later be used in their writing ■ Learn about spelling patterns that will help them better communicate with others through writing	Students who spell easily can use more of their brain power thinking about their ideas as they write (rather than having to concentrate on how to spell). Students learn to use higher-level vocabulary, which makes their writing more interesting.
Computer Work Station	■ Practice keyboarding ■ Compose, revise, and edit on the computer	Typing pieces on the computer can make it easier to read and facilitate the revising and editing processes.
Newspaper Work Station	■ Write news articles ■ Learn how news articles are written	Some students prefer to write informational text. This station offers this opportunity.
Grammar Work Station	■ Learn the rules of grammar to apply to their writing	Correct grammar improves student writing and helps the reader better understand the writer's message.
Handwriting Work Station	■ Practice writing in cursive	Legible handwriting makes it easier for the reader to comprehend the writer's message. Some students can write more fluently in cursive.
Poetry Work Station	■ Learn about different kinds of poetry ■ Write their own poetry	Some students, especially second-language learners, may thrive while writing poetry, because it requires fewer words to create mental images. Again, having a choice to write poetry may motivate some preadolescent writers.

Writing Research References

Dyson, A. H., and S. W. Freedman. 2003. "Writing." In J. Flood, D. Lapp, J. R. Squire, and J. M. Jensen, eds., *Handbook of Research on Teaching the English Language Arts*, 2nd ed.: 967–992. Mahwah, NJ: Erlbaum.
Graves, D. H. 1983, 2002. *Writing: Teachers and Children at Work*. Portsmouth, NH: Heinemann.
Langer, Judith A. 2002. *Effective Literacy Instruction: Building Successful Reading and Writing Programs*. Urbana, IL: National Council of Teachers of English.

Books I've Read in Grade _____

Name _____ Teacher _____

Title	Author	Date Done	Genre

Fiction Codes: RF (Realistic Fiction), HF (Historial Fiction), FT (Folk Tales, Fables), F (Fantasy), SF (Science Fiction)
Nonfiction Codes: IT (Informational Text), B (Biography)

Things I Want to Read

Name_____ Teacher _____ Grade _____

Title	Author	Why I Chose It (see Key below)	Library Section	Checked Out

What are you learning about yourself as a reader? As a writer?

Key:

R = Recommendation   A = Author I like
C = Covers (front and back)   T = Topic I'm interested in
G = Genre I like   RA = Read aloud by teacher

Practice with Purpose: Literacy Work Stations for Grades 3–6 by Debbie Diller. Copyright © 2005. Stenhouse Publishers.

My Library Plan

Name _____ Date _____

Books/Authors I Want to Read Next:

	Title/Author	Section of Library
1.	_____	_____
2.	_____	_____
3.	_____	_____

My Library Plan

Name _____ Date _____

Books/Authors I Want to Read Next:

	Title/Author	Section of Library
1.	_____	_____
2.	_____	_____
3.	_____	_____

Reading Response Rubric (Literary Letter)

Name _____ Date _____

Expectation	Achievement
1. Wrote as a letter and used correct form	
2. Book title included, spelled correctly, and underlined	
3. Author name included and spelled correctly	
4. Thoughtful responses	
5. Easy to read	

Scale: O = Outstanding, G = Good job, F = Fair, but could do better, N = Needs much improvement

Reading Response Rubric (Book Review)

Name _____ Date _____

Expectation	Achievement
1. Book title included, spelled correctly, and underlined	
2. Author name included and spelled correctly	
3. Summary of the book without giving away all that it's about	
4. Your opinion of the book included	
5. Interesting lead to hook the reader	
6. Easy to read	

Scale: O = Outstanding, G = Good job, F = Fair, but could do better, N = Needs much improvement

Practice with Purpose: Literacy Work Stations for Grades 3–6 by Debbie Diller. Copyright © 2005. Stenhouse Publishers.

Reading Response Rubric (Literary Letter—Historical Fiction Book)

Name _____ Date _____

Expectation	Achievement
1. Wrote as a letter and used correct form	
2. Book title included, spelled correctly, and underlined	
3. Author name included and spelled correctly	
4. Thoughtful responses	
5. References to historical events	
6. Easy to read	

Scale: O = Outstanding, G = Good job, F = Fair, but could do better, N = Needs much improvement

Reading Response Rubric (Literary Letter—Informational Book)

Name _____ Date _____

Expectation	Achievement
1. Wrote as a letter and used correct form	
2. Book title included, spelled correctly, and underlined	
3. Author name included and spelled correctly	
4. Thoughtful responses	
5. Discussion of what was learned and how you might use this information	
6. Easy to read	

Scale: O = Outstanding, G = Good job, F = Fair, but could do better, N = Needs much improvement

Writing Comment Sheet

Name _____ Date _____

Author's Name _____

Title of Writing Commented on _____

Dear _____,

I just wanted to comment on your writing. Something you did as a writer that I thought was outstanding is _____

_____

_____

Note: When filling out the comment sheet, be sure to include all information requested. Be positive and helpful with your comments. Include several thoughtful comments, please.

Writing Comment Sheet

Name _____ Date _____

Author's Name _____

Title of Writing Commented on _____

Dear _____,

I just wanted to comment on your writing. Something you did as a writer that I thought was outstanding is _____

_____

_____

Note: When filling out the comment sheet, be sure to include all information requested. Be positive and helpful with your comments. Include several thoughtful comments, please.

Abandoned Books

Name _____ Teacher _____ Grade _____

Date	Book Title	Why I Abandoned It

Look at your list. Do you see any patterns? Are you abandoning books for the same reason over and over? Use what you're learning to help you choose a better book the next time.

Status of Class for Writing at the Computer

Student Name	Title of Writing in Progress	Typing and Saving (Note File Name)	Revising and Editing	Ready to Print/Publish

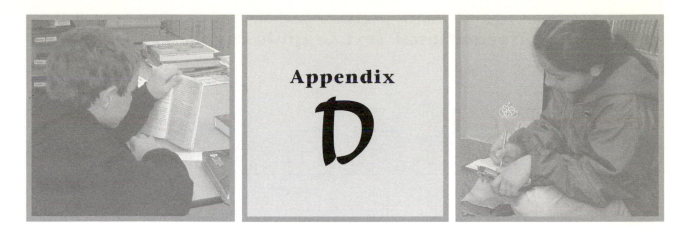

D

Resources for Easy–to–Set–Up Work Stations

Informational Text Graphic Organizer

Name _____ Date _____

Informational Text Title _____

Facts	New Words

Test-Taking Questions—Fiction

What do the main characters learn in this story?	**What do you think will happen next in the story? What information in the text helped you make that prediction?**
What will the main character probably do in the future?	**What is this story mainly about?**
What is the main problem in the story?	**You can tell in the story that . . .**
Why do the characters act like they do in the story?	**Choose a main character. How did he/she feel throughout the story?**
The story takes place at . . .	**The setting is important to this story because . . .**
This story was mainly written to . . .	**Why did the author probably write this story?**

Test-Taking Questions—Nonfiction

What is this article mainly about?	What conclusions can you draw from reading this? What information in the text helped you draw those conclusions?
What is the title of this article?	Which words tell you what _____ means?
On page ___ the word _____means . . .	Find examples of fact and opinion statements in the passage.
What are the most important ideas in the article? What information in the text told you that?	How is this article like another you read?
What is the most likely reason the author wrote this text?	The author organizes this information by . . .
The best summary of this article is . . .	The article gives you reason to believe that . . .

Listening Map—Fiction

Name _____ Date _____

Title _____

Author _____ Genre _____

What I Noticed in the Story:

Interesting Language/New Words:

After listening, go back to the "What I Noticed in the Story" box. Write a D beside each detail; circle the parts that tell what the story was mainly about. Then use the main ideas to write a summary below:

Listening Map—Fiction

Name_____ Date _____

Title _____

Author _____ Genre _____

Character:	Character Feelings	Character Traits
Character:		
Character:		

Setting 1: When and Where	Why It's Important to This Story
Setting 2: When and Where	

Most Important Events:

■

■

■

Conflict:

Resolution:

Author's Purpose:

Listening Map—Nonfiction

Name _____ Date _____

Title _____

Author _____ Genre _____

Listening Map—Biography

Title _____

Preview the text. What do you want to find out? _____

_____

Name of Person/Other Names for This Person	What This Person Is Known For

Important Information About This Person	Why It's Important	Character Traits	What Makes You Think This

Listening Map—Nonfiction

Name_____ Date _____

Title _____

Author_____ Genre _____

Listening Map—Informational Text

Title _____

Preview the text. What do you want to find out? _____
_____

Important Ideas	Words to Remember

Summary:

News Story Template

Type of News Story (circle one):

Event   Cartoon

Interview   Advertisement

Book Review   Other _____

Reporter Name _____

Date of Report _____

Title of News Story: _____

Newspaper Question Cards

You might copy the BEFORE READING cards onto one color, DURING READING on another color, and AFTER READING cards on a third color.

BEFORE READING
What is the title of the article? If there are any new words, jot them down and try to figure out what they mean. Use a dictionary, if needed.

BEFORE READING
What do the photos and captions tell you about this article?

BEFORE READING
Who is the author? Locate the byline.

BEFORE READING
Infer what you think this article will be about.

DURING READING
Read a paragraph or two. Then stop and think about what you read.

DURING READING
What connections are you making? What's this reminding you of?

Newspaper Question Cards

You might copy the BEFORE READING cards onto one color, DURING READING on another color, and AFTER READING cards on a third color.

DURING READING What are you visualizing? What questions are in your mind as you read?	**DURING READING** Highlight or circle new words. Figure out what they mean.
AFTER READING What are the big ideas you read about?	**AFTER READING** Tell what you thought was interesting in the article.
AFTER READING What will you do with the information you just read? Tell someone about it? Make something? Write a letter? Read more?	**AFTER READING** Summarize the article.

Newspaper Task Cards

Find and list ten proper nouns. Put them in columns by people, places, and things. Use proper nouns when writing news articles. Use capital letters!

Example:

People	Places	Things
Gary Smith	Washington, D.C.	Jeep

Cut out five or more strong verbs. Use these to write a new story. Glue your words onto the story you're writing.

Find an interesting photo. Read the caption and story to go with it. Cut out the photo and glue it onto notebook paper. Write a summary to go with it.

Read an article. Highlight the opinions in yellow. Highlight five or more facts in pink.

Read an article about someone in the news. List three or more questions you would ask in an interview of this person.

Find an ad. Highlight the parts that are opinions. Underline the facts.

Example:

This store makes it easy to sign up for free bonuses. Just come in and fill out an application today. Start saving soon. You'll be glad you did!

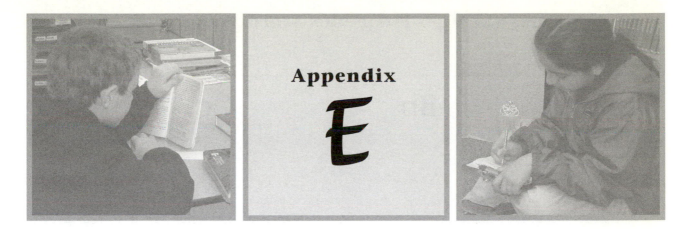

Resources for the Word Study Work Station

Personal High-Frequency Word Wall Pages

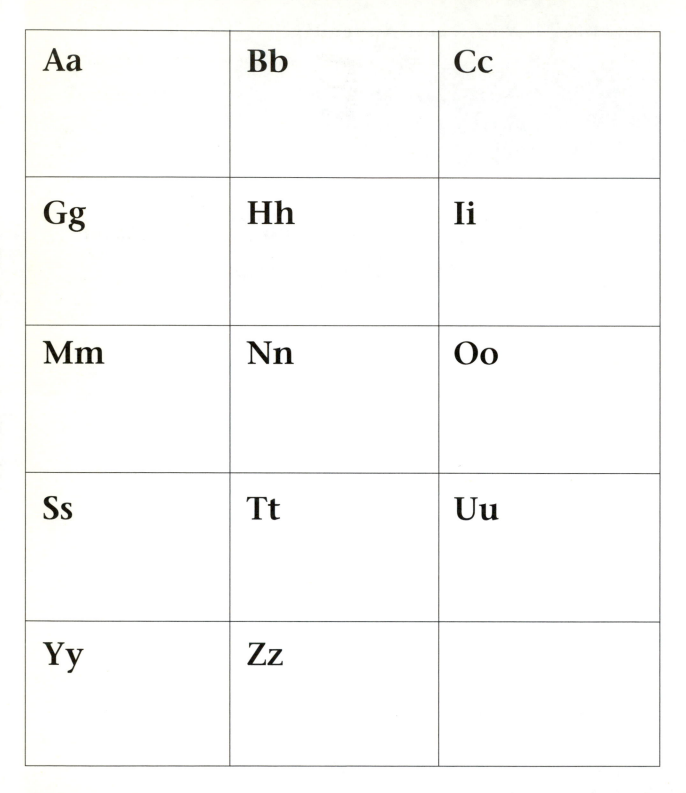

Aa	Bb	Cc
Gg	Hh	Ii
Mm	Nn	Oo
Ss	Tt	Uu
Yy	Zz	

Practice with Purpose: Literacy Work Stations for Grades 3–6 by Debbie Diller. Copyright © 2005. Stenhouse Publishers.

Personal High-Frequency Word Wall Pages

Dd	**Ee**	**Ff**
Jj	**Kk**	**Ll**
Pp	**Qq**	**Rr**
Vv	**Ww**	**Xx**

Planning Sheet for ABC Book

Name_____Date _____

ABC Book Topic _____

Brainstorm a word or phrase for each letter that relates to your topic. Use books to help with your research.

Aa	Bb	Cc	Dd
Ee	Ff	Gg	Hh
Ii	Jj	Kk	Ll
Mm	Nn	Oo	Pp
Qq	Rr	Ss	Tt
Uu	Vv	Ww	Xx
Yy	Zz		

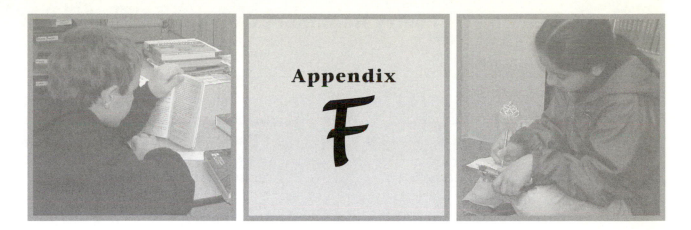

Resources for the Poetry
Work Station

Poetry Bookmarks

_____'s

Poetry Bookmark

I enjoyed the poem,

_____

by

_____

I think this is an awesome poem because

_____

_____

_____

This is the picture the poem creates in my mind:

_____'s

Poetry Bookmark

I recommend the poem,

_____

by

_____

Some words and phrases I like:

How this poem made me feel:

Poetry Task Cards

■ Which words feel important? Highlight them.
■ Read the poem again and emphasize these.

■ What does the poem make you feel?
■ Why?

■ Does the poem remind you of anything in your own life? What?
■ How does that help you better understand?

■ What pictures do you see in your mind as you read the poem?
■ Tell about what you also might hear, taste, smell, or touch.

■ What can you generalize from this poem?
■ This poem makes me think that . . .

■ Why do you think the poet wrote this poem?
■ What is the author's purpose?

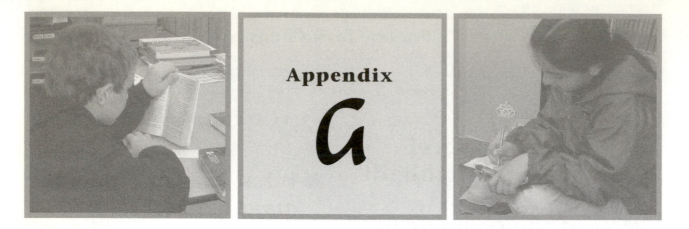

Resources for Content–Area Work Stations

Our Content-Area Connection

Book Title and Author	Our Connections	Page	Our Initials

New Words	Definitions

Culture Graphic Organizer

Student Names _____

_____ Date _____

_____ Culture _____

	Language	Religion	Music	Celebrations/ Traditions
Ethnic Groups				
Economy	Food	Schools/ Education	Housing and Transportation	Other

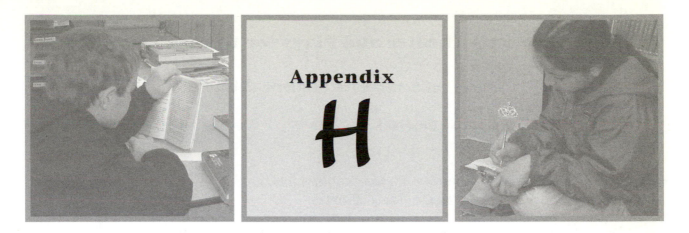

H

Resources for the Drama Work Station

Reader's Theater and Plays for Grades 3–6

Internet Sources for Reader's Theater

www.aaronshep.com/rt
www.teachingheart.net/readerstheater.htm
www.loiswalker.com
www.lisablau.com
cpanel.servdns.net/~readingl/Readers_theater/Scripts/scripts.html
www.literacyconnections.com/ReadersTheater.html

Professional Resources for Plays and Reader's Theater

Applebaum, M. 2003. *Colonial America: Read-Aloud Plays*. New York: Scholastic.
———. 2001. *Folk Tale Plays from Around the World That Kids Will Love!* New York: Scholastic.
Fry, E. 2000. *25 Mini-Plays: World History*. New York: Scholastic.
Glasscock, S. J. 1999. *10 American History Plays for the Classroom: Grades 4–8*. New York: Scholastic.
———. 2001. *10 Easy-to-Read American History Plays That Reach All Kinds of Readers*. New York: Scholastic.
Hanson-Harding, A. 2004. *Read-Aloud Plays: World War II*. New York: Scholastic.
Hollenbeck, K. M. 2003. *Easy-to-Read Folktale Plays to Teach Conflict Resolution*. New York: Scholastic.
Lewis, M. 2003. *Symbols of America: Read-Aloud Plays*. New York: Scholastic.
Murphy, D. 2000. *Read-Aloud Plays: Revolutionary War*. New York: Scholastic.
Nolan, T. 1999. *Read-Aloud Plays: Civil War*. New York: Scholastic.
Noll, K. 2003. *Read-Aloud Plays: Heroes in American History*. New York: Scholastic.
Rearick, J. 2002. *Read-Aloud Plays: Ancient Egypt*. New York: Scholastic.
Sanderson, J. 1999. *Middle Ages: Read-Aloud Plays*. New York: Scholastic.
———. 2002. *Read-Aloud Plays: Explorers*. New York: Scholastic.
Shepard, A. 2003. *Folktales on Stage: Children's Plays for Reader's Theater*. Olympia, WA: Shepard Publications.
West, T. 2001. *20 Terrific Mini-Plays That Build Reading Skills*. New York: Scholastic.
Wolf, J. M. 2002. *Cinderella Outgrows the Glass Slippers and Other Zany Fractured Fairy Tale Plays*. New York: Scholastic.

Highlighted Words

Name _____ Date _____

Read each sentence below, putting the emphasis on the highlighted word. Then write how the meaning changed in the box beside it.

That's a fancy new red car you're driving.	
That's a **fancy new red** car you're driving.	
That's a fancy **new red car** you're driving.	
That's a fancy new red car **you're** driving.	
I **don't** want to know what happened here.	
I don't want to know **what happened** here.	
I don't want to know what happened **here.**	

Question Cards to Use at the Drama Work Station

Mood	Character

Mood

■ What is the mood of this piece?

■ What do you feel as you read this piece or look at this picture?

■ What makes you feel that way?

■ Which lines and phrases describe the mood?

■ Show feeling as you read the piece aloud and dramatize it, or act out what is happening in the picture.

Character

■ Choose a character who is active and interesting. Become this character. Think, feel, and move like the character.

■ What is this character *really* like?

■ How would you describe this character?

■ Do you think he/she always acted this way?

■ If not, what may have made this character act this way?

■ What kinds of problems might this character have had in the past? In the future?

Dialogue, Plot, and Conflict Map

Names _____ Date _____ Title _____

Dialogue Notes (what you want to be sure the character says)	Plot Notes (main events to include in your dramatization)	Conflict Notes (what you want to communicate with and without words about the conflict)
Character		
Character		
Character		
Character		

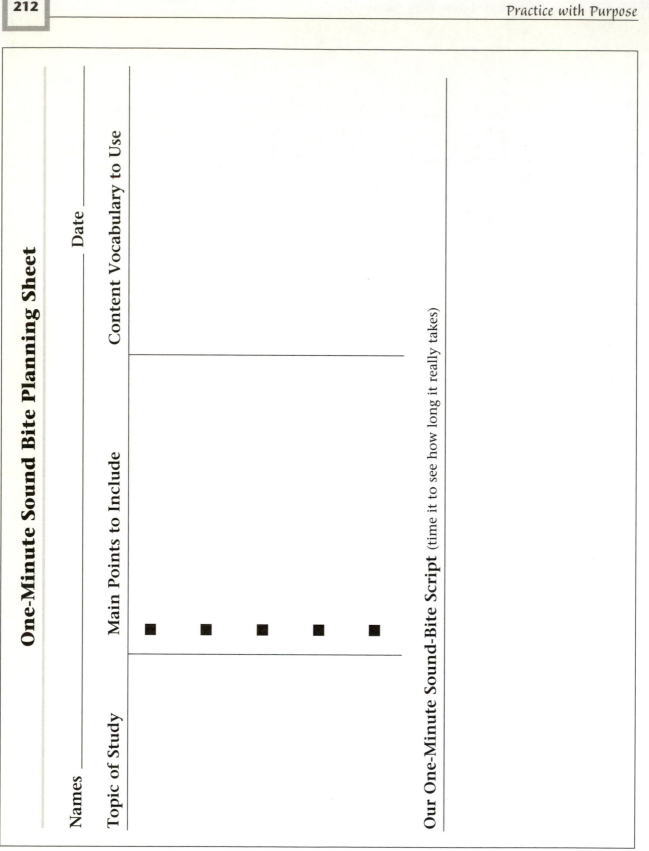

One-Minute Sound Bite Planning Sheet

Names _____

Date _____

Topic of Study

Main Points to Include

Content Vocabulary to Use

- ■
- ■
- ■
- ■
- ■

Our One-Minute Sound-Bite Script (time it to see how long it really takes)

Story Extension Planning

Name _____ Date _____

Read the story with a partner. Then jot down the main events of the story. Choose to plan an improv on what might have happened either before OR after the story. Jot down your ideas. Then act it out.

Before the Story

Think about what might have happened BEFORE this story.

During the Story

Jot down the main events of this story.

After the Story

Think about what might have happened AFTER this story.

Self-Evaluation

Names of Participants _____

Date_____ Improv/Dramatization of _____

Question	Our Response
1. Which were the best parts of our dramatization? What did we do to make the story or information clear?	
2. Which characters were most believable? What did we do to make them be so real?	
3. How did the dialogue sound? What made it interesting? Was there the right amount of dialogue?	
4. What did we do today that we will want to do again next time? How could we improve next time?	

References

Professional Sources

Allen, J. 2002. *On the Same Page: Shared Reading Beyond the Primary Grades*. Portland, ME: Stenhouse.

Angelillo, J. 2003. *Writing About Reading*. Portsmouth, NH: Heinemann.

Atwell, N. 1998. *In the Middle: New Understanding About Writing, Reading, and Learning*. Portsmouth, NH: Heinemann.

Bear, D. et al. 2004. *Words Their Way: Word Study for Phonics, Vocabulary, and Spelling Instruction*. Columbus, OH: Prentice Hall.

Brand, M. 2004. *Word Savvy: Integrated Vocabulary, Spelling, and Word Study, Grades 3–6*. Portland, ME: Stenhouse.

Brown, S. 2001. *All Sorts of Sorts 2*. San Diego: Teaching Resource Center.

Cambourne, B. 1988. *The Whole Story: Natural Learning and the Acquisition of Literacy*. Auckland, NZ: Ashton-Scholastic.

Cunningham, P. 1994. *Making Big Words*. Carthage, IL: Good Apple Books.

———. 1997. *Making More Big Words*. Carthage, IL: Good Apple Books.

Diller, D. 2003. *Literacy Work Stations: Making Centers Work*. Portland, ME: Stenhouse.

Enciso, P. 1990. The Nature of Engagement in Reading. PhD diss., Ohio State University.

Fountas, I. C., and G. S. Pinnell. 1996. *Guided Reading: Good First Teaching for All Children*. Portsmouth, NH: Heinemann.

Franco, B. 2005. *Conversations with a Poet: Inviting Poetry into K–12 Classrooms*. Katonah, NY: Richard C. Owen Publishers.

Gambrell, L. 1996. "Creating Classroom Cultures that Foster Reading Motivation." *The Reading Teacher* 50: 14–25.

Gardner, H. 1993. *Frames of Mind: The Theory of Multiple Intelligence*. New York: Basic Books.

Graves, D. 1989. *Investigate Nonfiction*. Portsmouth, NH: Heinemann.

Harvey, S. 1998. *Nonfiction Matters: Reading, Writing, and Research in Grades 3–8*. Portland, ME: Stenhouse.

Heard, G. 1998. *Awakening the Heart: Exploring Poetry in Elementary and Middle School*. Portsmouth, NH: Heinemann.

Jensen, E. 1998. *Teaching with the Brain in Mind*. Alexandria, VA: Association for Supervision and Curriculum Development.

Keene, E., and S. Zimmermann. 1997. *Mosaic of Thought: Teaching Comprehension in a Reader's Workshop*. Portsmouth, NH: Heinemann.

Miller, D. 2002. *Reading with Meaning: Teaching Comprehension in the Primary Grades.* Portland, ME: Stenhouse.

Moline, S. 1996. *I See What You Mean: Children at Work with Visual Information.* Portland, ME: Stenhouse.

Morgan, B., with D. Odom. 2005. *Writing Through the Tween Years: Supporting Writers, Grades 3–6.* Portland, ME: Stenhouse.

Morgenstern, J. 1998. *Organizing from the Inside Out.* New York: Henry Holt.

———. 2000. *Time Management from the Inside Out.* New York: Henry Holt.

Pearson, P. D., and M. C. Gallagher. 1983. "The Instruction of Reading Comprehension." *Contemporary Educational Psychology* 8: 317–344.

Pinnell, G. S., and I. C. Fountas. 2001. *Leveled Books for Readers Grades 3–6: A Companion Volume to Guiding Readers and Writers.* Portsmouth, NH: Heinemann.

Routman, R. 2000. *Kids' Poems: Teaching Third & Fourth Graders to Love Writing Poetry.* New York: Scholastic.

Robb, L. 2000. *52 Fabulous Discussion-Prompt Cards for Reading Groups.* New York: Scholastic.

Sibberson, F., and K. Szymusiak. 2003. *Still Learning to Read: Teaching Students in Grades 3–6.* Portland, ME: Stenhouse.

Sweeney, J. 1997. *Incredible Quotations: 230 Thought-Provoking Quotes with Prompts to Spark Students' Writing, Thinking, and Discussion.* New York: Scholastic.

Szymusiak, K., and F. Sibberson. 2001. *Beyond Leveled Books.* Portland, ME: Stenhouse.

Vygotsky, L. S. 1978. *Mind in Society: The Development of Higher Psychological Processes.* Cambridge, MA: Harvard University Press.

Wilhelm, J. 1996. *You Gotta BE the Book: Teaching Engaged and Reflective Reading with Adolescents.* New York: Teachers College Press.

Children's Books

Adoff, A. 1997. *Love Letters.* New York: Blue Sky Press.

Berger, M. 1985. *Germs Make Me Sick!* New York: HarperCollins.

———. 2000. *Scholastic Science Dictionary.* New York: Scholastic.

Codell, E. 2003. *Sahara Special.* New York: Hyperion Books for Children.

Crane, C. 2002. *L Is for Last Frontier: An Alaska Alphabet Book.* New York: Sleeping Bear Press.

Cullinan, B. E., ed. 1996. *A Jar of Tiny Stars: Poems by NCTE Award-Winning Poets.* Honesdale, PA: Boyds Mills Press.

Dadey, D. and M. T. Jones. 2001. *Mrs. Jeeper's Monster Class Trip.* New York: Scholastic.

Dakos, K. 1990. *If You're Not Here, Please Raise Your Hand: Poems About School.* New York: Macmillan.

Driscoll, M. 2003. *A Children's Introduction to Poetry.* New York: Black Dog and Leventhal.

Fisher, A. 2003. *I Heard a Bluebird Sing: Children Select Their Favorite Poems by Aileen Fisher.* Honesdale, PA: Boyds Mills Press.

Fleischman, P. 1988. *Joyful Noise: Poems for Two Voices.* New York: HarperCollins.

———. 2000. *Big Talk: Poems for Four Voices.* Cambridge, MA: Candlewick Press.

Franco, B. 2003. *Mathematickles!* New York: Simon & Schuster.

Franklin Institute Science Museum. 1995. *Ben Franklin Book of Easy and Incredible Science Experiments.* Indianapolis: Wiley.

Fritz, J. 1998. *Shh! We're Writing the Constitution.* New York: Putnam.

Garland, S. 1993. *The Lotus Seed.* San Diego: Harcourt Brace.

Garnett, S. et al. 2004. *The U.S. Navy Alphabet Book.* Watertown, MA: Charlesbridge.

Graham, J. B. 2003. *Flicker Flash.* Boston: Houghton Mifflin.

Grodin, L. 2004. *D Is for Democracy.* New York: Sleeping Bear Press.

Harley, A. 2000. *Fly with Poetry: An ABC of Poetry.* Honesdale, PA: Boyds Mills Press.

Harwayne, S., ed. 2002. *Messages to Ground Zero: Children Respond to September 11, 2001.* Portsmouth, NH: Heinemann.

Hines, A. G. 2001. *Pieces: A Year in Poems and Quilts.* New York: Greenwillow.

Holbrook, S. 1996. *I Never Said I Wasn't Difficult.* Honesdale, PA: Boyds Mills Press.

Hopkins, L. B., ed. 1994. *Weather: Poems for All Seasons.* New York: HarperCollins.

———. 1996. *Opening Days: Sports Poems.* Orlando: Harcourt Brace.

———. 2000. *Good Books, Good Times.* Orlando: Harcourt Brace.

Hughes, L. 1996. *The Dream Keeper and Other Poems.* New York: Knopf.

Janeczko, P. G., ed. 1996. *The Place My Words Are Looking For.* New York: Bradbury Press.

Kennedy, D. M., and X. J. Kennedy. 1992. *Talking Like the Rain: A Read-to-Me Book of Poems*. New York: Little Brown and Company.

Kneidel, S. S. 1993. *Creepy Crawlies and the Scientific Method: More Than 100 Hands-On Science Experiments for Children*. Golden, CO: Fulcrum.

Krach, M. S. 2000. *D Is for Doufu: An Alphabet Book of Chinese Culture*. Fremont, CA: Shen's Books.

Lobel, A. 1980. *Fables*. New York: Harper & Row.

Lyne, S. 1996. *Ten-Second Rainshowers: Poems by Young People*. New York: Simon & Schuster.

MacLachlan, P. 1987. *Sarah, Plain and Tall*. New York: HarperCollins.

McArthur, N. 1990. *The Adventure of the Buried Treasure*. New York: Scholastic.

Morrison, L. 2001. *Way to Go! Sports Poems*. Honesdale, PA: Wordsong/Boyds Mills Press.

Murray, S. 2001. *Eyewitness: Wild West*. New York: Dorling Kindersley.

Nesbitt, K. 2005. *When the Teacher Isn't Looking: And Other Funny School Poems*. Minnetonka, MN: Meadowbrook Press.

Pallotta, J. 1993. *The Extinct Alphabet Book*. Watertown, MA: Charlesbridge.

Pappas, T. 1991. *Math Talk: Mathematical Ideas in Poems for Two Voices*. San Carlos, CA: Wide World Publishing/Tetra.

Parker, S. et al. 1997. *Eyewitness Explorers: Rocks and Minerals*. New York: Dorling Kindersley.

Pelletier, D. 1996. *The Graphic Alphabet*. New York: Orchard Books.

Prelutsky, J., ed. 1983. *The Random House Book of Poetry for Children*. New York: Random House.

———. 1996. *A Pizza the Size of the Sun*. New York: Greenwillow.

Provenzo, E. F. Jr., and A. B. Provenzo. 1989. *47 Easy-To-Do Classic Science Experiments*. New York: Dover Publications.

Romanek, R. 2003. *Achoo! The Most Interesting Book You'll Ever Read About Germs*. Tonawanda, NY: Kids Can Press.

2001. *Scholastic Dictionary of Synonyms, Antonyms, and Homonyms*. New York: Scholastic.

Schmidt, G. D., ed. 1994. *Poetry for Young People: Robert Frost*. New York: Sterling.

Schwartz, D. 2001. *Q Is for Quark: A Science Alphabet Book*. Berkeley, CA: Tricycle Press.

Scieszka, J., and L. Smith. 1992. *The Stinky Cheese Man and Other Fairly Stupid Tales*. New York: Viking Penguin.

Silverstein, S. 1974. *Where the Sidewalk Ends*. New York: Harper & Row.

———. 1981. *A Light in the Attic*. New York: HarperCollins.

Stepanek, M. 2002. *Heartsongs*. New York: Hyperion.

Strasser, T. 1995. *Help! I'm Trapped in Obedience School*. New York: Scholastic.

Sutcliffe, J. 2004. *Milton Hershey*. Minneapolis: Lerner Publications.

Terban, M. 1996. *Scholastic Dictionary of Idioms: More Than 600 Phrases Sayings and Expressions*. New York: Scholastic.

Van Allsburg, C. 1987. *Z Was Zapped: A Play in Twenty-Six Acts*. Boston: Houghton Mifflin.

VanCleave, J. 1990. *Janice VanCleave's Biology for Every Kid: 101 Easy Experiments That Really Work*. Indianapolis: Wiley.

Van Leeuwen, J. 1992. *Going West*. New York: Penguin.

Wilbur, R. 2000. *The Pig in the Spigot*. Orlando: Harcourt Brace.

Wilder, L. I. 1953. *Little House in the Big Woods*. New York: HarperTrophy.

Young, Sue. 1997. *Scholastic Rhyming Dictionary*. New York: Scholastic.